Marketing Aspects of International Business

Nijenrode Studies in Business

Business administration is a broad field of study in which theory and practice should intersect for the analysis of old theories and the development of new ones. One of the main objectives of the Nijenrode Studies in Business is to provide an impetus to new developments in the multidisciplinary field of business administration, to serve modern managers as well as students and teachers of business administration.

Marketing Aspects of International Business

Gerald M. Hampton and Aart P. van Gent
Editors

Kluwer-Nijhoff Publishing
A member of the Kluwer Academic Publishers Group
Boston-Dordrecht-Lancaster-The Hague

Distributors for North America:

Kluwer Boston, Inc.
190 Old Derby Street
Hingham, Massachusetts 02043, U.S.A.

Distributors outside North America:

Kluwer Academic Publishers Group
Distribution Centre
P.O. Box 322
3300AH Dordrecht, The Netherlands

Library of Congress Cataloging in Publication Data
Main entry under title:

Marketing aspects of international business.

    (Nijenrode studies in business)
    1. Export marketing—Addresses, essays, lectures. I. Hampton,
Gerald M. II. Gent, Aart Pieter Van. III. Series.
HF1009.5.M358   1984   658.8'48   83–6272
ISBN 0–89838–136–3

Printed in the United States of America.

Contents

List of Figures and Tables

List of Figures

List of Tables

Preface

The old ways break down, times change, and new
life blossoms from the ruins.
Frederich Schiller

These words of a great poet express a basic fact of life—the inevitability of change. If marketers were asked to envision the future, they would not hesitate to answer that the entire globe is involved in a human revolution like no other in history. The changes now taking place, in both industrially developed and developing nations, are indications of the problems, challenges, and opportunities confronting future economic growth and development.

Perhaps the most prominent characteristic of this change is the growing economic interdependence of all nations. Today it seems quite unnecessary to point out that any nation's problems and opportunities anywhere are now every nation's problems and opportunities everywhere. This economic and business interdependence on a global scale is the new reality, regardless of whether we want to accept it. The task ahead for all corporate managers becomes one of adapting to this new international business reality. It also requires them to assume the leadership role in helping individuals of all nations to become more and more aware of their mutual need for another's products and services.

Today every corporation, whether confined within one nation or not, operates in this dynamic, changing, international business environment.

Those firms that conduct operations in several nations are simply more aware of the changes and dynamics. In the final analysis, it makes little difference, because the problems and challenges facing business have taken on an international dimension. As a result, business marketing is assuming an ever-increasing role. It seems reasonable to assume that no future business decision of importance will be untouched or unaffected by international marketing concerns.

As firms adjust their marketing activities to the changing international business environment, it becomes important to identify some of the problems and challenges that are currently influencing international marketing decisions. In doing so, we can understand what events are now shaping future decisions, and we should begin the thinking and planning needed to cope with emerging problems that are sure to arise during the remainder of this century. Finally, and to our good fortune, it must be remembered that most of our opportunities are the result of problems arising out of the rapidly changing world environment.

To begin such an effort, the research conference "International Marketing in the 1980s and Beyond: Problems and Challenges," was sponsored and hosted by the Netherlands School of Business in July 1982. The conference brought together a group of leading international marketing scholars from Europe and North America. Their task was to present papers that defined, explored, and discussed those problems and challenges that presently are, or will come to be, of concern to international marketing in the remainder of this century. This volume of the Nijenrode Studies in Business series contains a selection of papers presented at the conference.

The book begins with a chapter by Warren Keegan, who offers an assessment of the field in terms of its past, present, and future. Its purpose is to provide a new integrative framework, not only for this book but for the whole field of international marketing. Beginning with the past, Keegan outlines the major underlying forces that made it possible for business to grow and develop internationally. The six historical and positive forces include the international monetary framework, the world trading system, global peace, development of communication technologies, domestic economic growth, and the multinational corporation.

For the present, Keegan divides the field into four broad dimensions, the understanding and application of which he sees as essential for companies operating internationally. The first dimension is the need for a new conceptual orientation. This orientation includes the development of environmental sensitivity; an understanding of the unifying and differentiating influences, leverage, or experience effects; the product/market life cycle relationship; and the notion of learning. The remaining three dimensions consist of comprehending world markets, strategy, and international competition. In the future, Keegan forecasts a more balanced world in terms of economic power. He also expects that creativity, human resources, and professional skills will not be concentrated in just a few regions but will become more globally dispersed.

The chapter that follows, by Jan Van Rees, focuses on one aspect of the conceptual orientation discussed by Keegan, namely the notion, definition, or perception of international marketing. Professor Van Rees' concern is with the problem of bridging the gap between the work of scholars and international marketing practitioners. He asks marketers not to forget the past and urges us to begin anew, working from the premise of marketing as a process.

He argues that the process view of marketing takes us back to the essential fact that marketing is mainly interested in the stream of goods and services flowing through international society. For business, marketing is concerned with the buying and selling of raw materials, semi-manufactured goods, components and parts, capital goods, and consumer goods. The benefit derived from this view, according to Van Rees, is that we can see international marketing as the field in which we find the application of its total inheritance. The result is that the field must once again occupy itself with concepts and techniques not presently fashionable in modern marketing, but that are still very much a part of the problems and challenges faced by the international marketing managers and their staffs of experts in transportation, law, insurance, and so on, who form an important element of the international marketing mix.

The next chapter, by Helmut Soldner, like the previous one, is concerned with the conceptual orientation of the Keegan framework. His purpose is to focus on the essential elements necessary for international marketing theory building. Soldner's theme is that, when international firms are viewed as global systems for market development, the theoretical base of international marketing has to be broader than just internationalizing established marketing concepts. He advocates a holistic, interdisciplinary approach using international business theory as the conceptual base.

The Vern Terpstra chapter focuses on the importance of economies of scale for developing marketing strategies in the increasingly competitive international environment. Numerous examples are used to illustrate this concept, which is characterized by increasing market share, growing output, and declining cost. It is suggested that in the areas of marketing research; product pricing, distribution, and promotion policies; as well as marketing management, economies of scale, or the experience effect will exert increasing influence.

According to Jean J. Boddewyn's chapter, a constant challenge before international marketers is the regulation of worldwide advertising. To assess this challenge, Boddewyn focuses on the environmental factors, motivation of regulators, and the actors or forces at work. Boddewyn concludes that the net outcome for the 1980s will be a relative pause in advertising regulation. However, he warns that there are certain dangers during this period due to the recession-induced trade-protectionist measures that could lead to attacks against advertising under special circumstances. He suggests that during the 1990s we will return to the more traditional regulatory pressures on advertising but that business will be in a better position to anticipate problems, i.e., to fight restrictions and to self-regulate.

In Chapter 6, John K. Ryans examines the technological changes occurring in both internal and external communications. The focus is on how such changes will impact promotional and marketing strategies. The discussion provides a new perspective on the debate of using a standardized versus a market-to-market promotional campaign approach. His theme is that technological developments, especially television in Europe that makes possible trans-country coverage, suggest that current country-by-country market segmentation and strategic planning will be replaced by a multi-market approach leading to true international marketing plans.

Chapter 7, by S. Prakash Sethi and Hamid Etemad, addresses what many consider to be the most important problem and challenge facing international marketing—the role of marketing and its contribution to economic development. The purpose of this chapter is to highlight the significant role marketing has to play in the economic development process at both the theoretical and practical levels. It is argued that less-developed nations often define their problems in terms of inadequate supply. The authors show that this oversimplification of the question of adequate demand ignores the matching of product characteristics with consumer needs. The result is inefficient use of limited resources and failed development efforts. The theme is that the marketing process can be a potent catalyst that organizes, augments, and accelerates economic progress.

The chapter by Erwin Dichtl, et al. presents a comprehensive method for studying the export decision process of small- and medium-sized firms. The authors' contention is that to build good international marketing theory, more emphasis needs to be placed on the export decision process—the first and most innovative step in the internationalization process. Their method leads to the examination of (1) the main differences between exporting and nonexporting firms, (2) problems encountered by firms that have only recently begun to export, and (3) the risk perceptions and value trade-offs in evaluating export alternatives regarding markets, products, and strategies. This research framework facilitates an empirical examination of the exporting process and is an important contribution to the general theory-building efforts in the field.

In the next chapter, Malcolm McDonald identifies and evaluates the marketing planning process used by British industrial goods firms operating internationally. He also explores the validity of the conventional wisdom that formalized marketing planning leads to success. The findings demonstrate that the majority of firms do not conform to theory. McDonald concludes that while the process of marketing planning is universally applicable, it is the systematization of the process that makes it work successfully. This work demonstrates that designing and implementing systems and procedures for marketing planning is far more complex than present literature indicates, particularly in multinational firms.

The Matthew Meulenberg presentation is an attempt to assess how appropriate general theoretical aspects of marketing channels are for a theory of marketing channels in export marketing. Meulenberg contends that the distance to market, geographically and culturally, is the essential characteristic of export marketing. The impact of this variable is first analyzed within the framework of the Dorfman-Steiner model. It is then followed, in Chapter 10, with a more qualitative analysis of the impact of distance to market. The conclusion is that present marketing theory offers limited insights into the structure of export marketing channels.

Chapter 11, by Kenneth Simmonds, offers the insightful view that global corporations attempt control of complex international marketing strategies with overly simplistic control systems. He suggests that worldwide strategies with centralized objectives cannot be effectively implemented—much less controlled—when performance is basically decentralized on the basis of geographic markets (usually a country basis). The theme here is that complex strategies require equally complex control mechanisms.

Why is international marketing currently perceived by many academics to be an area of low interest? What are the important research topics of the future in international marketing? The final chapter in this book, by Gerald M. Hampton and Aart Van Gent, provides at least one set of answers. Using the participants of the 1982 International Marketing Conference as panel members, a Delphi study using three rounds explored these questions. The results were twelve reasons, grouped into four categories, as to why international marketing might be perceived to be an area of relatively low interest. In addition, the Delphi process developed a list of 50 possible international marketing research projects that span ten major subject areas. This contribution, will hasten to spread the international orientation much needed not only in marketing but in all areas of business study.

We would like to thank Dr. Gerard B. J. Bomers, Dean of the Netherlands School of Business, for his encouragement and moral support during the conference. We also extend our thanks to the administrative board of the school for providing the necessary funds for the conference. A very special thanks goes to the staff of the Management Development Center at Nijenrode for all their efforts during the conference.

1 INTERNATIONAL MARKETING: *Past, Present, and Future*

Warren J. Keegan

The field of marketing has undergone continuous change and development as the world's markets have responded to the rising income and productivity that have been the fruit of man's growing mastery of technology. This paper focuses on the evolution of the sub-field of international marketing, one of the fastest growing areas in marketing.

The Past—Where We Have Been

Let's begin with the past, or where we have been. As international marketers, we are part of what is one of the oldest if not the oldest profession in the world. Even the multinational corporation, which some people believe is

This chapter was the keynote address to the conference "International Marketing in the 1980s and Beyond, Problems and Challenges," which was part of the celebration of the "Bicentennial Nederland-Amerika 1982." I would like to acknowledge the conference co-chairmen, Professor Gerald M. Hampton of Seattle University and Professor Dr. Aart P. van Gent of the Netherlands School of Business, who had the vision to conceive of the conference and the energy to make it happen.

1

a recent invention, was well established as an institution by the beginning of this century. As Myra Wilkens has reminded us, the multinational company was alive and well before World War I. Companies like Ford, Singer, Westinghouse, GE, Philips, and IBM were operating internationally soon after they began operations in their home countries.

What has happened in this century, however, is truly remarkable in the context of world history. At the beginning of the century, there were local, regional, national, and international markets. The national and international companies were developing, but the size of international markets was still relatively limited. They grew, but the growth of the international markets was interrupted by World War I and was brought to a complete standstill by the Great Depression of the 1930s. The really explosive growth of international marketing and international business occurred after World War II. For almost all of the 37 years since 1945, international trade and investment have been growing faster than gross world product. This sustained growth over such a long period has transformed the world from a collection of relatively autonomous national economies to a highly interdependent world of international competition. This is true for all countries, even the formerly relatively isolated countries like the United States. In the United States today, international trade accounts for twice as much of the gross national product as it did in the 1960s. Exports generate one in six manufacturing jobs and keep one in every three acres of farmland active.

At the beginning of this century there were still domestic or national markets. Today, there are no national markets. There are, of course, still local and regional markets, but if a market is big enough to be a national market, it is either an international market or a candidate to become an international market. For example, the market for babysitting is a local market. There has been little international competition in this market, and none is expected. The market for almost all manufactured goods was a national or international market, and all of the goods in this market are candidates for international competition. George Weiseman of Phillip Morris used to say that there was no such thing as international marketing, only domestic marketing worldwide. The other side of this coin is that there is no such thing as a pure national market; all markets are either actual or potential international markets.

The past, then, has been characterized by a tremendous growth in the international economy and steadily increasing flow of product, people, and money across national borders. What about the future? One way of seeking to gain an insight into what the future holds for international marketing is to identify why the growth of the past four decades has been so great and to determine whether or not the underlying factors of the growth will continue to be present. The major underlying forces that have made it possible for business to grow and develop internationally are examined below.

Underlying Forces

The International Monetary Framework. The basic objectives of the architects of the post-World War II international monetary framework was to create a system of international liquidity that would facilitate economic growth and the transfer of goods and services between nations. These objectives have been met by a system that is far from perfect, but which has for over three decades functioned adequately. This evolving framework has every prospect of continuing to function adequately.

The World Trading System. The post-World War II world trading system was constructed out of a common desire to avoid a return to the restrictive and discriminatory trading practices of the 1920s and the 1930s. There was a commitment to the creation of a liberal world in which there would be a free flow of goods and services between countries. The system that evolved out of this commitment included the General Agreement on Tariffs and Trade (GATT), which provided an institutional framework and a set of rules and principles for efforts to liberalize trade. The most-favored-nation (MFN) principle, whereby each country agrees to extend to all countries the most favorable terms that it negotiates with any country, is an example of a GATT rule which contributed to the reduction of high tariff levels. Major reductions of tariff levels were accomplished by multilateral negotiations, such as the Kennedy Round of the 1960s and the Tokyo Round of the 1970s. The Tokyo Round, when fully implemented, will bring industrial country tariff levels down to roughly four percent by 1987, less than the sales tax in most U.S. states.

The major challenge to the trading system in the 1980s is not tariff levels, but the so-called non-tariff barriers (NTBs). These include safeguard actions in the form of quotas, exclusion orders, standards that either cannot be met in the case of natural products or that are very expensive to meet in the case of manufactured products and that have no real public welfare justification other than their effect on limited imports, exclusionary distribution, administrative delays (going by the *rules,* for example, at ports of entry). These actions are intended to protect domestic industries that are threatened by imports, sector arrangements for industries like textiles and steel, and attempts by the U.S. to impose its trade policy on its trading partners, as in the case of the high technology ban on exports to the

U.S.S.R. imposed by the Reagan administration in 1982. In the United States, these actions are administered by the International Trade Commission, the Treasury Department, and the Department of Commerce and are authorized by section 731 and 733(s) of the 1930 tariff act and sections 201, 301, and 406(a) of the trade act of 1974. The language of these acts, which refer to unfair competition, dumping (i.e., price discrimination), provides wide openings for appeals for protection from foreign competition. Only a renewed commitment to free trade and international specialization will avoid a creeping escalation of NTBs.

Global Peace. In spite of the continuous local and regional warfare that has occurred since the end of World War II, the global condition has been characterized by an absence of world war. There may be fighting in the Middle East, the South Atlantic, or wherever, but while this fighting takes place, the rest of the world carries on with everyday work in a peaceful way.

Communications. All of the developments that have increased the speed and reliability of data, voice, video, and physical movement have contributed to the shrinking of the globe and the development of international marketing. The rate of development of communications technologies continues to grow.

Domestic Economic Growth. A significant context for the growth of international marketing is the worldwide growth of domestic markets. The current slowdown and even standstill of the growth of domestic markets in most countries has put a real brake on the growth of international marketing. Until very recently, countries have been receptive to international participation in domestic markets because outsiders could enter the domestic market without taking away business from the local firms. Today, in no-growth markets, this is no longer possible. One company's success is at the expense of another company. When the one company happens to be foreign, there is understandably pressure to protect the domestic firms.

The Multinational Corporation. The multinational corporation (MNC), which is any business that seeks to participate in world markets using world resources, has been a major institution in expanding the role of international marketing in the world economy. These corporations have expanded from their once almost-exclusive base in the United States and Europe to the entire world, including the third world and the socialist bloc. The role of the MNC is strong and growing. The thrust of the MNCs is changing from a focus on serving national markets to a focus on serving global markets made up of segments that exist in many countries. This shifting focus is creating a new global corporation.

The Present

To assess the present status of international marketing, I have divided the field in four broad dimensions: conceptual, world markets, strategy, and competition.

Conceptual Orientation

There are two basic concepts that define international marketing as a subfield of marketing. One is that there is no such thing as international marketing. There is only one marketing discipline and that applies worldwide in every culture, under every system of government, and at every stage of development. To be sure, the relative importance of different aspects of the discipline may change from country to country, but this is merely a matter of emphasis, not of a different or distinctive discipline. Marketing is a universal discipline. There is not one kind of marketing for the home market and another for the international market. International markets are in fact domestic markets. What makes them international is the perspective of the observer, not the character of the market.

A second basic concept is that there are distinctive aspects to international marketing that must be understood and adapted to in order to succeed in international markets. These distinctive factors include the concept of environmental sensitivity, unifying and differentiating influences, leverage, the product/market life cycle relationship, and learning.

Environmental Sensitivity. The first of these distinctive factors is environmental sensitivity. Some products are more sensitive to cultural and economic factors in the environment than others. The need for adaptation of the marketing mix is a positive function of the degree of environmental sensitivity. The greater the sensitivity, the greater is the need for adaptation. As the world becomes smaller, the aggregate degree of sensitivity seems to be declining. Fewer and fewer products are produced in a unique national version. A good example is the American automobile, which used to be unique in world markets. This distinctive product was sensitive to a unique energy environment. The growing interdependence of the United States has eliminated this unique environment, and the unique product has given way to the world car.

Unifying and Differentiating Influences. The concept of unifying and differentiating influences, first suggested by Professor Fayerweather, has provided to be of durable significance. The successful international marketers are skilled at identifying what is the same and what is different in each national market. This skill enables them to profit from the economies of standardization and at the same time to adapt the marketing program where this is necessary in order to compete and meet the wants and needs of customers. One of the lessons of the past decade has been that the mastery of this skill is essential to success and indeed survival in the international marketplace. Philips discovered this in attempting to compete in the European TV markets with 14 different models on six different chasis, while their Japanese competitors were offering two models and one chasis for the entire European market. Philips had over-differentiated its product at cost and was not able to compete effectively with the Japanese because of its higher costs.

Leverage. Leverage is a term first introduced by Ralph Z. Sorenson, formerly Professor of International Marketing at Harvard, and then President of Babson College, and now President and CEO of Barry Wright Corporation. Basically, leverage is the sum of advantage that accrues to the international marketer who works smarter than his domestic counterpart. Leverage is in effect the international term for what the Boston Consulting Group has called the experience effect. This is the decline in costs that comes from increasing volume in well-managed firms. It includes the well-known scale economies, but goes beyond manufacturing to include the economies that come from working smarter in general management and marketing. Sorenson, in his classic study of competition in the detergent markets in Central America, discovered that the local companies, in spite of the fact that they were technically state-of-the-art (the general manager of one company had a Ph.D. in chemical engineering from MIT), were unable to compete with the international soapers like Colgate because the international soapers had the leverage of their accumulated marketing experience at their disposal and they used it effectively.

Product/Market Life Cycle. Understanding the product/market life cycle relationship is essential to the success of an international marketing plan. Companies that manage this relationship well do not make the mistake of unconsciously projecting their experience in the home or any market onto other target markets. The paradox of this factor is that the more successful the company, the greater is the danger that it will miss the turn on the product/market life cycle relationship. Polaroid, for example, in its attempt to enter the European market in the late 1960s, was unable to respond to the fact that the Polaroid concept was unknown in Europe, and that the entire marketing strategy that had been managed 20 years earlier in the United States was going to have to be managed again in Europe. Instead the company unconsciously projected its mature market strategy into the European marketing plans.

Today, IBM appears to be guilty of making this mistake in Japan. IBM, the world leader everywhere in the world except Japan, continues to behave like the market leader in Japan instead of like the underdog that it actually is. The company's share of market continues to erode, and its competitors continue to get stronger as their Japanese market positions strengthen.

Ethnocentric, Polycentric, and Geocentric. The terms ethnocentric, polycentric, and geocentric were coined by Howard Perlmutter of the Wharton School to describe the orientations of companies and individuals toward international business. These orientations are a valuable conceptual tool for international marketers because they help to identify unconscious assumptions about markets. Ethnocentric refers to a home country orientation or an unconscious bias or belief that the home country approach is best. An enthnocentric orientation may or may not work. It all depends on whether or not it is appropriate. If the home country product line is right for the world, then an ethnocentric product policy will be a successful policy. If it is not appropriate, then this policy will fail. American and Japanese companies have tended to be ethnocentric in their overall orientation, although the Japanese companies have rarely been ethnocentric in their marketing mix policy.

The polycentric orientation is the opposite of ethnocentric. It is the unconscious bias or belief that it is necessary to adapt totally to local culture and practice. Again, like the ethnocentric orientation, this orientation will be effective if it is appropriate. The major small country European multinationals have tended to be polycentric in their orientation.

The geocentric orientation is a synthesis of the ethnocentric and polycentric orientations. It is the belief or assumption that there are similarities and differences in the world and that these similarities and differences can be understood and adapted to in an integrated world strategy. The geocentric orientation does not assume that the home country approach is better, nor does it assume that there must be a total adaption to the local market and culture. It looks at issues of adaptation versus extension (no adaptation) on their merits, and seeks to come up with a design that maximizes customer value and at the same time minimizes company cost. Clearly, this approach is the ideal, it is fact rather than unverified assumption driven. Under the geocentric orientation, there are no unconscious assumptions. Both the ethnocentric and polycentric approaches are based on unconscious assumptions. The geocentric company and individual look at the facts and seek to create the greatest value for their customers at the least cost.

Learning.   Learning is the final concept that has distinctive importance for international marketing. Warren Bilkey, in his review of the export behavior of firms, identified the stages that firms go through in the process of becoming truly international export marketers [1]. The essential quality of this typology of stages is that each stage requires learning that prepares the firm for the next stage. Thus Bilkey recommends that firms begin their export activity with psychologically close or similar markets. The amount of learning required to market in the close markets is less, and the chances of success are greater since the firm is more comfortable and knowledgeable about the close markets. This corresponds to Perlmutter's ethnocentric, polycentric, geocentric schema, which describes the orientation of the firm towards international business and recognizes that the geocentric orientation is an ideal that can be reached, but that it must come from learning experience in the ethnocentric (home country), and polycentric (host country) orientations.

World Markets

Table 1–1 reports the location of global income and population. The countries and regions of the world are listed in descending order of GNP per capita in U.S. dollars in 1979. North America led the world in income per capita, a position it has enjoyed for more than a century. Japan is a close second, followed by Oceania and Europe, excluding the U.S.S.R. There is a striking concentration of wealth in the world; North America, Japan, Oceania, and Europe including the U.S.S.R. accounted for almost 84% of the world income in 1979.

This concentration of income has led to the formulation of market typologies that distinguish between the developed or industrialized countries, the developing or fast-growing industrializing countries, and the truly underdeveloped countries which have not yet reached the stage of self-sustaining growth. Each company must decide where it wants to focus its international marketing effort. In general, where there are large markets there is entrenched competition. Where the markets are smaller, there is greater risk and uncertainty. Some companies choose to compete in markets at every stage of development, and others have decided to focus on a single stage.

Table 1-1. Global Income and Population—1979

	GNP Par Capital (US$)	GNP (US$00 Millions)	Percent of World GNP	Population	Percent of World Population
North America	10,500	2,597	26	247	6.0
Japan	8,730	1,010	10	116	3.0
Oceania	7,000	154	2	22	1.0
Europe	6,760	3,546	35	524	13.0
USSR	4,040	1,067	11	264	6.0
Middle East[1]	4,310	207	2	48	1
South America	1,730	404	4	233	6
Central America[2]	1,620	172	2	106	3
Africa	700	322	3	456	11
Asia, Excluding Japan and Middle East	310	677	7	2,165	52
World	2,430	10,156		4,181	

Data Source: *1981 World Bank Atlas*, p. 10.

[1]Consists of Bahrain, Iraq, Israel, Jordan, Kuwait, Oman, Qator, Saudi Arabia, Synah Arab Republic, United Arab Emirates, Yemen Arab Republic, and Yemen (People's Democratic Republic of).

[2]Includes Mexico.

Source: Keegan, Warren J., *Multinational Marketing Management*, 3rd ed., 1984. Reprinted with permission from Prentice-Hall, Inc., Englewood Cliffs, N.J.

Strategy

One of the greatest illusions of the domestic company is that the national market defines the competitive field. International competition has become a reality for companies in a growing number of industries and fields over the past decades, and the trend continues. The three basic dimensions of strategy: environment, company, and values and aspirations have undergone a significant re-evaluation as companies have recognized the changing nature of the competitive environment and evaluated their own orientation and capability in relation to the demands and opportunities of international marketing and international competition. Companies in every corner of the globe have looked at themselves and looked at the world and concluded that they want to become international companies. In many cases companies recognized that they were ethnocentric (i.e., unconsciously home country oriented) in many respects and have set out consciously to try to become more geocentric (world oriented) in their attitude and operations.

The broad strategy alternatives are the mass market low-cost producer strategy that is based on going from maximum volume and getting costs down, and the market niche low-volume high-price specialist strategy. These alternatives are illustrated in figure 1–1. The strategy required to

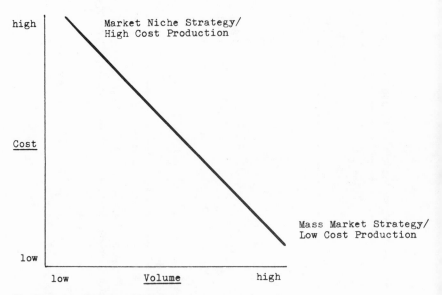

Figure 1–1.   Strategy Alternatives

penetrate and hold a market is to offer something more in total value to the customer than he/she is getting from his/her existing supplier. The advantage might be in price, product, promotion, or place, or any combination of the four.

Competition

The major development in international competition is the ascendency of the Japanese and their leadership and performance as the top performing national company group in the world today. With the Japanese rise, there has been the corresponding American fall from the position of world leadership.

Three Elements of Japanese Marketing Strategy   There are many factors that are part of the Japanese success in the world today. Not the least of these factors is Japanese marketing strategy. Kotler and Fahey have identified three stages of Japanese marketing strategies [2]:

1. Entry
2. Takeover
3. Sustaining or holding position.

Entry Strategy.   The key to successful entry is (a) enter the right markets, and (b) enter them right. The Japanese are skilled in both areas, but especially in the selection of markets to enter. In this area, they have done a number of surprising things, and in the process they have created a very useful example of how government and business can work together to set directions for development. A key element in this process is the selection of target industries and markets for development. Indeed, one of the most impressive innovations of the Japanese is their market selection strategy. Instead of relying exclusively on facts and the past, they also give weight and consideration to their own intuition about the possibilities for market growth and development. The motorcycle market is a good example. Before the Japanese entry, motorcycles were a mature market. After the Japanese entry, motorcycles became a growth market. Why? Because the Japanese made major investments in the industry to lower cost, raise quality and reliability, and generally offer more value to the customer. When they enter a market, the Japanese always offer the customer an advantage. Usually, it is product and price. Higher or greater quality, features, design advantages for the product, and a lower price. The combination is irresistible. This is elementary, but it is remarkable how many times companies enter a new market with nothing to offer.

Takeover.   When the Japanese enter a market, they commit to a long-term goal. One of the most overlooked elements of Japanese strategy is commitment. When the Japanese enter a market, they are not easily blown away by adversity. The Japanese auto companies provide excellent examples of commitment that has been an essential factor in their success. Toyota, for example, entered the U.S. market in 1969 with a model called the Toyopet. This product was such a disaster that, after a year of trying to sell the car, Toyota had to ship unsold cars back to Japan. This kind of experience would put an end to a sales-oriented organization's efforts. Toyota is, however, a marketing-oriented company, so when they realized that they could not compete in the United States with a product designed for Japan, they gathered all the information they could find about their experience and the U.S. market and went back to work designing a car for the U.S. market. Today, Toyota is a U.S. and world market leader in an industry where every year another follower drops by the wayside.

Twenty- and thirty-year plans for market takeover are not uncommon. Rome was not built in a day, and the Japanese know that taking over a market takes time and commitment. The quarter-to-quarter earnings measure is not applied to the evaluation of the performance of a management team that is pursuing a long-term goal of market takeover. Resolution, hard work, persistence, and all the basic *good* values are necessary. There is nothing new in this except the application of old principles.

Sustaining or Holding Position.   One of the most impressive aspects of the Japanese competitive approach is their ability to hold markets once gained. This requires a continuous application of marketing principles and discipline. The three basic principles of marketing are customer value, differential advantage, and concentration/focus. If you want to study an application of textbook marketing principles, study the action of Japanese competitors in the marketplace today.

Production—The Fifth P.   One of the distinctive contributions of the Japanese to marketing is their reminder that production, manufacturing, engineering, design, and quality are the essence of customer value for products. The new concept of marketing shifted the emphasis of marketing from the product to the customer, and in the process of implementing the new concept, the product (i.e., manufacturing, design, engineering, quality), was neglected. In effect, the Japanese have added a fifth P to the traditional four Ps of marketing. The fifth P is production, and the essence of production is quality as defined by the customer.

Probe—The Sixth P. The final distinctive contribution of the Japanese to marketing strategy is the addition of probe, or the sixth P, to the traditional four Ps of marketing. Probe stands for scanning or information acquisition, and the Japanese have demonstrated admirable prowess at gathering information about markets and competitors as a basis for formulating their marketing plan and program. In spite of the fact that there are formidable language barriers, the Japanese have scanned effectively for information on which to base their marketing strategy and plans.

The Future of International Marketing

Now that we have seen where we have been, where are we going? My prediction is that there will be continued growth and development of international marketing. I base this prediction on the pattern of underlying trends and factors that one can observe in the present situation. First, the international monetary framework will continue to serve its purpose, which is to enable companies to exchange currency for goods and services. Secondly, the global trading system will be threatened but not dismantled. It is too late now for any country to turn back. Thirdly, global peace as defined here will continue to prevail. Fourth, communications technologies will continue to develop. Capabilities will grow, and costs will continue to decline. The multinational corporation has turned out to be a worldwide institution and not just a U.S. and European device. One of the most significant trends of the past decade has been the rise of the third world multinational to take its place in the ranks of the first world multinationals. Finally, domestic economic growth will return one day. After the shocks and adjustments of the past decade are absorbed, the world will no doubt return to a growth cycle. This will support and encourage the growth of international marketing.

Two major trends will affect the role and future of all companies in the world today. The first is the trend toward symmetry in the relative importance of multinational corporations based in different parts of the world. Only a decade ago, there was a fear of an American takeover of the world economy, and today there is a fear of a Japanese takeover. Tomorrow, there will no doubt be another region or country that is on the ascendent. What is clear is that no country or region has a monopoly on drive, creativity, and energy for commercial effort. Today, there are major new multinationals emerging in third world countries.

A second trend of major significance is the emergence of an increasing number of world-scale industries serving global markets [3]. We are witnessing a shakeout of companies today that is comparable to the shakeout of regional companies that occurred in the countries of the world at the beginning of this century. Companies that find themselves in world-scale industries must choose between going for positions as high-volume low-cost producers for the volume markets of the world, or they must carefully position themselves as high-cost, low-volume premium price products in world markets. Each of these positions is a winning strategy. The companies that take these positions will be known as global enterprises in contrast to the multinational enterprises. The 1960s and 1970s were the eras of the multinational enterprise. The 1980s and 1990s will be the eras of the global enterprise. The losing strategy, which has been demonstrated by the now-defunct British motorcycle industry, is to be a high-cost producer trying to compete in the volume market against a low-cost producer.

Successful companies have demonstrated a great deal of skill in treading the line between the strategy alternatives. The future will require even more attention to insuring that the strategic position of the enterprise is aligned with the competitive realities of the world market.

References

1. Bilkey, Warren J. "An Attempted Integration of the Literature on the Export Behavior of Firms." *Journal of International Business Studies,* 9, Spring/Summer, pp. 33–46.
2. Kotler, Philip and Fahey, Liam. "The World's Champion Marketers: The Japanese?" Unpublished manuscript, November 1981, 22 pp.
3. Levitt, Theodore. "The Globalization of Markets." Harvard Business School Working Paper 83–24, Division of Research, Graduate School of Business Administration, Harvard University, Boston, Mass. 02163.

2 INTERNATIONAL MARKETING AS PART OF THE MARKETING PROCESS

Jan Van Rees

Introduction

This chapter is divided into two parts. The first part is about conceptions in marketing. In part two, the stress is on aspects of international management in a multinational corporation.

International Marketing and Marketing Thinking

There is a tendency in marketing to look with benevolent condescension upon the past and to think that the past has gone forever.

Today we have the management approach, and gone are the days of "bringing goods from producer to consumer" and of the commodity, institutional, functional and technique approaches. By making marketing identical with managerial marketing we lose, however, on practical as well as theoretical grounds, and this loss may well be at the root of the apparent difficulty to give marketing at the international level its right place.

This, in a sense, return to the basics of the marketing discipline has been inspired by over thirty years of activity in a multinational corporation.

15

Marketing as a Set of Specialisms. One wonders, as one wanders through the fields in the area of marketing, how it is possible for one word to be used, on the one hand, as a generic term, designating the flow of goods through society, while on the other hand it is also used for naming as little as only one of the elements of the marketing mix, thus instead of advertising, selling, distribution or product policy. It appears that words can be made to mean what one intends them to mean, and then one finds international marketing lumped together with real estate marketing or even grassroots marketing. To make matters worse, these concepts are also used specialisms and then we get direct marketing or retail marketing. These concepts are thus rewarded for the services they are providing by the recognition of an individual existence in their own right. This I find all highly confusing and I am, therefore, an adherent of recent strivings to take a more coherent or even holistic look at the field.

The Complete Marketing Scene. Certainly when we admit that marketing is basically concerned with the process of moving goods and services in the quantity and quality required by the final user, then we must admit at the same time that marketing activities occur at three levels of aggregation, briefly termed:

1.   the macro level or societal level;
2.   the meso level or branch-of-industry level;
3.   the micro level or level of the individual firm.

At each of these levels, sub-levels can be distinguished, and a quick conclusion is that it would be wrong to generalize broadly about the application of marketing techniques or instruments. One generalization seems justified, though, and that is: marketing means more than juggling with *the four Ps*, with some mathematics thrown in for good measure.

Figure 2–1 shows the field of our attention. When we look at the process that is going on there; how it is influenced, guided, steered, and assisted; and how it expands and contracts, and when we think, moreover, of what has to be done within companies to really develop and move the goods and services, we can conclude that marketing in our day has a place for everything the history of marketing thought has had to offer.

On the basis of this and the observations made under figure 2–1, I have formulated the following contentions and elaborations in international marketing.

The Significance of International Marketing Aspects. My first contention is that only by looking at the three levels at which the goods flow that we can give a logical place to international marketing, or rather marketing at the international level. What is usually termed international marketing is in fact international marketing management.

My second contention is that when we consider marketing to be the study of the marketing system and how it operates at all levels, the term *international marketing* is not necessary at all, since it is part of a system which has international aspects.

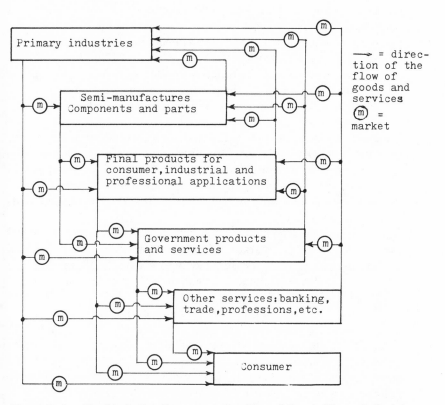

Figure 2–1.   The Marketing Process, or the Flow of Goods Through Society.

Figure 2–1 leads to some comments and observations:

1.   The flow of goods and services has many ramifications.

2.   There occur many reciprocal supplies between primary, secondary, and tertiary industries and government.

3.   The separation between the end of the industry push and the beginning of the market pull cannot be clearly indicated.

4.   All sales activities have a counterpart in purchasing activities.

5.   The international dimension has a place in this stream, but it cannot be unequivocally pinpointed, depending also on the size of a country.

6.   The consumer is really at the end of the marketing process.

7.   The differences between consumer and industrial marketing are not so sharply marked.

Elaborating mainly on the first contention and relating it to MNC practice, we find:

1. When a company is working to a certain degree under a system of backward integration, there exist clear relationships between the flows of goods in several stages of completion. These flows are part of a process to ensure continuous supplies towards the markets for final consumer products. This is the old and always discernible essence of marketing.

2. From the point of view of a MNC with headquarters in a small country, it is unthinkable not to work in terms of international purchase and sales and to be concerned with the different conditions and the different sets of rules and regulations in the several countries of operation. Here marketing is really in essence international marketing in the old as well as the new sense.

3. International business planning forces one to think about plans for different time periods ahead; for different levels of management in different sizes of operation; and for countries in different stages of development. This implies that the corporation must always have the whole body of marketing thought and technique in mind and at its immediate disposition.

4. International operations force a company to collect data about marketing (infra)structures, market forms and institutions, and about all conditions that have to be fulfilled before a market can really be entered. It is also essential to establish the values of the variables that influence the size of the market.

5. Finally, a great deal of attention must be paid to techniques which are not mentioned in most marketing texts but which are of crucial importance to get the products to their destination. In addition to product specifications, transportation, credit terms, packaging, insurance, and conditions of delivery are extremely important instruments and can be considered elements of the marketing mix or of the sales mix. Monetary considerations may determine whether there is a market at all.

This thinking is given some concrete shape in figure 2–1. It shows in basic form not only the flows of goods and services but also the levels at which exchanges take place. Businessmen at each level can see their position and know what action to base on it.

It can be just as well stated that international marketing does not have a place of its own, as that national marketing is a specal case of international marketing. To me, therefore, the label "complete marketing" can be tagged only to marketing at the international level. This statement demonstrates at the same time, however, how dependent marketing thinking can be on the size of the country in which one works and of the opportunities it offers.

In managerial terms, though, international marketing comes mostly after home marketing, and so it again can be concluded that much depends on the place of observation. In small countries, international marketing operations are not just performed by one department of a firm; the whole company must think in terms of international operations and that should make a big difference in practice as well as in teaching in small countries as compared with large countries.

International Marketing as a Term.   It is a curious phenomenon, in fact, that outside the United States—in the non-English-speaking countries—the term marketing was adopted slowly after 1950 and was identified with managerial marketing and to a large extent also with the marketing concept. This marketing concept, with its consumer-orientation, had its missionaries like a religion, and while it attracted many in the consumer product field, it had an antagonizing effect on companies in the non-consumer fields and, decidedly too, international marketing. In my country (The Netherlands), and in other countries as well, it is curious to observe that, with the exclusion of large companies, there exists more interest in international trade, exporting, or international business than in international marketing. Most governments, too, are more active in export promotion or something similar than in stimulating marketing at the international level.

This is significant, since it demonstrates that not only the factual or instrumental difficulties are considered more important than the considerations coming up in international strategy. We may infer from it that few if any exporters make a systematic analysis of world markets before deciding on a specific course of action. This reflects their attitude toward marketing in general and marketing internationally in particular. Most certainly one will find it among exporters of industrial equipment and supplies who still seem to hesitate using the term marketing.

So far my own attitude is to use the term international marketing at micro level in the sense of marketing management. At the macro marketing level, I have no use for the term, as marketing across frontiers is, in the whole process of actively moving goods, not clearly separable—conceptually at least.

I would prefer, instead, to refer to international marketing aspects, international trade, commerce, and exporting. A matter of semantics, one might say; but as far as I am concerned, not entirely so. When reading about the history of marketing, we are taught that the meaning of marketing has been changing all the time, and we get the impression that the past is little more than an interesting curiosity.

I would think, however, that—in practice in any case—the past is still very much with us; and, in particular, those who are engaged in activities across national frontiers go repeatedly through all the old phases. Descriptive marketing comes before managerial marketing; marketing systems remain important in relation to the marketing activities of firms in countries in differing stages of development; and one always has to perform within different cultural areas. This has been well demonstrated by at least some of those who are present on this occasion. One only wonders why that has not become a common preoccupation of marketing scholars. So the three arguments for taking an integrated or holistic view at marketing are based on (1) the flow of industrial products; (2) the practice of multinational corporations; and (3) the process approach or systems approach, which teaches us to look at operations and activities as guided and supported by institutions of all kinds according to time-dependent criteria and techniques.

International marketing is just an aspect of it, but still a matter deserving special attention.

Some MNC Experience

For the firm, the basic questions to be asked when trying to cross national frontiers are really very simple:

Do we sell the same products as in the home market?

Do we use the same advertising approach?

Do we ask the same price and do we use the same selling conditions?

Do we use the same distribution methods?

Do we approach the same target markets?

To solve the underlying problems no matters of principle are involved, since solutions depend on:

The local possibility to use our usual methods;

The firm's capacity and ability to take the methods abroad;

Specific local conditions;

The business climate;

The business infrastructure.

All admonitions and exhortations to take a global attitude in developing business abroad notwithstanding, international management must take a separate look at each individual country. Each country, moreover, must be judged mainly by its own standards, which is really another way of stating that international marketing is a different thing for different levels of a firm's international operations. They are, thus, in effect a sum of marketing efforts at local level which are very hard to compare indeed.

From my own experience I shall give a short description of two instances that illustrate how hard indeed it is to give guidance to certain international operations. The first one concerns overall management performance and in particular the sales performance. The second one is about advertising. These examples are not intended as a basis for generalization, though surely there will be firms that have had similar experiences on their path to international growth.

Commercial Award

In the particular MNC, an award was instituted not so long after World War II in order to start some competition among local managements with the dual purpose of (a) increasing turnover and (b) making these managements feel more a part of an internationally operating concern. The award was to be given on the basis of a year's performance in commercial and industrial management. A jury was appointed each year to select the winner according to strict criteria. There was a semi-permanent secretariat.

However, what seemed at the beginning a simple thing to do became always more complicated, because product ranges widened, turnovers reached upper limits, markets became saturated, companies had to work under changing and often difficult political situations, and so on. On top of that it appeared that some companies always outdid the other ones in terms of profit and, so as not to discourage these other ones, certain handicaps had to be introduced in order to give all concerned a chance of winning the award.

The question of *Who operates best?* can be answered fairly only by taking operating conditions into account. Since these changed all the time, the whole operation turned into a kind of Alice-in-Wonderland Caucus Race. Everyone wins, and if not by other people's criteria, then certainly by their own. And so the excercise died its own death, bringing international comparison no nearer than the usual comparison of profits and market shares, which is not enough for judging the real performance.

International Advertising Management

There has been an enormous concentration in the advertising world, so that the largest advertising agencies are now international agencies. They started going abroad in order to serve their internationally operating clients in the same way as at home and in order to be more able to design and operate international advertising campaigns. This development has indeed been welcomed by forms serving international markets.

However, the strange thing is that, with some notable exceptions, there seems to be little real advertising left in the sense of: identical advertising campaigns running in a number of countries while using more or less the same media and identical themes. I would even say that—the *Reader's Digest's* efforts notwithstanding—these international campaigns have not developed greatly. This I see as a consequence of:

Changed attitudes towards advertising,

The impossibility of using identical sales arguments and pictorials,

The unequal use that can be made of television,

The disappearance of family magazines, and

The reduced importance of the newspaper.

As a consequence, advertising has always to be adapted to the local situation and it is very hard, if not impossible, to direct from a central point, such as the headquarters of a multinational corporation.

During a period of five years, I have been involved in a succession of multinational advertising experiments, both as regards the theme of the advertising as the composition of the advertising budgets. The aim was to establish whether budgets of a certain size and composition improved the advertising effect in terms of sales, as well as of brand knowledge and product acceptance.

On the whole, the experiments and accompanying research were very instructive and helpful in the sense that they were instrumental in setting upper advertising expenditure limits. This was a gain, but the forecasting value was low and no important general tendencies were found, with one exception: the management of each country involved thought the findings from the other countries were very interesting, but gave no guidance for their own situation. When so much time and energy are spent on a project with so little impact, it will be dropped, of course. Still, this was not entirely the end.

Apart from the not-invented-here syndrome and the doubts about the relevance of international findings for one's own problems, the problem of international comparison remains. There do exist international statistics, but their degrees of comparability vary greatly. This may be particularly irksome for detailed analysis of factors determining market size, such as family or household size, income distribution, and a great many more, such as advertising expenditure. Even within a corporation there may exist differences in definition and hence incomparabilities between the affiliated companies. Given the reluctance to adopt suggestions from abroad by national affiliations, the central advertising people thought that by showing the differences in the composition of advertising budgets and expenditure, also in terms of a proportion of sales, they could still exert an influence, be it of an indirect nature, on expenditure. Unfortunately for the people who threw themselves on this work it proved a failure. No one in headquarters was able to prove local management wrong in the conduct of their advertising, and all comparisons made—though they often supplied interesting insights—did not lead to real policy recommendations, apart from what product management contributed.

The evident conclusion thus is: every country leads its own existence and therefore every country will have to be given its own treatment.

During my years of business travel abroad, I did not know that George Bernard Shaw had written somewhere: "I don't like to feel at home when I am abroad." It means, I think, do not get dulled by the familiarity of the surroundings and the people and keep your eyes open to all that is different from home and therefore more exciting. Still, I have tried to act in that sense and, being able to express myself in several languages, I have thoroughly enjoyed what I like to call the adventure of international communication, which is always an adventure since, though we may be speaking to all appearance the same language, people are still separated by the cultural area they live in.

The practice of marketing at the international level has, therefore, in addition to the typical marketing aspects at meso and macro level, important cultural anthropological dimensions and is therefore a field of application of wide knowledge.

In teaching marketing, I think that the international aspects of marketing are useful for demonstrating in a roundabout way how important it is not to take things for granted. Practice gives the best demonstration of how knowledge and experience from many areas can be combined to achieve objectives that are based on a multitude of stimuli, many of which come from preliminary research and intelligence.

Back in 1922, Cherington wrote that he could not find a satisfactory term that comprised all the activities that have to be performed for moving goods from primary producer to ultimate consumer. That satisfactory word still does not exist. We still make do with the term *marketing* and make it serve the development in our thinking. But let us not forget that it is basically about making goods and services flow, however complicated we make it through additional rules, regulations, norms, ethical considerations, politics, ecology, and other influences and developments. It then depends on the level at which we are thinking whether the term international marketing is really needed. In any case it should be a warning to let ourselves be more particular in the choice of our words, and let us try to reduce the dimension of adventure in the international communication about marketing.

3 INTERNATIONAL BUSINESS THEORY AND MARKETING THEORY:
Elements for International Marketing Theory Building

Helmut Soldner

State and Potential Directions of International Marketing Conceptualization

International marketing has been characterized repeatedly as one of the marketing areas in which work by practioners is often more advanced and insightful than its conceptualization by academicians.[1] The global marketing strategies implemented by successful multinationals, in particular, lend considerable support to such an assessment.

If we turn to the first part of the Delphi study conducted for this conference, it becomes obvious that theory development in international marketing is hampered already by a lack of a clear definition of what international marketing really is.[2] Defining the scope of international marketing appears to be at the heart of this problem. Sometimes one may even wonder whether we have sufficiently delineated the core of knowledge necessary to progress on the road of international marketing theorizing. Our methodological advances, frequently with a massive attention to data-analytic methods, may have been greater than our efforts to build the appropriate conceptual foundations.

How then can progress in international marketing conceptualization be achieved—even by way of discovering the existence of more black boxes than we have previously known? Chances are that the question about the particular features of international marketing and the special nature of idiosyncratic multinational marketing concepts has to be raised once more. One key to the answer will be a precise notion of the multifaceted nature of international marketing processes and structures. This will provide us with further insights into the breadth and comprehensiveness of study to develop a theoretical basis in international marketing. Toward this end, the participants, types of transactions, and strategies in international marketing are to be related to the multiproduct, multifunction, and multination parameters of international business activities. To date, the major conceptual bias of the international marketing community has been in the direction of internationalizing marketing (management) concepts, frequently with an even greater lopsidedness toward the international marketing practices of American multinationals. Thus, our primary concern has been with operational and micromarketing management decisions, as conditioned by the international task environment of the firm. International marketing operations are perceived as extensions of domestic marketing activities; international marketing conceptualizations are seen as extensions of domestic marketing concepts.

Recently, however, there is a growing awareness that we should look for a fuller range of international marketing specificities by adopting a stronger macro perspective.[3] For it is the overall macroeconomic—and general environment—parameters which govern a great many of the more basic strategic international marketing decisions, which in turn circumscribe or condition international marketing mix decisions to a fairly high degree. The more international firms can be viewed as global systems for market development and exploitation, characterized by a multiplicity of relationships with their environments or stakeholders,[4] the closer the attention we have to pay in our conceptualizations to the interplay of basic international marketing (strategy) decisions, general business policy[5] decisions, and firm-exogenous decision factors. Generally, the conceptual emphasis will shift not only toward the macro-environment of international marketing, but also toward the joint analysis of both micro and macro variables as interactive sets.

International marketing thus reads "internationalization and marketing." Following the research perspective adopted above, our major emphasis would be on marketing in the international macroeconomic environment. This suggests that we may want to turn, inter alia, to the disciplines explaining international economic relationships and exchange processes, in order to look for concepts and empirical results which might be integrated into more macro-oriented conceptualizations of international marketing. Of course, this synthesizing effort would be greatly facilitated if there would already be a stronger macro orientation also in recent marketing theorizing.

Marketing Theory

Indeed, the latest additions to the base of marketing theory lend considerable support to our perceived stronger conceptual macro orientation in international marketing. Specifically, we are talking here about the generic marketing paradigm, particularly in its social marketing variety, and the emerging area of macromarketing, including the notion of macromarketing management. The newest subfield of strategic (marketing) planning also reveals stronger macro connotations. Under the space constraints given, and before an audience of seasoned marketing scholars, a very brief characterization of these young branches on the marketing tree, and some of their links with the international marketing branch, will have to do.[6]

Generic/Social Marketing

In the *generic* definition, marketing is a social activity and technique to obtain desired responses from any audience targeted. Marketers are all parties/organizations relating to and exchanging values with their publics. This pertains directly to the international firm with its great variety of external relations, or stakeholders, and its high public visibility. More specifically, *social marketing*[7] implies the application of established marketing concepts and (economic exchange) techniques to the marketing of various socially beneficial (or at least sanctioned) ideas, causes, and practices. International firms, sometimes labeled as change agents or at least innovators, frequently are to effect social and economic change as a prerequisite for opening up new markets (LCD's!), by motivating and facilitating socially desirable and discouraging undesirable forms of living and behavior.

Macromarketing (Management)

Macromarketing analyzes marketing phenomena from a societal perspective, comprising the following:[8]

1. The impact of exchange systems and marketing operations on national/global societies with their various subsystems (educational, political, consumers, governments, etc.). International marketing

scholars will be particularly interested in the effects on socioeconomic developments, and the productivity and equity generated by various exchange modes and systems, primarily under societal welfare aspects.

2. The impact of environmental parameters on exchange systems and marketing practices. For the international marketer, this means especially constraints and opportunities associated with natural, technological, socio-political/legal, and cultural factors in host and home countries.

3. Respective comparative marketing analyses. In this context, reference to Boddewyn's excellent recent "state-of-the-art" review[9] must suffice.

4. Public policy issues, as related to exchange acts and systems, particularly with regard to objectives of social welfare/justice.

This is the notion of macromarketing management, comprising the administration of public policy in the framework of increased government-marketer interaction. Marketing is viewed as a socio-economic process that must be managed for private gain as well as for the public good.[10] Of special relevance for international marketing theorists: the more socially important the goods/services provided by international firms, the larger or more dominant international firms in individual markets, the higher their joint micro/macro responsibility—as in the case of LDC's.[11] Accordingly, macromarketing management theorizing would generate more normative models, providing guidance for plans whereby international (micro)marketing management might contribute to economic and social development and welfare on a regional, national, and supranational level.[12]

Strategic (Marketing) Planning

This latest expansion of marketing thought also reveals stronger macro connotations. Still beset by definitional and conceptual ambiguities, there is already a pronounced trend to move on from strategic planning to strategic management,[13] with its stronger business policy[14] and competitive strategy[15] orientation. At this juncture, we only need to reiterate that the merging of marketing with corporate planning and strategy formulation turned marketers more into corporate management generalists at the highest level of entrepreneurial decision-making. Here, numerous macro-environmental and macromarketing parameters have to be integrated when determining the strategic fit or dynamic adaptation[16] between the external firm environment and the organizational (internal) setup with its plurality of intrafirm coalition interests and critical resource factors.[17]

Altogether, by moving into these new directions, marketing is in line with a more pronounced environmental orientation in the field of business administration in general, evidenced also by the situational, contextual, and contingency approaches in management theorizing.[18] More specifically, the renewed and broadened macro orientation in marketing is a reflection of the increased societal expectations of marketing—growing with further economic development[19]—for meeting not only consumption needs, but also for acting in other ways in the public interest. "The task of marketing is the linkage between individual economic units themselves and with the social environment".[20]

From here, international marketing—particularly in its more strategic varieties—can expect conceptual support as to the recognition and satisfaction of the relevant societal national priorities. This pertains no longer just to host countries with regard to their national development planning and international economic relations.[21] Parent country priorities, too,[22] will be increasingly included in the analysis—priorities such as the determination of national R & D or sectoral policies,[23] improved export development programs,[24] or the future overall competitive posture of a country and its key industries[25] in a global industries marketplace (as exemplified by the Japanese MITI).[26]

International Investment/Business Theory

Next, the focus is on the second basic structural component of international marketing—the international macro environment—which can be approached along quite a few possible avenues of analysis. As suggested above, macromarketing, for example, implies conceptual links to the political and administrative sciences[27], to development/welfare economics and to cross-cultural studies, inter alia. For the sake of manageable proportions of our analysis, it will be confined to the international macroeconomic environment, with particular emphasis on international economic exchange processes and transfer structures.

Thus, one is referred to international economics and international business theory as the closest fields of exploration when aspiring to increase the paradigmatic diversity in international marketing theorizing via stronger interdisciplinary integration. As a first step in this direction, the question would have to be raised concerning how ready or amenable the related disciplines might be for such integrative efforts.

Economics, the mother discipline, still is quite often too readily discarded, due to our early adopted verdict of being much too abstract, macro-oriented, and technologically deterministic. After all, wasn't it for such reasons that marketing broke away from economics around the turn of the century?[28] But perhaps most of us have not been looking hard enough at the more recent developments "across the fence." Should we not have asked the following question: Just as marketing has adopted a stronger macro orientation (again), has economics—particularly its international branch— perhaps integrated more market-/marketing-related aspects?

Indeed, there is recent evidence for tendencies in (international) economics to move closer to reality, or at least to our realities. Consider the more pronounced lowering of the level of analysis not only to industries but also to singular economic units, e.g., in industrial organization theorizing.[29] Then you will recall the Linder or Vernon international trade theories, where emphasis is more on demand (factors) instead of the supply side.[30] Add Caves, as well as Grubel and Lloyd with their stress on differentiated (higher technology) products, advertising, and various types of economies of scale, to explain foreign direct investment[31] or intra-industry trade[32] (in our terms: MNC market interpenetration).

At this juncture, add to the picture the empirical verification that market/ marketing-related factors regularly are on top of foreign direct investment motives, as provided by a score of FDI studies.[33] Isn't it tempting, then, to look for more marketing elements and resemblances of marketing thought in international trade/investment theory and international business theorizing? And if we were to detect there even clues for sort of a marketing dominance—consistent with our MNC perception of global marketing systems—maybe it could be used as something like a unifying paradigmatic umbrella, under which we could reconsider, reinterpret, and integrate quite a few of the partial explanations provided by all the international trade/investment theories and conceptualizations of international business? Subsequently, those might be examined for use as building blocks for a more general and comprehensive theory of international marketing.

One word of caution may be appropriate with regard to such a pluralistic research strategy. There are numerous difficulties of comprehension already produced by the idiosyncrasies of the disciplines involved. When trying to integrate elements from long-separated bodies of thought, you are dealing with diverging scientific languages/terminologies[34] and varying levels of abstraction/aggregation. Operating in a holistic or eclectic fashion at the interface of various disciplines, our understanding is further complicated by the heterogeneous structure of the research heuristics applied, and the paradigms, theories, hypotheses, and conceptual frameworks used.[35] This will become readily discernible when we get now down to look in some greater detail at representative examples of recent theorizing in international economics/business.[36]

In the newer literature on international economics, a century-old brilliant research tradition obviously has made it rather difficult to supplement the time-honored institution of international trade by the more comprehensive and timely notion of international economic involvement. It comprises both international trade and international (direct) investment/production.[37] As suggested above, our analysis will concentrate on the latter by examining selected recent theories on international investment. Given the prevailing heavy emphasis on multinational enterprises, this implies the integration of elements from industrial organization theory, location theory, and particularly the theory of the firm. From here, it is a relatively short step to the most advanced conceptualizations of international business, with their stronger managerial orientation.

Long-Run Theory of the Multinational Enterprise (Buckley/Casson)

The Buckley and Casson theory[38] builds on the basic idea that enterprises tend to internalize markets which are difficult to organize—*imperfect* markets in economic terminology. In his seminal contribution to the theory of the firm, Coase already in 1937 had viewed the firm as an institutional alternative to the marketplace whenever corporate resources are to be marketed or less profitable via the free markets for tangible and intangible goods.[39] Management will then internalize markets, by way of vertical (forward and backward) integration and by subjecting to its control formerly independent customers/suppliers or competitors. This progresses to the point where marginal benefits equal marginal costs. When firms proceed to internalize technology, management know-how, integrated production and distribution, etc., across national boundaries, the multinational enterprise is created.

As marketing scholars, we will be particularly interested in the nature of the products or resources flowing accordingly within the expanded corporate system, instead of being exchanged on imperfect external markets— market imperfections, which for marketers translate into such business realities like a product's "unique selling proposition."

Primary products and the need to regulate their further supply are seen as the driving force of multinationalism until World War II. Since then, the rise of MNCs is determined primarily by corporate objectives to generate, profitably diffuse, and use technical and marketing know-how more in-house than externally. This is due to the difficulty of organizing markets in knowledge. Recently, the internationalization advantages for specialized technical know-how are seen to diminish relative to the advantages of internalizing general marketing expertise.

Such key intermediate products—management and marketing expertise and know-how—become manifest in firm-specific technological leads, patents, innovative marketing techniques, progressive organizational structures, etc. Above and beyond physical intermediate products (e.g., the technology incorporated in chips), it is particularly the streams of intangible intermediate products which link the corporate network of production, distribution, and particularly R + D units. To achieve such linkages through the imperfect (external) markets for intermediate products would be rather costly in terms of time and money—if at all possible.

Consider, for example, the not-patentable knowledge incorporated in innovative products. How do you negotiate an adequate price with a potential licensee between the Scylla of unveiling enough information for a good licensing fee and the Charybdis of excessive, imitation-prone disclosure? Consequently, the firm will tend to internalize this market via acquisition of prospective licensees (remember in this connection the well-known appropriability problems of R + D expenses, e.g., between MNC headquarters and subsidiaries). In international markets, the avoidance of national controls and governmental market interventions—in the form of taxes, earnings repatriations, and exchange regulations—appears as an additional internalization advantage.

The internationalization of firms, then, is a natural consequence of the internationalization of knowledge markets, inasmuch as corporate resources, like know-how and expertise, can be utilized by additional firm units without extra cost, nationally as well as internationally. The internal cross-border transfer of know-how is all the more advisable as the internalization of new knowledge generated by R + D regularly calls for corresponding expansions in the production and marketing areas. "Thus unless comparative advantage or other factors restrict production to a single country, internalization of knowledge will require each firm to operate a network of plants on a world-wide basis." "An MNE is created whenever markets are internalized across national boundaries."[40]

The authors' attempts for empirical verification center on regression-analytic data indicating that firms in R + D-intensive industries are among the most highly internationalized. (Of particular interest to our Dutch hosts: multinationals from the Netherlands and West Germany show the highest concentration on research-intensive industries.) Generally, multinational enterprises tend to predominate in highly concentrated industries in which intensive use is made of R + D, management, and marketing skills. Evidence of respective higher intra-firm exports—moving goods, parts, and components through the MNC global system—is strengthened by the recent comprehensive study by Dunning and Pearce on *The World's Largest Industrial Enterprises.*[41]

For a brief evaluation, let's return to the basic thought in the Buckley-Casson theory. With its emphasis on the cost-efficient, appropriation-oriented[42] internalization of resource flows and other transactions, the theory continues in the long-established cost orientation of conventional (international) economic theory. To be sure, the Buckley-Casson conceptualization pays a much greater attention to marketing factors than other work extending on Coases' central idea—notably the markets and hierarchies version by Williams, focusing on the economics of transaction costs.[43] But while featuring a certain amount of marketing terminology, Buckley and Casson remain supply- or production-oriented in the last analysis.

In the eyes of the marketing scholar, we would rather conceive the international firm as a global marketing system, which through coordinated multinational marketing strategies and integrated operations relate corporate resources to worldwide market(ing) opportunities. In this perspective, the internalization of intermediate markets for mainly intangible proprietory assets (such as knowledge) enters the picture more after the internationalization of markets for final products. Accordingly, we would hesitate to subscribe to the notion advanced by Buckley-Casson that the internationalization of firms is a by-product of the internalization of markets for intermediate products. One might be at greater ease viewing internationalization processes not as the incidental result of internalization, but to observe that today the internationalization of firms frequently progresses by way of internalization. For it is the international markets of final users which determine the chances of success for potentially internalizable knowledge. Part of this knowledge will also be generated by foreign units closely monitoring their country markets in harmony with a more interactive planning (Ackoff) relationship between MNC headquarters and subsidiaries.[44] Accordingly, the birth and rise of international firms would be primarily determined by the corporate rationale to profitably exploit product and process innovations via cross-border transfers in the international markets.

The firm's mode of entry into these markets is firstly conditioned by local (host country) market parameters, the overall environmental factors, and global synergy considerations. The decision between exporting, non-equity participating ventures (such as licensing), foreign direct investment (FDI), and combinations thereof, is then *also* influenced by internalization considerations. Here, above and beyond the original market imperfections, considerable weight has to be attached to the strong competitive posture achieved particularly by innovative and marketing-oriented firms in frequently oligopolistic markets through their product differentiation and promotional policies.

Generally, marketing parameters will have to be entered to a stronger degree into the equation of supply(cost)- and demand(revenue)-related factors, which eventually determines the appropriate degree of internalization (or externalization in times of growing international subcontracting[45]). Included are more macromarketing determinants accounting for increasing host-country government pressures toward joint venture-type operations, particularly in maturing industries. Considerations of such centrifugal political influences merge with a more differentiated, contextual view of the alleged economic advantages of vertical integration. Accordingly, our MNC research perspective will broaden from strongly centralized, globally integrated systems of international production to strategically flexible, market-oriented combinators of input and output factors when international firms strive to improve the appropriate situation-specific mix of sourcing and marketing parameters via varying internalization/externalization ratios.

Looking for some obvious conceptual links with recent marketing thought, the concepts of domesticated or administered markets[46] come to mind. An integration with additional theorizing on the structure and workings of horizontally and vertically integrated marketing systems[47] also appears increasingly feasible. The relatively strong emphasis placed by Buckley and Casson on industry-specific factors corresponds with a stronger differentiation between related aspects in consumer goods and industrial marketing—the latter being characterized more by longer-lasting relational situations instead of shorter-lived dealings at arm's length.[48] Refined conceptualizations on interfirm linkages, including findings about the combination of product and know-how relationships and their relation to technological and transactional dependence,[49] could yield further progress. Another avenue might be opened up by integrating the concept of psychic distance in international marketing[50] and the study of the effects of corporate experience as a type of time-related knowledge.[51]

Eclectic Theory of International Production (Dunning)

Before turning to another recent major contribution to international economics, let us re-emphasize our overriding objective of conceptual integration. Along these lines, the Eclectic Theory of International Production developed by John Dunning deserves special attention.[52] It tries to synthesize major strands of previous theorizing on international trade and investment, including the internalization theory by Buckley and Casson.

As we remember, the internalization approach (and the related markets and hierarchies school), by concentrating mainly on market imperfections/ failures and economies of interdependent activities, explains mainly the *how*, the mode of servicing foreign markets: exporting versus contractual arrangements versus FDI. Less attention is devoted to the *why*, while the *where* of international business activities is not explained at all.

Consequently, it appears logical to integrate the theory of the firm, as represented by the internalization paradigm, with the two other major lines of FDI theorizing: industrial organization theory, and trade and location theory. The former concentrates on firm-specific advantages (that create oligopolies), identifying the characteristics of international firms that give them a net competitive advantage over other firms that might supply the same foreign market(s). Superior technology, innovative capacity, and product differentiation appear to have the highest explanatory power, according to recent empirical testing.[53]

Trade and location theory traditionally emphasized resource availability and transportation costs as major decision factors for firms to produce in one country rather than another. As of late, market size repeatedly has emerged in statistical analyses among the most relevant variables identifying the host (and home) country-specific advantages directing FDI.[54]

Until recently, these and other international trade/investment theories—such as international trade theory in its classical comparative cost or modern product life cycle version, or capital and portfolio theories[55]—evolved by and large independently of each other. Thus they could add only partial dimensions to the understanding of the total FDI or international business phenomenon. The explanatory potential is greatly enhanced when the major strands of theorizing are integrated. Consequently, Dunning relates firm-specific, country-specific, and internalization advantages to each other. This, then, determines international firm preferences for the three basic modes of servicing international markets—exports, contractual resource transfers, and FDI:[56]

For all three of these international marketing modes, a firm-specific ownership advantage (e.g., innovative product) is deemed a necessary condition. It is a sufficient condition for contractual arrangements only. Overseas subsidiaries (FDI) will be preferred if a firm finds it more profitable to internalize its advantages (knowledge/know-how), and to use them in conjunction with the advantages offered by a foreign location.

The greater the ownership advantages of firms, the stronger the incentive for exploitation within the corporate system ("hierarchy") via internalization. The more the internalization-related economics of production and

Table 3–1.   Alternative Routes of Servicing Markets

	Advantages	Ownership	Internalisation	(Foreign) Location
Route	Foreign direct investment	Yes	Yes	Yes
of				
Servicing	Exports	Yes	Yes	No
Market	Contractual resource transfers	Yes	No	No

Source: Dunning, J. H.: INTERNATIONAL PRODUCTION AND THE MULTINA-TIONAL ENTERPRISE, London: George Allen & Urwin (Publishers) 1981. Reprinted with permission of the publisher.

marketing favor the domestication of international markets, the higher the propensity to establish foreign subsidiaries. The chances of internationalization for particular industries of a specific country are then determined by the degree to which its firms possess these advantages and by the locational advantages of that country relative to those offered by other countries.

Specifying the nature of these advantages in some greater detail, ownership advantages can be divided in a group of general ones, open to any firm, and special ones generated by the firm's multinationality. Additionally, we can separate synergetic advantages for subsidiaries of established international firms over new entrants. The following summary of the general advantage categories relates them to major types of international business activities and representative industries:[57]

In a further refinement of Dunning's conceptualization, the more specific varieties of advantages in our general categories of ownership, location, and internalization are shaped by company-specific, industry- and country-specific parameters. This can be illustrated by integrating some elements of the international product life cycle. Ownership advantages, by their very nature, are firm-endogenous at a specific point in time. However, in a longer-run perspective—as demonstrated by Vernon—they also depend, inter alia, on the demand structure of the firm's home country, and the R + D-intensity of the industry.[58]

In the last analysis, then, type and intensity of international business activities are determined by the interaction between the three categories of advantages with the structural parameters of firms, industries, and coun-

Table 3–2. Types of International Production: Some Determining Factors

Types of International Production	Ownership Advantages (The why of MNC activity)	Location Advantages (The where of production)	Internalisation Advantages (The how of involvement)	Illustration of Types of Activity which Favor MNEs
Resource based	Capital, technology, access to markets	Possession of resources	To ensure stability of oil supply at right price. Control of markets	Oil, copper, tin, zinc, bauxite, bananas, pineapples, cocoa, tea
Import substituting manufacturing	Capital, technology, management and organizational skills; surplus R & D and other capacity, economies of scale. Trademarks.	Material and labor costs, markets, government policy (e.g., with respect to barrier to imports, investment incentives, etc.)	Wish to exploit technology advantages, high transaction or information costs, buyer uncertainty, etc.	Computers, pharmaceuticals; motor vehicles, cigarettes
Rationalized specialisation (a) of products (b) of processes	As above, but also access to markets	(a) Economies of product specialization and concentration (b) Low labor costs, incentives to local production by host governments	(a) As type 2 plus gains from interdependent activities (b) The economies of vertical integration	(a) Motor vehicles, electrical appliances, agricultural machinery (b) Consumer electronics, textiles and clothing, cameras, etc.

Table 3-2. Continued

Types of International Production	Ownership Advantages (The why of MNC activity)	Location Advantages (The where of production)	Internalisation Advantages (The how of involvement)	Illustration of Types of Activity which Favor MNEs
Trade and distribution	Products to distribute	Local markets. Need to be near customers. After-sales servicing, etc.	Need to ensure sales outlets and to protect company's name	A variety of goods, particularly those requiring close consumer contact
Ancillary services	Access to markets (in the case of other foreign investors)	Markets	Broadly as for types 2 and 4	Insurance; banking and consultancy services
Miscellaneous	Variety—but include geographical diversification (e.g., airlines and hotels)	Markets	Various (see above)	Various kinds (a) Portfolio investment in properties (b) Where spatial linkages essential, e.g., airlines and hotels

Source: Dunning, J. H.: INTERNATIONAL PRODUCTION AND THE MULTINATIONAL ENTERPRISE. London: George Allen & Unwin (Publishers) 1981.

tries. This is shown by table 3–3, which also serves to illustrate to which degree this branch of international economics has actually gotten down to international business and marketing aspects:[59]

Before isolating some potential links with international marketing theorizing, it appears advisable to deal with Fayerweather's conceptual framework of international business. Once the conceptual relationships between Dunning and Fayerweather have been established, a synoptic look at the stepping stones for further international marketing conceptualization contained in the work of these authors will be more rewarding.

Conceptual Framework of International Business Management (Fayerweather)

Among the contributions to a foundation for international business theory,[60] Fayerweather's Conceptual Framework[61] excels with regard to the level and breadth of conceptualization. This automatically renders it a prime prospect for our synthesizing efforts.

Fayerweather explicitly erects the framework of his analysis on the basis of international trade theory (comparative advantage), supplemented by cultural anthropology and political science aspects. This already suggests a certain affinity to the explanatory concepts considered so far. We discover it in the first, bi-national dimension of Fayerweather's conceptualization, where he perceives the international firm as the institutionalization of the inter-nation transfer of varied economic resources. These transfers are governed by the economic exchange relationships between two countries, which are caused by economic differentials (like natural resources, skills, and demand structures), and conditioned by political and cultural factors. The final determination of corporate transfer possibilities, however, depends on the structural characteristics of the international firm. Combining these factors, the transfer of skills—technological, managerial, and entrepreneurial skills above and beyond raw materials, labor and capital— emerges as the primary motive for international business activities.

Reduced to the formula "resource transfer (capabilities) to economic differentials," we can now detect strong similarities with Dunning's corresponding formula "ownership advantages as related to location advantages." Thus, it would be the common denominator of both explanatory concepts that international firms utilize their strongest resources, ownership advantages, in countries offering the most favorable economic conditions location advantages.

Table 3-3. Some Illustrations of How Ownership-Location-Internalization (OLI) Characteristics May Vary According to Structural Variables

OLI Characteristics	Structural Variables Country Home—Host	Industry	Firm
Ownership	Factor endowments (e.g., resources and skilled labor), market size and character. Government policy towards innovation, protection of proprietary rights, competition and industrial structure. Government controls on inward direct investment.	Degree of product or process technological intensity. Nature of innovations. Extent of product differentiation. Production economics (e.g., if there are economies of scale). Importance of favored access to inputs and/or markets.	Size, extent of production, process or market diversification. Extent to which enterprise is innovative or marketing-oriented, or values security and/or stability, e.g., in sources of inputs, markets, etc. Extent to which there are economies of joint production.
Internalization	Government intervention and extent to which policies encourage MNEs to internalize transactions, e.g., transfer pricing. Government policy towards mergers. Differences in market structures between countries, e.g., with respect to transaction costs, enforcement of contracts, buyer uncertainty, etc. Ade-	Extent to which vertical or horizontal integration is possible/desirable, e.g., need to control sourcing of inputs or markets. Extent to which internalizing advantages can be captured in contractual agreements (c.f. early and later stages of product cycle). Use made of ownership advantages. Cf. IBM	Organizational and control procedures of enterprize. Attitudes to growth and diversification (e.g., the boundaries of a firm's activities. Attitudes towards subcontracting—contractual ventures, e.g., licensing, franchising, technical assistance agreements, etc. Extent to which control procedures can be built

	quacy of technological, educational, communications, etc., infrastructure in host countries and ability to absorb contractual resource transfers.	with Unilever-type operation. Extent to which local firms have complementary advantages to those of foreign firms. Extent to which opportunities for output specialization and international division of labor exist.	into contractual agreements. Type of transactions undertaken, e.g., the degree of uncertainty or idiosyncrasy attached to technology transfers. The frequency with which transactions occur.
Location	Physical and psychic distance between countries. Government intervention (tariffs, quotas, taxes, assistance to foreign investors or to own MNEs, e.g., Japanese government's financial aid to Japanese firms investing in South East Asian labor-intensive industries).	Origin and distribution of immobile resources. Transport costs of intermediate and final good products. Industry-specific tariff and non-tariff barriers. Nature of competition between firms in industry. Can functions of activities of industry be split? Significance of *sensitive* locational variables, e.g., tax incentives, % energy and labor costs.	Management strategy towards foreign involvement. Age and experience of foreign involvement (position of enterprise in product cycle, etc.). Psychic distance variables (culture, language and commercial framework). Attitudes towards centralization of certain functions, e.g., R & D, regional office and market allocation, etc. Geographical structure of asset portfolio and attitude to risk diversification.

Source: Dunning, J. H.: INTERNATIONAL PRODUCTION AND THE MULTINATIONAL ENTERPRISE. London: George Allen & Unwin (Publishers) 1981. Reprinted with permission of the publisher.

In Fayerweather's second, multi-nation dimension of conceptualization, the international firm synergistically utilizes its specific skills in a globally integrated corporate system of production and marketing. The most efficient transmission of firm resources (particularly knowledge and skills) is achieved by means of a sophisticated corporate communication and control system. Constituting a special strength of multinationals, it counterbalances the fragmentation effects of environmental parameters like cultural variables and governmental interventions.

In these determinants, we frequently recognize the causes of market imperfections of the Buckley-Casson model, prompting internalization by way of foreign subsidiaries. This already reveals stronger conceptual links between the theory of internalization and the unification-fragmentation theme in Fayerweather's multi-nation dimension. In a more comprehensive comparison between Fayerweather's Conceptual Framework and Dunning's Eclectic Theory, a high degree of conceptual similarity can be established.

Another similarity between Dunning and Fayerweather lies in the conceptualization of the specific efficiency gains arising from internationalization. Just as Dunning establishes a special category of related multinational ownership advantages,[62] Fayerweather stresses the access of individual subsidiaries to the totality of resources within the global corporate system. When Fayerweather emphasizes the necessity of corporate structural homogeneity (unification) as a new dimension of the firm's resource transfer capabilities,[63] this corresponds with *step two* of the internalization concept: internalization per se produces only part of the MNC advantages—others, as well as the related international business modes, are determined by the increase in efficiency achieved through unification via internalization.

A Dunning/Fayerweather Synopsis: Cues for Integrated International Marketing Theorizing

A stronger eclectic orientation in international investment/business theorizing suggests a more comprehensive and eclectic conceptualization of international marketing as well. In the following discussion, the quest for greater conceptual integration is illustrated by drawing various perspectives for future international marketing theorizing developed from a synthesis of the Dunning and Fayerweather theories.

The basic lesson we may want to draw from Dunning and Fayerweather can be related to the challenge already mentioned above: to recognize and to structure more explicitly those international marketing problems or deci-

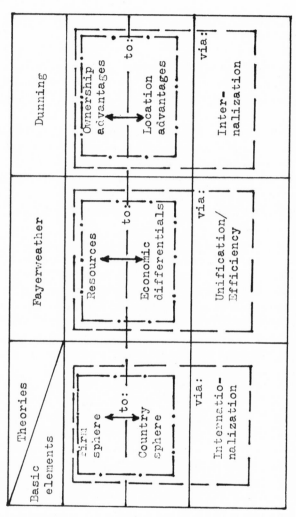

Figure 3–1. A Comparison of the Fayerweather and Dunning Conceptualizations

sions pertaining primarily to the multinational macro-environment. More precisely: to arrive at a better integration of firm-internal micro-management aspects with the external parameters prescribed by the firm's market and non-market macro-managerial environments. Couched in some other, perhaps more familiar, terms: more focus on the interrelationships between the international firm's task environment and global general environment, which translates into more attention to the interplay between strategic, managerial, and operational decision-making in international marketing.

Adopting a holistic and synergistic corporate systems view under the auspices of global competition, the international firm first will determine its basic position with regard to the relevant patterns of economic relations between countries and their industries, including the major competitors. Numerous strategic modifications will have to be made, accounting for the multiple internal and external stakeholder interests to be observed in the wider multinational cultural, social, political, and technological firm environments. Only then the conceptualization will proceed from the overall global strategy to the national marketing program as the specific MNC approach for individual country markets.

Thus, we would account for significant changes in the nature of international business as the extent of multinationality of international firms has widened and deepened. From exporting more or less modified products and overseas investments primarily to utilize local resources (initially raw materials), international firms developed into worldwide production and marketing systems, culminating in MNCs striving for global rationalization and competing in world-scale industries. Regional or global product/process specialization and world product mandating[64] are today among the critical strategic choices in the world business arena.

Both horizontal and vertical specialization and the related intrafirm flow of intermediate and final products is facilitated by advanced telecommunications and computer technologies.[65] Scale economies, integrated markets (internalization efficiencies), and differentials in critical input factors (natural and human resources as host country-specific advantages) yield advantages secured by horizontal specialization. Different final products are produced in different countries (by Philips in the EEC) where the foreign production units specialize in parts of the total product range and supply all other subsidiaries region- or worldwide. Specialization along the verticals of production, in the framework of regionally or globally integrated networks of sourcing, has assigned certain stages in the production process to units in countries with low labor/production costs: e.g., Ireland in Europe, Southeast Asian countries for European, American (e.g. micro-electronics offshore production), and particularly Japanese multinationals. (See Kojima's theory below).

Under these auspices, we may profit the most from the Dunning/Fayer-weather conceptualizations by injecting some degree of multinational/global marketing strategy philosophy. Accordingly, we would superimpose more demand-oriented global corporate strategy objectives on the rather static supply-side/production factors or cost orientation still prevailing in international trade/investment theorizing. To paraphrase in the Chandler tradition, it is today not so much "strategy follows structure," as dictated by country resource differentials, with automatically ensuing flows of corporate skill transfers. Instead, we would view the international firm more in a proactive than reactive role. Under the primacy of market development and protection motives, ownership advantages are nowadays actively created in the marketplace, in order to be related subsequently to worldwide location advantages via appropriate global corporate structures. In this sense, MNC "structure follows strategy." Along these lines, international firms create, alter, and transfer production and distribution factors around the world, sometimes influencing the local conditions of operation to a considerable degree. This implies a strong rationale for opening up new (partial) markets or to restructure them, preferably by a combination of new product introduction and market segmentation policies, resulting in new market imperfections (e.g., via innovative/promotional product differentiation, exclusive dealings, etc.).

As a matter of fact, Fayerweather in his latest writings seems to move over to some degree to this global marketing network perception of the international firm. Besides introducing the notions of product-delivery system and production-marketing system, he refines his overall conceptual scheme by differentiating between an MNC-developed nation model and an LDC-MNC model.[66]

LDC subsidiaries frequently cannot be considered as economically viable within the MNC's global scheme. For them, the needed satisfactory combination of host country cost and demand factors (scale disadvantages!) or a constructive role in the MNC global logistic system are often hard to achieve. Therefore, Fayerweather feels that much of the conceptualization must rest on political distortions (e.g. national development priorities) of MNC-relevant resource flows away from the basic economic differentials (macromarketing connections!).

MNC activities in developed countries are then explained in a "marketing plus scale/learning curve economies" context. Basic is the concept that each firm occupies a distinct market niche, created by market differentiations resulting from marketing mix variations. By way of specialization in the requirements of each niche, and international expansion, economies of scale and learning curve advantages[67] are secured for the international firm. When the market area is expanded from national to global, there are greater opportunities for more firms to compete economically, with a higher number of (world) market niches for feasible exploitation. This is the conceptual basis for mutual marketing area interpenetration by MNCs, as motivated by profits in general and the quest for market position in particular.

With this refined conceptualization by Fayerweather, we have obviously moved into the vicinity of business portfolio and strategic marketing planning concepts. Consider the well-known product-market strategy definition. Let's roughly equate broadly defined *products* with firm-specific advantages, the former constituting the marketing-relevant manifestation of the latter. Substitute country for market. Then it becomes evident that in a broadened, more strategy-oriented conceptualization of international marketing, a third category should be added, as an equivalent for the notion of internalization in international economics.

Advantages of internalization were directly related to what can now be introduced as modes of entry in international business, or more specifically as international marketing modes. Accordingly, we arrive at the combination products—markets—international marketing mode. It constitutes the marketing-strategic equivalent[68] to the above, more general international investment/business combination of firm-specific, country- and internalization-specific advantages. From here, moves to more detailed levels of analysis should follow when trying to determine the role of each specific country market in a global portfolio perspective.

Apart from that, work on integrated global marketing strategy, and the application of portfolio analysis[69] and strategic planning[70] concepts to the international domain are in a rather embryonic stage. In the future, greater attention has to be given to the internationalization of portfolio concepts employing larger variable sets with a stronger environmental input, e.g., the SSP: Strategy-Structure-Performance paradigm (Thorelli/Preston), relating corporate strategy, internal and external firm environment.[71]

Within such a broader conceptual framework, the refined micro categories of the Wind/Douglas matrix[72]—with its undifferentiated *country* category—could be integrated with the home country—host country variables of the Dunning conceptualization. The latter might be supplemented with a third country category to take care of export platform perspectives,[73] making it more compatible with, e.g., international product policy classifications. Leroy's differentiation between country of R + D efforts, country of production, and country of market could provide a springboard in this direction.[74] Under the macromarketing aspects of increasing firm-government interaction or even cooperation,[75] the enacted environment concept by Weick,[76] expanding on Emery/Trist, might suggest a division of country-specific parameters into the ones to be influenced or not by the international firm.

Against this background, also, some less comprehensive perspectives can be pursued. A few examples may illustrate how, in parts of the overall conceptualizations considered above, future research might progress in a more holistic way.

Among the empirical tests to which Dunning has subjected parts of his theory, the ones pertaining to the FDI positions of countries and the international competitiveness of their industries[77] deserve mention in this context. Not only can we witness the emergence of global industries, but also the carving-out of global market niches by industries of particular countries.[78] The more this is the result of close (home) government-business interaction, starting already with joint global scanning efforts in the case of Japan Inc., the more macromarketing connotations are involved. (Cf. Kojima's theory below).

In the Delphi study, the question of how international marketing could contribute to progress in developing countries appears as one of the most challenging for the profession.[79] Part of the assistance to be given to LDCs will be directed at improved marketing programs for products from their frequently mixed economies in the world market. What would be appropriate exchange structures and international marketing modes (as well as for dealing with the Eastern countries)? Which corresponding roles are to be assumed by MNCs in general[80] and in consideration of their global marketing networks and logistic schemes in particular? More sophisticated conceptualizations will also be needed for stronger moves toward tapping the LDC mass markets via products specifically tailored to the average living conditions, as well as national development priorities,[81] instead of the traditional MNC product-extension strategies directed at upper-LDC market segments.

International marketing analysis will thus extend to a broader range of economic, cultural, and socio-political macro factors. At the same time, it will be increasingly integrated with strategic (marketing) management, in order to play a stronger role in international business decisions. But broader international marketing conceptualizations will be required to structure the evaluation process not only of the economic relationships between alternative investment projects in different countries within the global MNC system. What might be, e.g., the relevant host country parameters when trying to examine a foreign market investment not just in a narrow bargaining power perspective[82] but also through the eyes of the local government planning authorities,[83] as suggested by the macromarketing management approach? In quite a few third world countries, industrial as well as demand structures may be subject to a varying degree of development planning. To this extent, not only macromarketing but also social marketing perspectives are involved. Consequently, international marketing efforts will have to start in many cases with selling ideas and programs, causes and priorities.

One could continue for quite a while to establish additional linkages between the above broader international investment/business conceptualizations and the related subfields of a broadened international marketing theory base. While this has to be done elsewhere, we would just leave it with the observation that there is good support for such efforts offered by a wealth of additional analyses published recently in international economics (e.g., development and welfare economics) publications. Many results of these—also empirical—studies fit in quite nicely into particular cells of our broader conceptual schemes.

Macroeconomic Theory of Foreign Direct Investment (Kojima)

The special position of the Kojima theory in international business theorizing is established by its emphasis on the variations in investment behavior of firms from different countries. It focuses on the compatibility of the investments or activities of international firms with the comparative advantages of host and also home countries.[84]

Kojima contrasts the investment and marketing policies in Southeast Asian (less developed) countries by American MNCs on the one and Japanese international firms on the other side. Japanese international business activities so far showed a relatively strong concentration on low-technology, labor-intensive production processes (such as textiles)—generally industries for which Japan recently lost her comparative advantage (if it ever had one). By establishing subsidiaries in countries with respective location advantages (e.g., South Korea), Japanese firms transfer their ownership advantages (capital, technology), in order to produce there at low cost. These subsidiaries export heavily to third countries (e.g., Indonesia) and the home country. Japan in turn concentrates on comparatively more advantageous higher-technology industries with a strong export potential. Thus a complimentarity between international investments and international trade is established.

This Japanese-type, trade-oriented investment is fundamentally different from the American-type, anti-trade investment behavior. U.S.-American foreign investors are usually in high-technology industries. They transfer comparative advantages to the host countries, where they exploit their leads in knowledge and oligopolistic positions by producing primarily for the local market. Thus, no contribution is made to the development of local comparative advantages and LDC export activities. To the extent that U.S. subsidiaries export back to the home market, they further undermine the comparative advantage of the parent country. Accordingly, such foreign investments tend to forestall or reduce international trade.

As marketing scholars, we have no difficulty to discover quite a few macromarketing (management) perspectives in this theory with its stronger normative overtones. Otherwise, let's reconsider it again from our global corporate marketing system perspective.

From this angle, a stronger rationale than macroeconomic trade or anti-trade aspects will be the position of the individual corporate unit within the synergistically structured world enterprise. While comparative advantage and Japan Inc.[85] aspects are not neglected, they will be subordinated to the leitmotiv of worldwide marketing network efficiency. Accordingly, we have recently come to view the true advantage of Japanese multinationals and their far-spread trading companies[86] as lying in their sophisticated, highly developed marketing systems—in others words, in the possession of international markets.

To open up and defend these markets takes a lot more than just excellence in playing the *4 Ps* game in the international arena. Under orderly marketing auspices, for example, Japanese corporate strategists will presumably view their offshore subsidiaries in Taiwan or Singapore less under Kojima's harmonious trade aspects rather than as an opportunity to circumvent U.S. or European import restrictions against true Japanese products with price-aggressive "Made in Taiwan (Singapore)" lines. Such an evaluation of the Kojima theory seems the more opportune as the protection against low-technology imports (at the bottom of the product cycle) and encouragement of FDI in high-technology industries persists as common denominator of American international trade policy—a relationship which is reversed for Japan and (parts of) continental Europe.[87]

The dominance of global marketing strategy considerations is further suggested by Mason's research: there are no significant differences with regard to ownership and market entry strategies between Japanese and U.S. firms with similar product lines.[88]

Kojima's theory appears to hold promise for further international marketing conceptualization when rendered more dynamic by merging it with, e.g., the (updated) international product life cycle. It may hold still greater potential when drawing greater attention of international marketing theorists to the increased significance of coordinating sourcing and marketing factors in international firms as synergistic global production and (even more) marketing networks—not the least under macromarketing (management) auspices.

Some Future Perspectives of International Marketing Theorizing

In a short résumé, this preliminary overview can be characterized at best as an attempt to isolate some relevant conceptual threads, to structure some of the issues, and to open up some promising perspectives for further advances in international marketing theorizing. Hopefully, the interdisciplinary integration of additional concepts of a more general nature can assist us in making progress toward a broader, more universal conceptual framework for international marketing.

In the future, the hitherto cherished concentration on American international business/marketing will be less and less adequate to capture the already existing, much more complex reality of a truly global international business community. Responding to this challenge, we are on the verge of much-needed greater conceptual or paradigmatic diversity: this with regard to international firms from countries of a different size, stage of economic development, and politico-economic philosophy[89]. The name of the game is no longer just multinationals *from* different home countries but also *in* host countries or regions[90] which vary accordingly.[91] International firms also differ with regard to ownership and size as well as sectors (international marketing for services!) and industries (plus related levels of technology).[92]

Varying degrees of firm internationalization make for strategy variations between initial international investments and moves in a well-established global corporate marketing system.[93] There is offensive-defensive and leader-follower investment behavior.[94] Differences in the overall strategic logic, exemplified by the global-centered versus country-centered MNC continuum (Porter)[95] or other strategy models[96] reflect a broad spectrum of resource strengths and global capabilities[97] owned by international firms of a widely varying nature.

Eventually, the classical MNC, or FDI through wholly-owned production subsidiaries, is losing in dominance as the typical way of engaging in international business, in favor of a greater diversification in international business involvement with a growing non-equity bias. The trend is toward more flexible varieties of ownership, management, and control strategies, resulting in novel forms of participation, coordination, and cooperation in inter-firm relations, based increasingly on contractual arrangements. Appropriate middle-range theories in international marketing, as well as lower explanatory concepts, appear the more feasible as the recent plea[98] for introducing an intermediate meso-marketing level of analysis (e.g., industry studies between micro and macro[99]) are carried over to international marketing theorizing. The obvious conceptual links to corresponding or related work in international economics could also broaden the basis for expanded, stronger interdisciplinary comparative marketing research,[100] which additionally integrates newer results from comparative (strategic) management.[101]

Instrumental will be a stronger multi-cultural approach (e.g., via further "de-Americanization"),[102] yielding more universal building blocks for a theory base of international marketing. "Interscience" comparisons[103] could provide the overall guidance for such synthesizing efforts within a global network of international research cooperation.

The resulting lower or middle-range conceptualizations will have to find their proper place within the broader framework of the more general theoretical schemes outlined above.

Notes

1. In a recent survey among U.S. marketing academicians, international marketing was among the marketing areas ranked last in terms of perceived progress toward theory development. See: Chonko, L. B. and Dunne, P. M. "Marketing theory: A Status Report." In: R. F. Bush and S. D. Hunt (eds.), *Marketing Theory: Philosophy of Science Perspectives.* Chicago: American Marketing Association, 1982, pp. 43–46.

2. Hampton, G. M. and Van Gent, A. "International Marketing in the 1980s and Beyond: Research Frontiers. See: Chapter 12 in this volume.

3. See, for instance, Wind, Y. and Perlmutter, H. "On the Identification of Frontier Issues in Multinational Marketing." *Columbia Journal of World Business* 12 (Winter); 131–39, 1977.

4. Boddewyn, J. "International Public Affairs." In: I. Walter and T. Murray (eds.), *Handbook of International Business.* New York: John Wiley, 1982, Section 42. Gives a detailed account of MNC "non-market" relations. For the management of related conflicts, see Gladwin, T. N. and Walter, I. *Multinationals Under Fire.* New York: John Wiley, 1980.

5. Rowe, A., Mason, R. and Dickel, K. *Strategic Management and Planning: A Methodological Approach.* Reading, MA: Addison-Wesley, 1982, presents the major approaches reported in the literature of the field.

6. Soldner, H. "Marketing's Future in Theory and Practice." *European Journal of Marketing* 17(5), 1983; and Sheth, J. N. and Gardner, D. M. "History of Marketing Thought." In: R. F. Bush and S. D. Hunt (eds.), *Marketing Theory,* pp. 52–58, provide a broader background.

7.   Lazer, W. and Kelley, E. *Social Marketing*. Homewood, Ill.: R. D. Irwin, 1973, covers the societal dimension. For a broader definition, see Spratlen, T. H. "A Conceptual Analysis and Framework for Social Marketing Theory and Research." In: O. C. Ferrell, S. W. Brown, and C. W. Lamb, Jr., (eds.), *Conceptual and Theoretical Developments in Marketing*. Chicago: American Marketing Association, 1979, pp. 166–83.

8.   See the contributions by S. D. Hunt, D. L. Shawver and W. G. Nickels, P. D. White, R. Chaganti, and S. Heede in: "What is Macromarketing: A Colloquium," Parts I and II. *Journal of Macromarketing* 1(1): 7–13, and 1(2): 56–61, 1981.

9.   Boddewyn, J. J. *Comparative Marketing: the First Twenty-five Years*. *Journal of International Business Studies* 12(1): 61–80, 1981.

10.   Bartels, R. *Global Development in Marketing*. Columbus, OH: Grid, 1981. p. 66.

11.   Terpstra, V. "On Marketing Appropriate Products in Developing Countries." *Journal of International Marketing* 1(1): 3–15, 1981.

12.   Behrman, J. N. "Transnational Corporations in the New International Economic Order." *Journal of International Business Studies* 12(1): 29–42, 1981, gives an illuminating account of emerging international sectoral/industrial structures.

13.   Schendel, D. E. and Hofer, C. W., (eds.). *Strategic Management*. Boston: Little, Brown, 1979.

14.   Leontiades, M. "The Confusing Words of Business Policy." *Academy of Management Review* 7(1): 45–45. 1982.

15.   Porter, M. E. *Competitive Strategy*. New York: The Free Press, 1980.

16.   Chakravarthy, B. S. "Adaptation: A Promising Metaphor for Strategic Management." *Academy of Management Review* 7(1): 35–44, 1982.

17.   McDonald, M. H. B. "International Marketing Planning." *European Journal of Marketing* 16(2): 3–32, 1982; Shuptrine, F. K. and Toyne, B. "International Marketing Planning: A Standardized Process." *Journal of International Marketing* 1(1): 16–28, 1981.

18.   Koontz, H. "The Management Theory Jungle Revisited." *Academy of Management Review* 5(2): 175–87. 1980.

19.   Bartels, R. *Global Development and Marketing*, Columbus, OH: Grid, 1981, pp. 2–12.

20.   Meyer, P. W. "The Marketing Functions in the Framework of the Integrative Marketing Concept." *European Journal of Marketing* 14(1): 72, 1980.

21.   See: Rutenberg, D. "Multinational Corporate Planning and National Economic Policies." Paper presented at the annual meeting of the Academy of International Business, Washington, D.C., October 1982.

22.   In greater detail, Hörnell, E. *Foreign Direct Investments and the Home Country Interests*. Working Paper 1982/6, Centre for International Business Studies, University of Uppsala.

23.   Cf. Pugel, T. A. "Comparative Industry Growth Rates in the U.S. and Japan: The Role of Technological Change and Technology Transfer." Paper presented at the annual meeting of the Academy of International Business, Washington, D.C., October 1982.

24.   Czinkota, M. R. *Export Development Strategies: U.S. Promotion Policy*. New York: Praeger, 1982.

25.   See: Dunning, J. H. "Domestic and National Competitiveness, International Technology Transfer and Multinational Enterprises." Paper presented at the 8th Annual Conference of the European International Business Association, Fontainebleau, December 1982.

26.   Ozawa, T. "Japan's Industrial Groups." *MSU Business Topics* 28(4):33–42 1980.

27. See: Arndt, J. "The Political Economy of Marketing Systems: Reviving the Institutional Approach." *Journal of Macromarketing* 1(2): 36–47, 1981.

28. Lazer, W. "Some Observations on the Development of Marketing Thought." In: O. C. Ferrell, S. W. Brown, C. W. Lamb, Jr. (eds.), *Developments in Marketing.* pp. 652–64. Corrects the widespread notion of marketing as just an extension of economic thought: "The study of marketing began on an interdisciplinary basis and later in the 1950s and 1960s returned to the interdisciplinary approach."

29. For a concise summary, see Dunning, J. H. *International Production and the Multinational Enterprise.* London: George Allen and Unwin, 1981, p. 77; and Vernon, R. "Theories of Foreign Direct Investment Taken from the Field of Industrial Organization." In: S. Raveed and Y. R. Puri (eds.), *1977 Proceedings of the Academy of International Business* (Chicago: Academy of International Business, 1978), pp. 115–18.

30. Vernon, R. "The Product Cycle Hypothesis in a New International Environment." *Oxford Bulletin of Economics and Statistics* 41(1): 255–67, 1979. Updated version. For Linder's preference similarity theory, see the brief account in Hood, N. and Young, S. *The Economics of Multinational Enterprise.* London: Longman, 1979, p. 141.

31. Caves, R. E. "International Corporations: The Industrial Economics of Foreign Investment." *Economica* 38(February): 1–27, 1971.

32. Giersch, H. (ed.). *On the Economics of Intra-Industry Trade.* Tübingen: Mohr, 1978.

33. See, for instance, Hood, N. and Young, S. *Multinational Enterprise.* p. 79; Ajami, R. A. and Ricks, D. A. "Motives of Non-American Firms Investing in the United States." *Journal of International Business Studies* 12(3):25–34, 1981.

34. Brodbeck, M. "Recent Developments in the Philosophy of Science." In: R. F. Busch and S. D. Hunt (eds.), *Marketing Theory,* pp. 1–6, discusses language problems in theorizing.

35. See: Anderson, P. F. "Marketing, Strategic Planning and the Theory of the Firm." *Journal of Marketing* 46(2): 15–26, 1982, for divergent research traditions (ontologies and philosophical methodologies) in these domains.

36. Part III draws heavily on an earlier German version written by the author in 1980 as "Neuere Erklärungsansätze internationaler Unternehmensaktivitäten" ("Newer Explanatory Concepts of International Business"). In: W. H. Wacker, H. Haussmann, B. Kumar (eds.), *Internationale Unternehmensführung* ("International Business Management"), Berlin: Erich Schmidt Verlag, 1981, pp. 71–94. Since then, the following review articles on FDI/MNC theories have appeared: Buckley, P. J. "A Critical Review of Theories of the Multinational Enterprise." *Aussenwirtschaft* 36(I): 70–87, 1981; Calvet, A. L. "A Synthesis of Foreign Direct Investment Theories and Theories of the Multinational Firm." *Journal of International Business Studies* 12(1):43–59, 1981; Grosse, R. *The Theory of Foreign Direct Investment.* South Carolina Essays in International Business, No. 3. Columbia, S.C: University of South Carolina, 1981.

37. Dunning, J. H. *Multinational Enterprise.* p. 24, 98.

38. Buckley, P. J. and Casson, M. *The Future of the Multinational Enterprise.* London: Macmillan, 1976.

39. Coase, R. H. "The Nature of the Firm." *Economica* 4(Nov.):386–405, 1937.

40. Buckley, P. J. and Casson, M. *Multinational Enterprise.* p. 45.

41. Dunning, J. H. and Pearce, R. D. *The World's Largest Industrial Enterprises.* Farnborough: Gower, 1981, p. 113.

42. This is the centerpiece of Magee's closely related appropriability theory: by transferring new product/process technology more efficiently within an internationally expanded

corporate system ("hierarchy," cf. 43) than through markets, the MNC solves the fundamental problem of appropriating technological leads completely to itself, in the face of potential imitators. The latest version is Magee, S. P. "The appropriability Theory of the Multinational Corporation." *The Annals of the American Academy of Political and Social Science* 458, November 1981.

43. Williamson, O. E. *Markets and Hierarchies: Analysis and Antitrust Implications.* New York: Free Press, 1975.

44. Hedlund, G. "The Role of Foreign Subsidiaries in Strategic Decision Making in Swedish Multinational Corporations." *Strategic Management Journal* 1(1):23–36, 1981.

45. Hörnell, E. and Vahlne, J. E. *The Changing Structure of Swedish Multinational Corporations.* Working Paper 1982/12, Centre for International Business Studies, University of Uppsala; Germidis, D. (ed.) *International Sub-Contracting: A New Form of Investment.* Paris: OECD Development Centre, 1980.

46. Arndt, J. "Toward a Concept of Domesticated Markets." *Journal of Marketing* 43(4):69–75, 1979.

Arndt, J. "The Market is Dying: Long Live Marketing." *MSU Business Topics* 27(Winter):5–13, 1979.

47. Stern, L. W. and Reve, T. "Distribution Channels as Political Economies: A Framework for Comparative Analysis." *Journal of Marketing* 44(3):52–64; Arndt, J. "The Political Economy," pp. 36–47.

48. Håkansson, H. *International Marketing and Purchasing of Industrial Goods: An Interaction Approach.* New York: Wiley, 1982.

49. Jansson, H. *Interfirm Linkages in a Developing Economy: A Model.* Paper presented at the AIB/EIBA Joint International Conference, Barcelona, December 1981.

50. Hallen, L. and Wiedersheim-Paul, F. *Psychic Distance in International Marketing: An Interaction Approach.* Working Paper 1982/3, Centre for International Business Studies, University of Uppsala.

51. Davidson, W. H. *Experience Effects in Internal Investment and Technology Transfer.* Ann Arbor: UMI Research Press, 1980.

52. Dunning, J. H. *Multinational Enterprise.* (Especially chapters 2–5, which constitute revised versions of Dunning's earlier publications stressing the eclectic approach.)

53. *Ibid.*, p. 78.

54. For Example, *ibid.*, pp. 59–66.

55. See the literature listed in 30 and 36.

56. Dunning, J. H. *Multinational Enterprise*, p. 111.

57. *Ibid.*, p. 49.

58. Vernon moves to a more differentiated analysis in his PLC-re-evaluation (cf. 30).

59. Dunning, J. H. *Multinational Enterprise*, p. 113.

60. Robinson, R. D. "Background Concepts and Philosophy of International Business from World War II to Present." *Journal of International Business Studies* 12(1):13–21, 1981; Macharzina, K. *International Business Theory Development: Remarks on Concepts of Research.* Hohenheimer Betriebswirtschaftliche Beiträge Nr. 9 (Hohenheim Contributions to Business Adminstration), University of Hohenheim, 1980.

61. Fayerweather, J. A. "Conceptual Framework for the Multinational Corporation." In: W. H. Wacker, H. Haussmann, and B. Kumar (eds.), *Internationale Unternehmensführung*, pp. 17–31, is the most recent version. For a broader background, see Fayerweather, J. *International Business Strategy and Administration.* Cambridge, MA: Ballinger, 1978.

62. Dunning, J. H. *Multinational Enterprise.* p. 27, 79.

63. Fayerweather, J. *International Business Management.* p. 216.

64. Etemad, H. "World Product Mandating in Perspective." Paper presented at the annual meeting of the Academy of International Business, Washington, D.C., October, 1982. For adequate financial controls systems, see Simmonds, K. "Global Strategies and the Control of Market Subsidiaries," Chapter 11 in this volume.

65. See: Flaherty, M. T. and Graham, M. B. W. "The Effects of New Communications and Computer-Related Technologies on the Management and Competitiveness of International Manufacturing." Paper presented at the 8th EIBA Annual Meeting, Fontainebleau, December 1982.

66. Fayerweather, J. *Conceptual Framework.* pp. 22–31.

67. See also Terpstra, V. "The Role of Economies of Scale in International Marketing." Chapter 4 in this volume.

68. Luostarinen, R. *Internationalization of the Firm.* Helsinki: Helsinki School of Economics, [2]1980, p. 31, 94.

69. Larréché, J-C. "The International Product/Market Portfolio." In: H. Thorelli and H. Becker (eds.), *International Marketing Strategy.* New York: Pergamon, 1980 (rev. ed.), pp. 296–305.

70. Channon, D. F. and Jalland, M. *Multinational Strategic Planning.* London: Macmillan, 1980.

71. Preston, L. E. Strategy-Structure-Performance: A Framework for Organization/Environment Analysis; and Thorelli, H. B. "Introduction to a Theme." Both in: H. B. Thorelli (ed.), *Strategy + Structure = Performance,* Bloomington, IN: Indiana University Press, 1977, pp. 30–49 and pp. 3–29.

72. Wind, Y. and Douglas, S. "International Portfolio Analysis and Strategy: the Challenge of the 80s." *Journal of International Business Studies* 12(2): 69–82, 1981.

73. See: Moxon, R. W. *Export Platform Foreign Investments in the Theory of International Production.* University of Reading Discussion Papers in International Investment and Business Studies, No. 56, September 1981, for a stronger conceptual orientation.

74. Leroy, G. *Multinational Product Strategy: A Typology for Analysis of Worldwide Product Innovation and Diffusion.* New York: Praeger, 1976, p. 24.

75. Doz, Y. L. *Government Control and Multinational Strategic Management.* New York: Praeger, 1979, especially pp. 37–43.

76. Weick, K. *The Social Psychology of Organizing.* Reading, MA: Addison-Wesley, 1969, p. 64.

77. Dunning, J. H. *Multinational Enterprise,* particularly p. 109, *et sq.*

78. Hout, T., Porter, M. E., and Rudden, E. "How Global Companies Win Out. *Harvard Business Review* 60(5): 98–102, 1982.

79. Hampton, G. M. and Van Gent, A. International Marketing in the 1980s and Beyond: Research Frontiers. See chapter 12 in this volume.

80. See: Dunning, J. H. "Multinational Enterprises and Trade Flows of Developing Countries," In: Dunning, J. H., (ed.), *Multinational Enterprise,* pp. 304–20, for an economic analysis.

81. See: Sethi, S. P. and Etemad, H. "Marketing: The Missing Link in Economic Development." Chapter 7 in this volume.

82. Fagre, N. and Wells, L. T. Jr. "Bargaining Power of Multinationals and Host Governments." *Journal of International Business Studies* 13(2): 9–23, 1982.

83. Dunning, J. H. "Evaluating the Costs and Benefits of Multinational Enterprises to Host Countries: A *Tool-Kit* Approach," In: Dunning, J. H., (ed.), *Multinational Enterprise,*

pp. 357–84, is representative for a rich literature. See also: UNCTC. *Transnational Corporations Linkages in Developing Countries.* New York: ST/CTC/17 E.81 II A 4, 1981.

84. Kojima, K. *Direct Foreign Investment: A Japanese Model of Multinational Business Operations.* London: Croom Helm, 1978.

85. Drucker, P. F. "Behind Japan's Success." *Harvard Business Review* 59(1):83–90, 1981.

86. Tsurumi, Y. *Sogoshosha: Engines of Export-Based Growth.* Montreal: Institute for Research on Public Policy, 1980.

87. Bergsten, C. F., Horst, T., and Moran, T. H. *American Multinationals and American Interests.* Washington, D.C.: Brookings Institution, 1978, p. 297.

88. Mason, R. H. "A Comment on Professor Kojima's *Japanese Type Versus American Type of Technology Transfer.*" *Hitotsubashi Journal of Economics* 20(2):42–52, 1980.

89. From the rich literature already reporting on these variables, just one representative publication each can be quoted here: Agmon, T. and Kindleberger, C. P. *Multinationals from Small Countries.* Cambridge, MA: MIT Press, 1977; Keegan, W. J. and Heenan, D. A. "The Rise of Third World Multinationals." *Harvard Business Review* 57(1):101–09 1979; Zurawicki, L. *Multinationals in the West and East.* Alphen a.d. Rijn: Sijthoff and Noordhoff, 1979.

90. Baumer, J-M. and von Gleich, A. *Transnational Corporations in Latin America.* Diessenhofen: Rüegger, 1982; Takamiya, M. "Japanese Multinationals in Europe: Internal Operations and their Public Policy Implications." *Columbia Journal of World Business* 16(Summer): 5–17, 1981.

91. Neff, N. H. and Farley, J. U. "Advertising Expenditures in the Developing World." *Journal of International Business Studies* 11(2):64–79, 1980.

92. Again, for each variable just one example is listed: Vernon, R. "The International Aspects of State-owned Enterprises." *Journal of International Business Studies* 10(3):7–15, 1979; Steinmann, H., Kumar, N. B. and Wasner, A. "Some Aspects of Managing U.S. Subsidiaries of German Medium-sized Enterprises." *Management International Review* 19(3):27–37, 1979; Turnbull, P. W. "International Aspects of Bank Marketing." *European Journal of Marketing* 16(3):102–05, 1982; Katz, J. H. *Does Foreign Direct Investment Theory Reflect Reality: The Case of the American Multinational Food Processors.* M.I.T. Working Paper 1354–82, October 1982.

93. Soldner, H. "International Marketing: A Typology of Strategies and Attitudes." In: S. Raveed and Y. R. Puri (eds.), *1977 Proceedings of the Academy of International Business,* Chicago: AIB, 1978, pp. 81–83.

94. Knickerbocker, F. T. *Oligopolistic Reaction and the Multinational Enterprise.* Boston: Harvard University Press, 1973.

95. "Why Global Businesses Perform Better." *International Management* 38(1):40, 1983.

96. Behrman is more specific with his *home-market, host-market* and *world-market* firms, to supplement the earlier *resource/market/efficiency seeker* MNC-classification. Behrman, J. N. and Fischer, W. A. "Transnational Corporations: Market Orientations and R + D Abroad." *Columbia Journal of World Business* 15(3):55–60, 1980.

97. Fayerweather, J. and Kapoor, A. *Strategy and Negotiation for the International Corporation.* Cambridge, MA: Ballinger, 1976, pp. 7–24. Focuses on the strategy models of dynamic high- or low/stable-technology, advanced management skills and unified-logistics labor-transmission.

98. Arndt, J. "The Conceptual Domain of Marketing: Evaluation of Shelby Hunt's Three Dichotomies Model." *European Journal of Marketing* 16(1): 27–35, 1982.

99. Hunt, S. D. and Burnett, J. J. "The Macromarketing/Micromarketing Dichotomy: A Taxonomical Model." *Journal of Marketing* 46(3):11–26, 1982.

100. Boddewyn, J. J. *Comparative Marketing:* The First Twenty-Five Years. Journal of International Business Studies 12(1): 62, 73, 1.

101. See, for instance, Negandhi, A. R. (ed.). *Functioning of the Multinational Corporation: A Global Comparative Study.* New York: Pergamon, 1980. More integrative and synthesizing efforts in comparative/international management were already advocated by Schöllhammer, H. "Current Research in International and Comparative Management Issues. *Management International Review* 15(2–3):29–45, 1975.

102. See, for example, Skully, M. T. (ed.). *A Multinational Look at the Transnational Corporation.* Sidney: Dryden Press Australia, 1978.

103. In recent German literature, attention has been called to the fact that the study of economic phenomena in different countries has produced particular national approaches, conceptualizations, and theory structures used, e.g., by *business administration, managerial economics,* or the German-Dutch *Betriebswirtschaftslehre/Bedrijfskunde.* Accordingly, it is a prerequisite for integrative international research to compare the systems of thought, values, and research traditions of the respective disciplines, in the context of their national operational parameters. For comparative marketing and accounting, see: Perridon, L. "Bedeutung der Vergleichenden Betriebswirtschaftslehre für die Führung internationaler Unternehmen" ("Significance of Comparative Business Administration for International Business Management"). In: W. H. Wacker, H. Haussmann, B. Kumar (eds.), *Internationale Unternehmensführung,* pp. 157–69. For marketing, see: Soldner, H. Marketing (wissenschafts) Vergleiche— Vergleichbares and Unvergleichbares ("Marketing (science) Comparisons—Comparables and Non-comparables"). *Marketing ZFP* 2(4):285–90, 1980. For a practical example of thoughtful Anglo-Dutch research integration, see: Van Gent, A. P. *Marketing-Ontwikkeling* ("Marketing Development"). Leiden: Stenfert Kroese, 1976.

4 THE ROLE OF ECONOMIES OF SCALE IN INTERNATIONAL MARKETING

Vern Terpstra

The best strategy is always to be very strong, first generally, then at the decisive point ... there is no more imperative and no simpler law for strategy than to keep the forces concentrated.

—Karl von Clausewitz

Clausewitz is proclaiming here a classic military strategy that has a parallel in economics—and international marketing. We find, for example, two McKinsey people discovering that "Critical Mass is the Key to Export Profits."[1] The idea that critical mass or economies of scale are important in economics is at least as old as Adam Smith. He declared that specialization and the division of labor are the source of the wealth of nations and that specialization is limited by the size of the market.

More recently we have learned that economies of scale are a source of comparative advantage for nations in international trade and a factor in the rise of large oligopolistic enterprises, including multinational firms. Perhaps the newest and most sophisticated manifestation of the idea of economies of scale is the development of the experience curve phenomenon, which has been particularly applied to explain the success of Japanese firms. The internalization theory of foreign direct investment is also related to this idea.

Economies of scale is the general expression to describe the phenomenon we are considering. There are, however, other terms with similar connotation, i.e., critical mass, the experience curve, synergy, leverage, entry barriers, and breakeven point. What do we mean by economies of scale? There is no standard dictionary definition we can draw on, but the concept is generally understood by both economists and business people. Put most simply, it is the idea that in some situations, increasing output leads to decreasing costs per unit.

Some of the sources of economies of scale have been identified as: (1) indivisibilities of various factor inputs, (2) economies from specialization and the division of labor (as noted by Adam Smith), and (3) the learning or experience effect. These factors have been recognized and discussed in the literature but almost entirely in the context of production economies as opposed to other aspects of the firm's activities. Thus we have the example of Henry Ford's wonderful assembly line bringing down the price of automobiles. Or the illustration of the experience curve to explain the success of Japanese companies in world markets. In this chapter we will show that the logic and necessity of economies of scale can be as important in the firm's international marketing as it is in its production operations.

Economies of Scale in International Marketing

Economies of scale have been briefly defined above. International marketing can be defined as the activities undertaken by the firm to relate to its foreign markets. The major activities usually included are: (1) market research, (2) product development and management, (3) pricing, (4) distribution, and (5) promotion. Our approach will be to take these marketing activities one by one (except for pricing) and show how important economies of scale can be in their performance. We begin with international market intelligence.

International Market Intelligence

Knowledge of the market is a prerequisite to successful marketing. Unfortunately, knowledge is not a free good equally distributed to all producers. Therefore, firms invest significant sums to study their domestic markets. Market knowledge is equally essential for marketing internationally, but it requires relatively greater investment than domestic market research. Information costs internationally may be higher for several reasons: (1) the firm is further away from foreign markets, (2) the firm is less familiar with the foreign culture and marketing, (3) statistics are often less available and reliable in foreign markets, (4) language differences compound the problem. Furthermore, the value of the information may be less because of the smaller size of many foreign markets compared to the domestic.

Because of the sizable investment in knowledge required for International marketing, many firms have been deterred from marketing abroad. Various studies of exporters versus non-exporters have shown that ignorance of foreign markets and marketing is a major deterrent to engaging in export. Knowledge costs are an entry barrier. Another indicator of the importance of knowledge for international marketing is the fact that firms generally begin their marketing abroad in countries which are most like their home market, thus attempting to minimize their knowledge investment. This practice is in accord with Linder's trade theory which suggests that most international trade takes place between countries with similar income levels and consumer preferences.[2]

We have suggested that foreign market intelligence is a lumpy, indivisible kind of investment which is a prerequisite for international marketing. This has two implications. One is that knowledge costs are a barrier to entry in international marketing. Another is that once the investment has been made, there are economies of scale in exploiting it. A firm that has made the initial investment in foreign market knowledge can exploit it at little or no incremental cost by expanding its own international marketing or by selling the knowledge to others.

There are several illustrations of firms exploiting the scale economies from their investment in foreign market knowledge. In a general sense, this knowledge is part of the advantage of the multinational firm and part of the internalization process. As Williamson says, the firm must be an efficient information processor.[3] More specific examples are the export management company (EMC) and the Japanese trading company (JTC). One of the major arguments for using an export management company is that it offers the producer instant foreign marketing and market know-how. The EMC has already made the knowledge investment. It effectively sells its knowledge to a number of producers who buy it on an incremental basis. This way of buying foreign market knowledge is moderate and manageable compared to the producer's having to make the whole investment by itself.

The Japanese trading company is similar to the EMC in nature except that the EMC pales in comparison to the size and scope of the JTC. The JTC is the preeminent model. Indeed, it has stimulated imitators in many other countries. The United States will also be an imitator if the Export Trading Company Act ever passes Congress. While the JTC provides many services it is perhaps most famous for its information-gathering activity. The author visited the computer communications center at Mitsui, which must be one of the largest such facilities in the world. Additionally, JTC's do extensive intelligence abroad. The Pan Am building in New York "is an anthill of intelligence activity." Mitsubishi has two floors and a small army of people gathering intelligence.[4] The tremendous investment in intelligence made by the JTCs is made available at a modest price to their thousands of Japanese clients. Except for the grander scale of operations, they are similar to the EMC in this service. Both the EMC and the JTC sell their intelligence not as a separate item but as part of the package of services they offer.

Although the EMC and the JTC are particularly good examples of the important role of the intelligence function, it is also evident in many other situations. Indeed, in most cases where the firm enters a foreign market in some cooperative venture, the high cost of local knowledge is usually an important reason for the cooperation. In "cooperative ventures" I include using a distributor or licensee as well as the traditional joint venture, because in all three cases one of the motivations in choosing the entry method is to obtain the local partner's knowledge of his market. For example, many firms use the United Africa Company (UAC) as a distributor when selling to African markets. UAC has been in Africa since colonial days and knows the territory extremely well. Outside firms coming into those markets would need to make a relatively big investment to get satisfactory knowledge about them. By using UAC as their distributor, they can avoid making that invesment in market intelligence.

Product Development

Product development involves many functions within the firm, including engineering, finance, and production, as well as marketing. However, it is, theoretically at least, essentially a marketing function wherein the firm seeks to maintain and enhance its market franchise. It is the product which brings the firm and its market together. A glance at any marketing text will confirm the central role of product development in marketing.

For our present purposes, we must identify that this marketing activity involves fixed costs, which lead to economies of scale. This is not hard to do as there are many up-front costs in product development that have been well-identified in the literature. Most of these are personnel costs for new product departments or committees, research scientists, and so on, but there are further costs for laboratory equipment and testing, and legal costs including, eventually, patent protection. Kotler cites the example of a company which estimated its costs of finding one successful new product at $14 million.[5]

Product development for international marketing has the same costs as for domestic marketing, but they are even larger because some of them must be carried on in foreign markets as well as at home. For example, gathering and screening of ideas, product and/or market testing, and patent protection are all activities that must be carried out multinationally. In the case of the Hovercraft, ten percent of the development costs were spent just on getting patent protection around the world. Ford and General Motors are developing what they call a world car. The costs of this activity are greater than the already large amounts required to bring out a new model domestically.

Product development is an expensive activity and therefore favors large firms, including multinationals. Indeed, multinationals have an advantage compared to other large firms which are not multinational, because they can conduct the multicountry activities required for product development more efficiently than purely national firms. Even large multinationals, however, often find product development costs so large that even they cannot afford to develop new products alone. Some of the world's biggest enterprises are getting together or finding some cooperative ways to share the costs of developing new products, as illustrated in the following examples:

1. In the aircraft industry, McDonnell Douglas has joined with Fokker of the Netherlands to develop a new generation of airplanes. Fokker is also seeking ties with large Japanese firms like Fuji, Kawasaki, and Mitsubishi.
2. In developing a new engine for tomorrow's aircraft, General Electric, Rolls Royce, and Pratt and Whitney are all seeking partners to share the development costs. Generally, the cooperative ventures will include firms from three countries—United States, Japan, and one from Europe. Rolls Royce already has entered a consortium with IHI, Kawasaki and Mitsubishi in Japan.
3. In the computer industry, ICL of Britain is collaborating with Fujitsu of Japan to improve its mainframe computers. Intel has been a go-it-alone success story, but now it has signed a ten-year agreement with Advanced Micro Devices for joint design and development of future products. There are several aspects to the agreement but the "main reason for the joint venture is to improve R + D efficiency."[6]
4. In the automotive field, there have been numerous joint ventures of European firms for the development of new models, engines, and

components. Even mighty General Motors has a joint venture with Suzuki Motors of Japan, part of which will involve joint development of a new small car, which will be part of GM's worldwide strategy.

5. In the watch industry, Seiko, one of the industry leaders, recently acquired a Swiss watch company to further Seiko's development of high-cost luxury watches for world markets.

6. In the new industry of robotics, General Electric is somewhat of a latecomer. To help it move rapidly into this field, GE will be assembling Hitachi robots for sale in the U.S. market and later will begin developing its own models, getting a start with Hitachi technology. GE had earlier signed an agreement with DEA, an Italian producer of robots.

Product Line. Another aspect of product policy is the search for a profitable and complementary family of products to offer to the market. Complementarity may be defined in terms of market expectations, channel requirements, and/or the firm's production or marketing situation. The product line issue is related to our previous discussion on product development because the traditional way of getting a family of products was through internal development. Because product development is increasingly a strain on the firm's resources and because it often is a very slow process, more and more firms are trying to get an appropriate product mix by joining with other firms. In recent years, acquisition of other companies has been a popular way to expand the firm's product line. Acquisition reduces the time required to get a product addition and, all things considered, is probably also cheaper than internal development.

Apart from acquisition of another company, there are less expensive ways of joining with other firms to reduce the cost of assembling a product family. We will cite several examples of firms joining together to establish a desired family of products. Underlying all the examples is the same theme, the need to overcome the cost barriers in assembling a product mix. This is accomplished by realizing the economies of scale of sharing in the efforts and products of other firms. All of the examples involve multinational firms, highlighting the point that the development of an international family of products is another activity lending itself to economies of scale. Economies derive from two sources: one is reduced development costs; the other is in production costs avoided by getting products from another firm, paying incremental versus fixed costs. For example:

1. Japan has been the world's largest user of facsimile machines because these more easily transmit the complex ideographs of the Japanese language than do telex machines. Partly because of this, some Japanese firms have become leading producers. Siemens of Germany and Bur-

roughs and 3M of the United States are all marketing high-speed facsimile machines from Japan. Even Xerox imports its high-speed model from its Japanese affiliate. Explaining their rationale, a 3M executive said, "We simply can't cover all ranges of machines ourselves," so they fill gaps in their product lines by buying from the Japanese.[7] Even giant IBM markets small copiers from Minolta for similar reasons.

2. The automobile industry provides other illustrations. The General Motors tie with Suzuki includes the likelihood that GM will round out its product line with very small models made by Suzuki. Britain's BL will enrich its product offerings by selling a British-produced version of Honda's mid-sized Ballade. One aspect of the AMC-Renault link is that AMC will have a reasonable range of products to offer from Renault, perhaps allowing AMC to survive in the U.S. market.

3. In the pharmaceutical industry, internal product development is an extremely costly and slow process. Therefore, it is standard practice by multinationals in this industry to round out their product line by some other method such as licensing, joint ventures, or acquisitions. Warner Lambert has relied on licensing of others' products for a major part of its pharmaceutical sales. Merck is a giant in the industry, but it still markets in the United States a number of drugs developed by a relatively small Swedish firm, A. B. Astra. Pfizer is expanding its medical systems division offerings by marketing diagnostic gear from the Japanese Aloka company.

Distribution

Distribution in international marketing often involves an extra step not found in domestic marketing. In domestic marketing, the task is to get the product from the producer to the consumer via some distribution channel. The extra step in international marketing is that the product often starts from another country and must be exported into the target market. Thus, distribution in international marketing is usually a two-stage process, international and domestic. It is worthwhile to examine each stage of this distribution to see the role economies of scale might play.

Exporting. There are several aspects to the international distribution or exporting task, most of which lend themselves to economies of scale.

The first task in exporting is making appropriate organizational arrangements for this new kind of marketing for the firm, such a setting up an export department. This tends to become a fixed-cost operation to a large degree, thus lending itself to economies of scale. For example, an American packaged goods marketer began exporting to Europe. The new export department persistently had high selling costs as a percent of sales. As the firm could not significantly expand sales of its own products in Europe, it sought economies of scale by carrying to Europe complementary products of other U.S. firms—a piggyback arrangement. Trading companies and EMCs offer another way for firms to avoid the fixed-cost barrier of an export department. Selling to these organizations is like a domestic sale and no special administrative overhead is necessary.

Another early task in exporting is market research, learning what foreign customers want and how to reach them. The important scale economies in this market intelligence function have already been discussed.

Another job in exporting is the *physical distribution* of the goods. Shipping is an area where the economies of scale are recognized explicitly in the vocabulary of the business—"less-than-carload-lot," and so on. Whether the exporting be done by truck or train, ship or plane, there are obvious savings in matching as closely as possible the technical and economic specifications of the carrier. Many exporters have less than optimum-sized export shipments and are forced to pay higher rates unless they can combine shipments somehow to get economies of scale. There are several mechanisms which offer these economies to exporters: trading companies, export management companies (EMCs), and piggyback exporting. Trading companies and EMCs were discussed earlier. Piggyback exporting is when a manufacturer will carry another firm's products into foreign markets along with its own. All three of these approaches offer combined shipments and transportation savings as part of their attraction. In contrast, firms that can't find economical shipping may be noncompetitive in foreign markets.

Related to physical distribution are the documentation, insurance, and financing tasks in exporting. These require specialized skills and contacts and also lend themselves to economies of scale, as evidenced by the existence of the specialized agency, the foreign freight forwarder. Foreign freight forwarders handle documentation and other aspects of export shipments for many firms, both large and small. Because of their internal economies of scale, they assured their survival. Most of their clients find it more expensive to perform their functions in-house than to use their services. The Japanese trading company provides similar economies for its clients. For example, insurance costs can be less when the trading company has a special department and expertise to handle it. As one illustration, Mitsui in the United States has a large master contract with the Foreign Credit Insurance Association for its shipments from the United States. This means each client enjoys coverage at less cost than doing it alone.

Distribution Within the Foreign Market. Exporting is getting the product from the producer's country to the customer's country. Now we shall examine distribution within the customer's country. This is the traditional task of distribution as discussed in marketing texts where scale economies are indicated as a major rationale of distribution channels. Corey notes that "A distribution system . . . is a key external resource. Normally it takes years to build and is not easily changed."[8] Kotler says middlemen are used because most producers lack the financial resources to embark on a program of direct marketing and because middlemen offer superior efficiency based on their experience, specialization, contacts, and scale.[9]

The rationale of distribution systems applies in any country, whether the producer's home market or foreign markets. The producer's reliance on this external resource is often greater in foreign markets, however, because most international marketers operate on a smaller scale in their foreign markets than they do at home. Many firms feel that they cannot get an adequate presence in foreign markets merely by relying on the existing distribution channels there. Although these channels offer scale economies, these firms believe that an even greater impact is necessary so they join with national firms to get the critical mass desired. The contemporary world market scene offers innumerable illustrations of exporters joining with national firms to achieve an effective scale of distribution penetration. The examples come from all countries and all industries, for instance:

1. In the auto industry, Mitsubishi joined with Chrysler to be able to reach the U.S. market through the thousands of Chrylser dealers. Similarly, Renault's major reason for joining AMC in the United States was to gain access to AMC's established dealer network. Renault figures it would have taken ten years to build a comparable network. Renault worked the same way in Sweden by joining with Volvo to distribute some of its models through Volvo's dealers there. In the auto industry especially, establishing a dealer network is a large investment, so scale economies are particularly important.

2. In the food industry, General Foods tried to operate its own distribution system in Japan for about 20 years. Insufficient volume and unsatisfactory profits forced the company to join with Ajinomoto, a company 20 times its own size. Resultant economies led to both greater market share and profits for General Foods-Japan. In a similar manner, Quaker Oats was unsuccessful going it alone with its pet foods in Germany, so Quaker Oats decided to piggyback with Henkel, the detergent firm, which has one of the best distribution organizations in Germany. McDonald's now has over 1,000 outlets overseas. Having started a

decade ago, they are now starting to achieve economies of scale that their competitors can't begin to enjoy until they spend much more time and money building up a critical mass abroad. One of the major arguments favoring the Nabisco-Standard Brands merger is the synergy the firms will achieve in their distribution in foreign markets.

3. Savin and Olivetti have joined together to sell copiers and other machines for the office of the future. Each claims that the venture will bring greater penetration in the market of the other partner. Neither partner felt it could make it alone in the foreign market.

4. Many Japanese producers enjoy production economies of scale but have problems getting a critical mass in foreign market distribution. Therefore, they frequently piggyback or otherwise cooperate with a national firm to gain economies in distribution. The Mitsubishi-Chrysler connection was noted above. Minolta sells copiers in the United States through IBM, even though it has its own U.S. marketing subsidiary. The latter organization is too small to have the desired market coverage. Hitachi is a major force in Japan but didn't feel able to market its robots in the United States by itself. Hitachi is working with General Electric as the major way to establish a market presence in the United States. Major Japanese firms are using the same strategy to enter European markets. For example, Mitsubishi is marketing high-speed copiers in Europe via Siemens' marketing organization. Fujitsu will market computers in Europe through ICL, the British computer company. Nissan has links with several car manufacturers in Europe and Suzuki's tie with General Motors gives it access to GM's *worldwide* sales network. In the drug industry, Japanese and Western firms are piggybacking with each other to penetrate each others' markets.

Promotion

Promotion is another major task in marketing, sometimes called the communications job. Knowledge is assumed to be free and universally available in the theory of perfect competition. Because that is not true in the real world, the producer must communicate with potential customers to inform them of his or her offerings and to persuade them to buy. The major forms of marketing communications and persuasion are advertising and personal selling. Sales promotion and publicity can also be important in some circumstances. We will consider the role of economies of scale in communications or promotion in international marketing.

Advertising is the most visible of the promotional tools used by marketers. Customers may be reached by radio and television or a variety of print media. Advertising and the consumer franchise it helps to achieve are explicitly recognized as barriers to entry by economists. This means that advertising expenditures by existing firms create a high-cost hurdle for a newcomer. The new firm, for example, cannot spend one-hundredth of the ad budget of existing firms and expect to get a one percent market share. Advertising is another lumpy expense item which lends itself to economies of scale. Procter & Gamble and General Motors are the leading advertisers in the U.S. market. Each has an advertising budget near $500 million! A new competitor for either of these firms would have a hard time making his or her voice heard unless he or she had lots of money—or lots of help.

Personal selling is the major promotional tool in the industrial market. When one considers the sales force of DuPont, a General Electric, or an IBM, it is obvious that personal selling can be another high-cost hurdle for a new competitor. Establishing and managing a sales force is also usually a fixed cost activity, lending itself to economies of scale.

The costs of promotion to establish a market franchise are an entry barrier in domestic markets. They are generally a greater barrier in foreign markets because international marketers operate on a smaller scale abroad than at home. It can be said that many firms, especially multinationals, have successfully hurdled these barriers abroad. That illustrates the point precisely. It is because these firms are large and have the resources that they can overcome the cost hurdles and buy into foreign markets. It is said, for example, that Procter & Gamble entered European markets and bought a 15 percent market share in a short time with heavy advertising campaigns. Procter & Gamble has the resources to do that.

The promotional task of gaining product/brand recognition and a market franchise in a country requires a critical mass as do the other international marketing activities discussed above. Nissan provides an unusual example of this. The company wants to change its brand name from Datsun to Nissan, the company name. One observer estimated this would cost $60 million in the United States. Small firms may find the promotional costs of foreign market entry too great and remain domestic marketers only, or they may try to find ways of sharing promotional costs, such as using a trading company or other cooperative ventures. Large firms may be able to achieve the critical mass required, as in the Procter & Gamble illustration or the Nissan case. Even large firms, however, often find it desirable to avoid or lessen the costs of buying market position in a foreign country, for example:

1. In the consumer packaged goods industry, Colgate has an experienced marketing staff in many countries, plus international advertising know-how and contacts. To take advantage of Colgate's economies, various producers used Colgate to market their products abroad, including

Wilkinson blades and DuPont (for a consumer product). General Foods-Japan could not afford a large enough sales force to cover Japanese retail outlets. By joining with Ajinomoto, General Foods was able to dismiss its own salesforce and piggyback on the large staff of Ajinomoto.

2. It is worthwhile to note how the Japanese, those very successful international marketers, have frequently used the established market position of national firms in place of, or alongside of, their own promotional efforts. Japanese tractor makers specialize in models of less than 40 horsepower. Six of seven U.S. tractor manufacturers market these smaller models under their own brand name through their marketing organizations.

3. Sony and Matsushita are the leading producers of videotape recorders. In the United States, the majority of these are sold under such brand names as RCA, Zenith, and Sears and by the marketing organizations bearing these names.

4. In copiers, Minolta and other Japanese producers are selling in the United States under such names is IBM, Savin, Pitney Bowes, and 3M and through their marketing organizations.

5. In the new field of robotics, Hitachi chose to enter the United States using not only the marketing force of GE but also the GE brand name on its equipment.

In all these cases, international marketers are capitalizing on established brand names and marketing organizations. They can gain a significant volume of business without high start-up costs. This business allows them production economies of scale and. may provide a foothold for future business under their own brands.

Conclusions and Implications

We have suggested that to be successful, many international marketing activities require a critical mass or economies of scale. To illustrate this, we examined the various functions of marketing. Obviously, the elements of the marketing mix are interrelated and economies in one function are affected by economies in another. For example, gaining a critical mass in distribution may influence economies in market intelligence or promotion. This was evident in some of our examples. Our analysis is consistent with all those who stress market share as important to profitable operations.

Economies of scale can be significant in domestic marketing also, but they are usually more critical and harder to achieve in international marketing. This has implications both for firms and for countries.

For firms, the implication is that a massing of resources may be necessary to cross the threshold to effective international marketing. In a recent case, AT&T wants to market to Nippon Telephone and Telegraph, which has just opened its business to non-Japanese firms. In 1981, therefore, AT&T opened a Tokyo office at a first year cost of over $250,000. This is not necessarily a typical example, but it illustrates the problem. Smaller firms may avoid international markets because of their lack of resources, or they may join in some kind of cooperative venture to gain the necessary critical mass. These cooperative ventures range from trading companies, export management companies, and piggyback exporting to licensing and joint ventures.

Large companies may have adequate resources to make a sufficient impact by themselves, as in the AT&T example. Many large companies, however, also face problems of diseconomies of scale. Even AT&T is uncertain about maintaining its Tokyo office. Numerous examples were given earlier of other large firm's cooperative efforts to avoid big cost outlays and gain economies. The Japanese examples are especially noteworthy, because the Japanese have been so successful in their international marketing. Part of that success derives from their recognition that in many areas, quicker and more effective market penetration may be achieved by joining with national firms to share the benefits of their already-established economies of scale. As a result, they have been more active in cooperative ventures than the Americans and the Europeans.

An implication for managers is that they must recognize the scale problem in international marketing and consider it in their strategic planning. That may mean avoiding markets or product areas where the firm cannot achieve a critical mass. Alternatively, it could mean the firm must seek ways to achieve the critical mass by sharing in the efforts and resources of other firms. There are many different ways of sharing, as was evident in the examples cited earlier.

For nations wishing to expand their economies and their exports, the implication is that to achieve their goals, more cooperation between firms both domestically and internationally should be allowed and encouraged. Even proud France is seeking foreign help in key industries. Many countries are forming or considering models of the Japanese trading company. In some cases tax, competition, or other laws might have to be reviewed to allow or encourage such cooperation. Those who favor free trade stress the benefits of international interdependence. What we have been discussing is similar, except that the interdependence is more firm and industry-specific and therefore has implications for managers as well as national planners.

Notes

1. Robert S. Attiyeh and David L. Wenner, "Critical Mass: Key to Export Profits," *Business Horizons,* December 1979, pp. 28–38.

2. Staffan B. Linder, *An Essay on Trade and Transformation* (New York: Wiley, 1961).

3. Oliver Williamson, "Transaction-Cost Economics: The Governance of Contractual Relations," *Journal of Law and Economics,* 22 (October, 1979), pp. 233–62.

4. *Business Week,* December 14, 1981, p. 52.

5. Philip Kotler, *Marketing Management* (New York: Prentice Hall, 1980), p. 314.

6. *Business Week,* October 19, 1981, p. 47.

7. *Business Week,* November 2, 1981, p. 104.

8. E. Raymond Corey, *Industrial Marketing* (Englewood Cliffs, N.J.: Prentice Hall, 1976), p. 263.

9. Kotler, op. cit., p. 417.

5 THE REGULATION OF ADVERTISING AROUND THE WORLD IN THE 1980s AND BEYOND: Precipitating Circumstances, Motivations, and Forces

Jean J. Boddewyn

A traditional way of analyzing a major phenomenon such as advertising regulation consists of focusing on three variables: (1) environmental factors or precipitating circumstances; (2) objectives or motivations; and (3) actors or forces at play. For example, the precarious financial situation of the regional press in France (= precipitating circumstance), coupled with the interests of local politicians who depend on it for their visibility (= motivation), has led to the latter successfully opposing the development of commercial radio and television in that country (= force). While these categories are not absolutely airtight, they can be applied to the likely development of advertising regulation around the world in the foreseeable future.

Environmental Factors

Consumer Dissatisfaction and Complaints

There are three major indications of dissatisfaction with advertising:

1. Polls of the Gallup and Yankelovich types usually reveal fairly high degrees (as high as 70%) of dissatisfaction with advertisements in terms of being misleading, boring, tasteless, useless, and the like. Such high

73

proportions, however, usually result from direct questions of the type, "Do you find advertisements to be informative?" If the question is more indirect (e.g., "What do you talk about most with your friends and relatives?"), the salience of advertising takes a downward plunge to two to eight percent and is hardly a major source of concern for most people.

2. Sample studies of actual advertisements in terms of their compliance with regulations and industry guidelines have found that some four to seven percent of them are problematic—particularly in terms of being misleading. While this percentage is low, it applies to tens of millions of ads each year and thus represents a large number of unsatisfactory advertisements.

3. Complaints filed by consumers and competitors with advertising self-regulatory bodies and with government agencies are relatively few, numbering in the hundreds or the thousands per country each year. While we know that only a small portion of people do bother to complain, such statistics reveal far less dissatisfaction with advertisements than with advertising. A sizable proportion of these complaints deal with matters of taste (e.g., about deodorizers, toilet papers, feminine-hygiene products, ethnic jokes) but also with misleadingness (e.g., the ad failed to specify some significant data).

Altogether, there are some legitimate gripes extant about advertising and advertisements. While their number and salience may be relatively low and are probably decreasing on account of both regulatory and self-regulatory efforts, they remain a primary precipitating circumstance for the development of regulation around the world.

New Media Technologies

Until recently, mass-media advertising was dominated by newspapers, magazines, radio and television, followed more recently by cable television, which already reaches some 30–35% of U.S. households and much more in some European countries (e.g., 65% in Belgium). During the 1970s, videocassette recorders, pay cable television, and automated telephone services entered millions of households. Over the next few years, subscription television, interactive cable, personal computers, Viewdata and Teletext services, as well as direct satellite broadcasting will increase the array of media choices available to these same households as well as to advertisers. There are problems, however.

Interactive two-way communication systems such as QUBE and Viewdata permit consumers to place orders electronically after viewing a presentation by the seller; while pre-recorded telephone calls and the use of toll-free numbers in conjunction with TV advertisements allow consumers to order from their home. These techniques are clearly convenient, but they may deprive consumer of the time needed to consider their purchases and therefore require new cooling-off periods. Besides, video sales pitches using a longer format could blur the distinction between advertisement and information, which may lower consumer defenses that would otherwise be used to evaluate a seller's message. Moreover, the relatively high costs—capital, operating, and learning—of some of the new media may limit access to these novel sources of information for some groups of consumers, thereby increasing the gap between the information-rich and the information-poor publics.

Furthermore, some of the new interactive media will allow the collection of various demographic, viewing, and purchasing-pattern data. While some consumers may be willing to sacrifice privacy for the convenience of direct-mail ordering, this practice will generate new private data banks useful to marketers but potentially encroaching on personal privacy. (A similar problem exists in the case of the direct-mail industry which sells or rents consumer lists.)

On the other hand, many of the new media could be of great benefit to consumers by increasing and improving their access to marketplace information in terms of variety (because of multiple data sources), specificity (because better targeted to some audience), greater detailing of information, and timeliness. Hence, cable television, Viewdata system, and home computers could both improve consumer information and cause governments to re-evaluate the traditional notion that all information about a product must appear in advertisements for that product, since consumers may be able to obtain the details they need more easily from their Viewdata terminals at home before they shop or even from a computer terminal at the point of sale.

Altogether, these media innovations are creating new consumer-protection problems that are bound to generate additional regulations, although they may also reduce the need for others since consumer information is being increased.

Recession and Inflation

Economic activity around the world is stagnating, and forecasts of recovery are generally reserved; while inflation is way above normal in most countries. Such recessionary conditions typically lead to trade-protection measures. Thus, the French government's intent to legalize comparison advertising has recently been stopped by the fear that Japanese carmakers would use it to widen their penetration of the troubled French automobile market. While the outcome for comparison advertising may thus become problematic, demands for more information in advertisements are likely to increase.

On the other hand, recessionary conditions are frequently associated with less regulation (except for trade protection) because of the higher business and consumer costs connected with burdensome rules. The present deregulatory movement in the United States, the United Kingdom, and Norway evidences this development, although it is more likely to result in a regulatory pause rather than in any major dismantling of existing rules. But enforcement is also going to be more lax on account of reduced budgets for regulatory agencies and departments.

Objectives

Consumer Protection

This remains the prime objective of politicians, regulators, consumerists, and assorted experts, even though it encompasses both protection of consumers against business practices and against themselves since quite a few regulators believe that consumer cannot quite resist advertising—even perfectly legal ads. Its principal manifestation is in general requirements that ads be truthful and not misleading/deceptive nor unfair. This has led to: increased demands for ad pre-substantiation and pre-clearance; reversal of the burden of proof on the advertiser; clamors for more informative ads; the banning of various claims and wordings; the mandatory inclusion of certain messages, and corrective advertising. There are no reasons to doubt that such requirements will remain applicable in the foreseeable future. What is likely to grow, however, is a more targeted attack against advertising instead of a broad frontal assault on the ground that such a broad assault is economically useless or generally false or misleading.

In brief, the argument is that advertising may be acceptable and even desirable in general but that it should be prohibited or at least severely controlled when it comes to such vulnerable groups as the young, the old, the sick, the recently bereaved, and the ignorant. Recent attacks against advertising to children and the promotion of breastmilk substitutes to relatively uneducated women in less-developed countries exemplify this trend.

The tastelessness charge is also growing, namely, that many advertisements offend various groups of people in terms of real or fancied slurs on their race, ethnicity, religion, age, sex, convictions, and the like, or simply that they embarrass the viewers. Clearly, these are real and valid concerns to which regulation and particularly self-regulation have addressed themselves and will continue to pay attention in the light of changing mores and values. The danger of this more targeted attack, however, is that it can end up restricting or even prohibiting quite a few advertising targets and bases of appeal. After excluding: (1) the young, the sick (which includes many of the old), the recently bereaved, and the ignorant (let us remember that some three-fourths of the world population live in LDCs, and most of them have not received much in the way of formal education), and (2) appeals based on fear, superstition, and the seven deadly sins (lust, envy, pride, gluttony, etc.). there would not be much left for advertising to do except produce informative announcements.

This is precisely the goal of some consumerists and regulators, but it would radically change the nature of advertising, which is traditionally defined as salesmanship in print and which also tries to persuade people by playing on their emotions—besides providing them with some information. The more likely outcome is that we will witness more pre-clearance (preventing)—both mandatory and voluntary—of ads as a way of coping with the clamor about vulnerable groups and tastelessness. On the other hand, the advent of narrow-casting to reach better targeted audiences will help alleviate some of the problems which result from the right advertisement or commercial being read, seen, or heard by the wrong people.

Similarly, attacks on advertising are likely to focus on particular groups of products or services. Besides the breastmilk-substitute issue already mentioned, the entire pharmaceutical industry is being targeted for playing on fear; while the food industry is being challenged on claims linked to health and nutrition, and the toy industry for being targeted at children.

Therefore, even without any overall objective of destroying or shackling advertising per se, it is possible to shrink its scope by what used to be called the salami approach, that is, by slicing it away progressively on partial grounds. This danger will loom large in coming years.

Trade Protection

Concern with consumer protection frequently obscures the fact that advertising regulation is frequently designed to protect competitors against attacks from other businesses. A prime example is, of course, comparative advertisements which name names, but most arguments about unfair advertising emanate from businessmen rather than from consumerists (except in the case of advertising to vulnerable groups).

Here, worsening economic conditions are likely to maintain or further restrictions against unfair ads as competition becomes more desperate. This will probably take the form of allowing more class action on the part of both business and consumer associations.

Nationalism, Culturalism and Conservatism

The desire to keep or create jobs for local labor and to preserve the nation's cultural heritage has generated a definite tendency to ban or restrict the use of foreign languages and materials in advertising. Thus, "English *not* spoken here" is a growing reaction in France, Malaysia, Mexico, and the Philippines, where the use of foreign languages, expressions, and copy is closely watched or restricted. Besides, there is an evident reaction abroad against U.S. and Western cultural influences, of which advertising represents a highly visible and vulnerable manifestation. What has happened in Iran and other Islamic countries points to a likely growth of opposition to liberated or Western approaches in advertising.

Even in developed countries, one can detect a return to more traditional and conservative beliefs and attitudes. This happens every generation or so and is likely to follow the permissive wave of the 1960s and 1970s. The growing number of complaints about taste in advertising corroborates this development.

Actors

The Consumerist Movement

It is difficult to get a good reading of the strength of that movement. Even in Sweden, which is considered avant-garde in this field, one finds several associations with conflicting constituencies (e.g., trade unions, families, cooperatives) and interests (e.g., product testing), and with no single leadership and unified goals. Besides, it has been argued that pro-consumer regulations tend to flourish in good economic times when the economy can absorb their cost. This is hardly the case nowadays.

Still, the movement remains supportive of further regulation of advertising. For one thing, it is precisely its lack of unity and political representation that makes it engage in guerilla tactics that nettle business. Besides, its advocacy of consumer rights (information, voice, redress, etc.) has been largely successful among broad segments of the consuming public, the electorate, and politicians.

Last but not least, it has shrewdly chosen to fight on issues where a more emotional case could be made against advertising (e.g., about ads directed to children and to poor and uneducated women in LDCs). More of the same can be expected.

Governments and International Organizations

The overall political scene remains confusing as socialist and conservative governments keep playing musical chairs in many countries. However, one can argue that even leftist governments will have to keep a wary eye on the cost of increased regulation and on the growing public reaction—not just business reaction—against over-regulation. On the other hand, revenue shortages are bound to result in the increased taxation of advertising, whatever the demerits of the case.

One area where government will certainly react is that of cross-border satellite advertising. Threats to the press, potential loss of revenues, and fears of cultural invasion and of foreign propaganda will fuse and result in international agreements to limit unwanted "footprints." Besides, nations are better organized nowadays to discover and exchange foreign regulatory experiences. (Some nations, such as the United States, the United Kingdom, and Sweden, serve as pilots in many cases.) This factor is normally conducive to the spread of advertising regulations around the world, although the spirit of deregulation will spread, too.

Finally, more international or supranational organizations, such as the United Nations, the EEC Commission, and the Council of Europe, have joined in the act. They are increasingly focusing attention on advertising and coming up with various directives, codes of conduct, reports, and resolutions. Most of these bodies are relatively uninformed and prejudiced about the working of advertising and of its self-regulation. This means that they are most dangerous at the ideological level because their reports are often broadly diffused; they are quoted as authoritative, and they provide governments with various ideas about regulating advertising. On the other hand, their lack of sophistication makes them vulnerable to business counterattacks, which have often resulted in their modification, postponement, and ultimate death.

The Advertising Industry

Advertising self-regulation is growing around the world, reaching a minimum of 35 nations and resulting in a number of codes and voluntary guidelines besides those of the International Chamber of Commerce. The major power of these self-regulatory bodies, which either group some segment of the advertising industry (e.g., agencies) or all advertisers, agencies, and media, is that the lack of prior approval (when pre-clearance is required, as is common in broadcasting and for certain products such as medicines and drugs) normally results in the media member refusing to print or broadcast a controversial advertisement. Ads found to be violating guidelines are usually modified or stopped, but they can also be referred to the appropriate authorities if the advertiser refuses to change or discontinue the message. By publicizing their guidelines and decisions, and by inviting complaints from consumers, these organizations (e.g., in Canada, France, the United Kingdom, and the United States) also put indirect pressure on potential violators.

In Japan, the Philippines, Singapore, and the United Kingdom (as far as radio and television are concerned), there is a fairly explicit delegation of quasi-regulatory power to some self-regulatory bodies in lieu of formal mandatory regulations. In Canada, South Africa, the United Kingdom, and the United States, among others, it is more a case of associations trying to preempt further regulations by proving that industry can do as good a job or better than any government agency could. Some observers see in this phenomenon another example of the resurgence of corporatism whereby control is not so much exercised by government or the firm but by the industry itself, which is considered to be the appropriate repository of knowledge about what constitutes proper business behavior. Corporatism, however, has its problems, too, since it can act conservatively, collusively, or in disregard of the public interest.

Many governments and now the EEC Commission favor the growth of self-regulation, whether as a major substitute for further laws and decrees or as a desirable complement to the existing regulatory system, because it lightens their own burden and is done by people with advertising experience. Some of these bodies have suggested that codes be developed in cooperation with consumer associations. However, consumerist groups have been rather lukewarm toward self-regulation since few consumer or even independent representatives sit on advertising policy making and complaint boards. Hence, they suspect that too much soft-pedalling and whitewashing takes place within voluntary groups. Consequently, many developed countries witness a race between consumer groups trying to set up a stiff legal framework and the advertising industry (where organized) attempting to produce a self-disciplinary system which is effective and looks credible. Unfortunately, both groups tend to go on working in a vacuum, without any cooperation, as though the other does not exist.

Businessmen themselves are not wholly behind self-regulation. Many of them like to operate with minimum restraint, prefer to trust their judgement

Table 5–1. Factors Affecting Advertising Regulation and Their Likely Future Impact

Precipitating Circumstances (=Environmental Factors)	*Predictions of Impact on Regulation*
1. Dissatisfaction with advertising and consumer complaints	STABLE regulation
2. New media technologies	LESS regulation
3. Recession and inflation (assumed to last until around 1990)	LESS regulation
Motivation (=Objectives)	
4. Consumer protection against false, misleading, and unfair advertising	LESS regulation in general
5. Trade protection (e.g., comparison advertising and cooperative advertising)	STABLE regulation
6. Nationalism, culturalism, and conservatism	MORE regulation
Forces (=Actors)	
7. Consumerist movement	LESS general regulation but MORE specific ones
8. Governments and international organizations (UN, ECOSOC, EEC, Council of Europe)	LESS regulation in terms of new general laws; MORE regulation on account of an ideological and technical spread of information against advertising
9. Advertising-industry reactions (mainly, lobbying and self-regulation)	STABLE regulation

or that of their lawyer, and are willing to assume the risk of having broken some law or guideline. Some of them suspect that self-regulatory bodies can be biased, old-fashioned, and/or overcautious, as in the case of comparison advertising, which has been opposed by a number of self-regulatory bodies and media. Besides, they fear—at least in countries like the United States— the antitrust implications of associations attempting to impose their standards on the entire industry in a cartel-like manner. (Actually, United States industry codes cannot be mandatory.) Moreover, self-regulation tends to be stronger at the national than at the local level; and it excludes various categories, such as personal ads, which can be equally misleading if not downright false.

Regionally and worldwide, the advertising industry is increasingly organizing itself to monitor, influence, and even oppose various regulatory developments emanating from the EEC Commission, the Council of Europe, and such United Nations bodies as UNESCO and ECOSOC. The International Chamber of Commerce is waking up to this threat.

Conclusion

The net outcome of these environmental factors, objectives, and actors/ forces is likely to be a relative pause during the 1980s in the growth of advertising regulation in terms of broad frontal assault on its falsity, deceptiveness, and unfairness. The immediate dangers, however, lie in recession-induced trade-protectionist measures and in piecemeal attacks against its use in numerous special circumstances (e.g., vulnerable groups, pre-clearance in matters of taste, and cultural/conservative reactions). Broad economic recovery in the 1990s would then reanimate the more traditional regulatory pressure on the practice of advertising.

The industry, fortunately, is better equipped and more determined to anticipate problems, to fight criticisms and restrictions, and to volunteer self-discipline and self-regulation in lieu of regulation or as a complement to it. Hence, the projected regulatory developments are not likely to be as successful and virulent as was the case during the previous consumerist phase.

Bibliography

Boddewyn, J. J. and Marton, Katherin. *Comparison Advertising: A Worldwide Study*. New York: Hastings House, 1978.
Boddewyn J. J. "Advertising Regulation, Self-Regulation, and Self-Discipline Around the World." *Journal of International Marketing* I (1): 46–55, 1981.

Boddewyn, J. J. "The Global Spread of Advertising Regulation." *MSU Business Topics,* 5–13, Spring 1981.

Boddewyn, J. J. "Advertising Regulation in the 1980s: The Underlying Global Forces." *Journal of Marketing,* 27–35, Winter 1982.

Business International. *Europe's Consumer Movement: Key Issues and Corporate Responses.* New York and Geneva: December 1980. For an abbreviated version of this study, see: "Consumerism Issues: How Companies Will Feel the Pinch," *Business Europe,* 265–72, 22 August 1980.

Clutterback, David. "Is the Writing on the Wall for Advertising?" *International Management,* 20–24, August 1980.

Dunn, S. W. "The Changing Legal Climate for Marketing and Advertising in Europe." *Columbia Journal of World Business,* 91–98, Summer 1974.

Dunn, S. W. "The United Nations as a Regulator of International Advertising." Mimeographed. University of Missouri/Columbia: 13 pp.

Evans, J. R. (ed.) *Consumerism in the United States; An Inter-industry Analysis.* New York: Praeger, 1980.

Federal Trade Commission, Office of Policy Planning and Evaluation. *Media Policy Session: Technology and Legal Change.* Washington, D.C.: 3 December 1979.

International Advertising Association (New York). Various studies since 1978 on the regulation and self-regulation of advertising (J. J. Boddewyn, main author).

LaBarbera, Priscilla. "Analyzing and Advancing the State of the Art of Advertising Self-Regulation." *Journal of Advertising* IX (4):27–38, 1980.

Miller, Mark. "Can Advertising Regulate Itself?" *Marketing and Media Decisions* XVI (7):37 ff., July 1981.

Molitor, G. T. T. "Environmental Forecasting: Public Policy Forecasting." In: Lee E. Preston (ed.), *Business Environment/Public Policy 1979 Conference Papers.* St. Louis Mo: American Assembly of Collegiate Schools of Business, 139–51, 1980.

Neelankavil, J. P. and Stridsberg, A. B. *Advertising Self-Regulation: A Global Perspective.* New York: Hastings House, 1979.

Westen, Tracy. *Consumerism in the 1980s—New Roles for Government.* Washington, D.C.: Federal Trade Commission, 8 February 1980.

6 HAVE TECHNOLOGICAL DEVELOPMENTS MADE CURRENT INTERNATIONAL MARKETING PRACTICES/STRATEGIES OBSOLETE?

John K. Ryans, Jr.

By 1985, Honeywell expects to raise minicomputers to 40% of its computer revenues by concentrating its marketing efforts in carefully selected niche markets as well as in its customer base.

—*Business Week,*
February 15, 1982, p. 84.

While much of marketing's attention is being directed toward the area of strategic planning (and tactics), an overriding presumption is that the marketer can effectively segment its market(s). So effectively in fact, that a Honeywell can be certain it can identify niches that will achieve its future share-of-market (SOM) objective. In fact, marketing warfare that has recently titillated the business community has as its underpinning the firm's ability to segment its markets so accurately that it can employ a counteroffensive defense [21] and other sophisticated military tactics [9]. And, of course, there is much evidence to support the presumption that the marketer can (and does) marshal its product planning and marketing research resources in order to carefully identify its target markets (real and potential). To a great extent, such efforts in the international marketing area, however, have been limited to individual national markets due to (1) the firm's overriding belief in cultural sovereignty, (2) its subsidiary-oriented organizational style, and (3) its system of profit center measures (and accounting/control requirements). Such an approach even prevails in Europe, although some marketers now suggest that a pan-European strategy is long overdue. Still, some research in the international marketing area would indicate that even the national level is too broadly based for segmentation purposes and has focused on " . . . significant within-nation differences . . . " that influence consumer buying patterns [18].

A corollary to this expectation regarding the firm's ability to effectively segment its market(s) is the presumption that it can also effectively communicate (promote) to buyers within the tight parameters established for the particular segment(s). In other words, the marketer expects to have media available that will permit reaching the potential buyer with a message designed especially for him/her. Such an expectation is held, in fact, regardless of whether we are talking about consumer or industrial products or are concerned about domestic or international markets, including Western Europe.

Wind and Douglas [23, p. 72] have stressed the importance of the international portfolio approach to strategic planning, which necessitates a data collection procedure that provides a continuous inflow of product information by market segment for each country. Or, in other words, they suggest that the ability to view segments across national markets is essential to their portfolio system, although presumably the segments themselves could have some intermarket variation in terms of consumer identification. Their approach is compatible with the *Eurobrand,* a trendy term that has been defined as " . . . a single product for a single market embracing 12 or more countries . . . " [2, p. 3], but still their system is not dependent on (nor does it suggest) such a multimarket orientation.

So, in effect, what we have typically witnessed is an ever-increasing effort to improve on market segmentation techniques within national markets and an occasional reference to the possibility of a multimarket brand, one that is often seen as a Coke-like product embracing an extremely broad segment. But, what of the *Eurobrand* movement, what of those who say, "With the coming of international media, branders will have the tools to promote transnational brands . . . "? [2, p. 9] Are these individuals, who for starters advocate pan-European campaigns, suggesting that international marketers, including academics and practitioners, have been guilty of what Bonoma [4, p. 115] recently described as marketing inertia, or the failure to move from what is comfortable in the past? Are we in fact on the threshold of major technology and media/advertising regulatory changes which render useless the international marketing segmentation and promotional approaches that have succeeded in the past? In this chapter, the author will discuss the earlier views regarding a standardized promotional approach to certain markets, including Western Europe, and will identify some of the technological changes that will directly impact on marketers. In addition, the constraints implied by current (and proposed) media and advertising regulatory change will be explored. Finally, the author will address the basic issue of whether the international marketer is prepared to alter its strategies, which have traditionally accounted for market-to-market differences, in light of the vast array of new multi-market media and the suggestion that country cultural differences have been over-emphasized.

Some Background on Standardized Campaigns Versus A Marketing-To-Market Approach

The concept of employing standardized campaigns (worldwide) and directing the firm's promotional campaigns from a central base (often home office) is not new. Beginning with Esso's putting "A Tiger in Every Tank" [15, p. 69], the question of standardized campaigns had been much debated [11–13, 16], and the debate continues today [6, 10, 11, 34]. In fact, the dialogue and debate have been feverish and continuing; the space devoted to the standardized advertising issue here is in no way reflective of the amount of discussion that has been leveled by both its proponents and exponents.

At the heart of this issue, of course, is culture or the relative importance that is assigned to cultural differences between countries. And the basic issue typically has not been "Can we offer the same exact advertisement in every market?" but rather "Can we employ the same basic theme (and appeal) so we have a consistent image in every market?" Contrasting views on this question were recently reflected by actions taken by two jeans competitors in Europe: a Levi spokesman said, "Consistency in image (in Europe) is a priority, . . . " [6, p. 34] and took action to centralize its approach; while Blue Bell International (Wrangler) shifted to a market to-market approach to gain " . . . the individual needs of each market. . . . " [6, p. 36]

While a centralized approach and some modification of a standardized campaign theme have many advantages, such as cost-savings, the opportunity to exercise leverage over the agency, etc. [13, pp. 16–17], the real issue has always revolved around cultural differences. And while the debate on this issue continues, there has been recent evidence to suggest that for many marketers (and their products), the differences within Western Europe are either minimal [19, p. 12] or have little or no impact. (The latter is especially true for industrial marketers.)

Of course, there are a number of firms that subscribe to some version of the centralized control/standardized communications approach. These include companies such as Henkel KGaH, Novo Industri, Goodyear International, IBM, 3M, Digital Equipment Corporation, Texas Instruments, and Cessna Aircraft. Such firms are perhaps best prepared to respond to the technological changes described in the next section. The comments of an advertising agency director (and Eurobrand proponent) are worth noting: ". . . part of the key to a Eurobrand is to seek similarities between Europeans in each product market, not to be led astray by the differences." [2, p. 9]. What this individual and other proponents of the Eurobrand are saying is that basic differences may simply have impeded or have made it impossible for some MNCs to employ a multi-market strategy, but that other MNCs may not have attempted to determine if their particular segment has similar attributes in multiple markets. The marketing services director of *Scientific American,* talking about the results of a pan-European survey of leading European business readers that indicated high ratings for his publication and *Time, Newsweek,* the *Financial Times,* and *The Economist,* says

> . . . the 6,400,000 upmarket, educationally elite readers of those five magazines have more in common with each other than with their fellow countrymen who are less well off . . . over 70% of them speak English in their business lives and therefore have a common means of communication. [2, p. 9].

This illustrates the type of segment that has a cross-border orientation, rather than the market-to-market orientation suggested by the more traditional international marketing approach to segmentation, which relies heavily on the sovereignty of culture.

Rampant Technology

A special client/in-house publication of Benton & Bowles, Inc. suggests that " . . . the age of transnational advertising via satellite in Europe will not become a full-scale reality before the 1990s." [22, p. 3] But, such a projection does not reflect accurately the current technology boom in Europe, which, according to the Mackintosh Report, will reach $3 billion annually by 1985. [3, p. 11] Nor does it suggest the impact that cable television is already having on certain markets. The potential problems of cable television are perhaps best illustrated in Canada, where 53 percent of the homes already have cable and where the dominance of U.S. television is becoming a major concern. [7, pp. 16–17] Cable television brings the Canadian consumer in contact with U.S. television and, in effect, reduces the need for U.S companies to advertise on Canadian stations. In other countries, such as Denmark, where television advertising is not permitted, there is a different dilemma. The technology developments may force the Danish government to permit advertising on television as a defense against their own firms going outside the country in order to advertise back to the home market. [1, p. 6]

Naturally, there has been extensive inter-country media overlap in Europe long before the advent of cable, the immediate concern for satellite television, and other video developments. For years, it has not been uncommon for a Dutch viewer to have a favorite German or Belgian television program; and the print media, as suggested by the quote from the *Scientific American* director above, have long shown a remarkable tendency to cross borders. To some extent, such media overlap has resulted in redundancy—viewed favorably by some companies and negatively by others. To a firm seeking to confine a particular maketing theme or approach to a single national market segment, however, this overlap has always presented problems and affected media selection. In the future, as the technology advances further and the European countries respond to pressure for wider use of cable and then satellite television, the problem of narrow market identification will become more formidable.

Let us return to satellite television, which earlier was suggested as not becoming a full-scale reality until the 1990s. Will it become a force—an important advertising medium opening the entire European market—prior to that date? Luxembourg's RTL (Radio-Tele-Luxembourg) is scheduled to begin by the mid-1980s; and RTL has demonstrated a capacity in the past to create waves, as it carried broadcasts to neighboring countries. It has been estimated that its start-up costs will be $350 million; it plans to broadcast three services, French, German, and Dutch or English. (12, p. 1). Understandably, therefore, most forecasters seem uncertain regarding the date that satellite television will become a force. One estimate is that there could be as many as 60 TV satellites in orbit by the year 2000 [20, p. 33], but this appears to be the extreme position. What is more realistic is the view that satellite TV will be an important promotion medium in the next decade. Nestle's Keith Monk has indicated that his company views it as a future reality and sees the issue " ... is really whether product advertising now handled (by Nestle) on a country-by-country basis can be adapted to international standards."(2, 5)

Clearly, the variety of electronic media in the future is imposing [8, p. 24], but only those that cross borders, such as satellite TV and cable TV, impact on the questions raised here.

Regulation

There are really two dimensions to the regulatory concerns regarding the new TV technologies. The first concerns the regulation of satellite television and cable television—the former is regulated under the resolution adopted by WARC in Geneva in 1977 [14, p. 14] and the latter on virtually a state-to-state basis. Many countries, such as Germany, seem to be moving slowly on both fronts, although they will clearly feel the impact of the introduction of RTL. The second regulatory dimension concerns the regulation of the advertising message content. This is an area that is likely to create many problems, since the countries of Western Europe vary greatly in terms of what products (and messages) may appear on television. RTL has indicated that it will attempt to follow various advertising codes and to ban all alcohol and cigarette advertising [12, p. 1]. However, research on the impact of consumerists' efforts regarding advertising in Europe suggests that there will be numerous problems, since each country has unique advertising rules and, even in the E.C., these have not as yet been harmonized. [17]

National regulations range from a total ban on television advertising (Denmark and Sweden) to some extremely specific regulations regarding claims (Germany), and the use of children in television advertising [12, p. 15]. As Monk has suggested, "the overall affect of all these different rules and regulations is perhaps the ... most serious issue facing everyone—advertisers, viewers, and the media owners alike." [5, p. 2] He feels that companies like Nestle, which are fairly decentralized in their promotional efforts, " ... may find they will need to have more control over advertising programs, setting up guidelines within which the national companies can operate." [5, p. 2] Of course, the variety of national regulations will undoubtedly lead many advertisers to respond to the guidelines in the most restrictive markets in order to insure the acceptance of their commercials in all markets via satellite television.

Are Changing Practices/Strategies Needed?

Earlier, the debate over the importance of culture in international marketing strategy was mentioned. While it continues to rage, there is much to suggest that evolving socio-economic patterns, increasing technology, and advancing marketing regulatory measures may make the discussions superfluous. There is much to suggest a broader, cross-market view of market segmentation—even though the perceived product niche may be narrower in terms of customer/buyer characteristics. The aggregate market provides the necessary size to make the niche viable. Marketing strategies that have been based on the independence of markets—with each country a profit center—will need to be modified to permit intermarket synergism, and all stages of planning will have to focus on customers that may not have a common language or single national purpose. Their main similarity, in fact, may revolve around the characteristic(s) that makes this group a valuable niche for your product.

It has been suggested that some companies do view Western Europe as a single market, while others are considering the advocacy of such an approach. And, clearly, all products will not be able to ignore serious market-to-market differences; food has been the most cited exception.

At issue are questions concerning how international firms should respond to the new problems/opportunities resulting from this revised media mix and whether this is actually just part of a larger transition away from the cultural constraints imposed on international marketers in the past. Do these international marketers need to revise their definition and approach to their markets(s)? Should they explore the potential of a Eurobrand and/or single European marketing strategy? Should companies such as Xerox and Hoover be concerned with identifying niches (or gaps in the market) based on intermarket rather than market-to-market analyses? And, perhaps more pointedly, are international marketing academics preparing to meet the challenges offered by these changes? Are improved macromarketing strategies and tactics needed—along with new marketing research techniques that accommodate to more rapid data collection and assimilation? It would appear the answer is *yes*. As a senior vice president of Doyle Dane Bernbach recently stated, "If a marketer wants to be in a position to utilize pan-European broadcasting via satellites, he is not only going to need a uniform product and uniform packaging across Europe, but uniform positioning, too. Today there are very few advertisers in Europe who are in a position to use satellites." [24, p. M–22] In fact, many are faced with multiple overlapping and often conflicting images such as recently plagued Pan Am planners [24, p. M–22].

Can it also be stated that few international marketing academics are prepared to accommodate to an evolving Western European intermarket environment—where market-to-market approaches may in some instances even be dysfunctional? Most discussion to date still indicates a prevalence of the market-to-market perspective, even among strategic planners. Such a view not only fails to recognize current technology and evolving market patterns, but costs marketers the opportunity for intermarket leveraging as well.

Summary and Some Conclusions

During the next decade, marketers in Western Europe will experience the first shockwave of the rapid technological developments—satellite TV and expanded cable television—that will dramatically change their promotional efforts. Traditionally accustomed to segmenting their markets on a country-by-country basis and employing national media that have offered relatively minimal market overlap, they will be faced with television that is trans-country in coverage.

The earlier debates regarding centralized advertising planning and standardized promotional programs were centered on the relative importance of culture; proponents seeking consumer commonality and opponents stressing market-to-market differences. Still, the resulting standard plans were implemented on national media programs. More recently, Digital Equipment Corporation, Henkel, and others, who recognized the need for a single European corporate image, have targeted messages to reach specialized trans-Europe audiences. To do so, they have pre-tested advertisements in multiple country markets to arrive at programs that have intermarket acceptance. Then, these advertisements are used in media that cross borders to reach their target audience. The European business press and the international editions of U.S. publications provide such print media for reaching corporate influentials.

Current research by the Swiss-based International Research Institute of Social Change (RISC) has suggested that national cultural differences within the European Community may be overstressed today; "... the growing awareness of shared 'lifestyle' traits, transcending national boundaries, may well usher in a new era of Europe-wide marketing and advertising strategies." [19, p. 12] If so, this fact, coupled with the television technological developments, suggests that current country-by-country market segmentation and strategic planning will need to be replaced by a multi-market approach to segmentation and strategic planning. If so, the question raised earlier—"Are international market practitioners and academicians prepared (or preparing) for such a change?"—is most appropriate, and to date the answer, with few exceptions, is *no*. However, to reiterate Monk's earlier point, the issue is not whether such change will occur, but rather how the marketer can respond best to it. While the centralized/standardized communications approach (or some modification of it) seems to be the best alternative to date, the need to develop more effective promotion strategy is apparent.

References

1. Arnold, Peter. "Satellites May Alter Danish TV." *Advertising Age/Europe,* November 1981, Vol. 3, Issue 10, p. 6.
2. Bacot, Eugene. "Eurobrand: A New Approach to Marketing." *Advertising Age/Europe,* October 1981, Vol. 3, Issue 9, pp. 3, 9.
3. Bacot, Eugene. "Europe's Video Boom: Sales to Top $3 Billion." *Advertising Age/Europe,* March 1981, p. 11.
4. Bonoma, Thomas V. "Market Success Can Breed *Market Inertia." Harvard Business Review,* September/October 1981, Vol. 59, No. 5, pp. 115–19.
5. "Can Product Advertising Adapt to Satellite TV?" *International Advertiser,* January/February 1982, Vol. 2, No. 4, p. 2.
6. Chase, Dennis and Bacot, Eugene. "Levi Zipping Up World Image." *Advertising Age,* September 14, 1981, Vol. 52, No. 39, pp. 34, 36.
7. Hardingham, Tony. "New Technologies Fracture Canada's TV Market." *International Advertiser,* Vol. 2, No. 2, September/October 1981, pp. 16–20.
8. Hartley, Robert F. and Moore, Thomas A. "New Video Technology Poses Perils for Some Advertisers." *Harvard Business Review,* September/October 1981, Vol. 59, No. 5, pp. 24, 26, 28.
9. Kotler, Philip and Singh, Ravi. "Marketing Warfare in the 1980s." *Journal of Business Strategy,* Vol. 1, No. 3, Winter 1981.
10. LaFolette, Joseph O. "Centralized International Advertising and Promotion in a Decentralized Environment." Unpublished paper presented at the International Advertising Clinic, A.N.A. Annual Meeting, November 7–10, 1981, San Francisco, California.
11. Mellor, Simon. "Single Market Strategy in Europe?" *Advertising Age/Europe,* October 1981, Vol. 3, Issue 9, pp. 3, 11.
12. Newman, Barry. "European States Face Problem of Controlling Their Neighbors' TV," *Wall Street Journal,* Vol. LXII, No. 110, March 22, 1982, p. 1, 15.
13. Peebles, Dean M. and Ryans, John K., Jr., "Using Multinational Advertising Strengths in National Markets." *Advertising and Marketing,* Vol. 17, No. 1, pp. 12–17.
14. Roth, Peter. "German Television on the Verge of Change." *International Advertiser,* January/February 1982, Vol. 2, No. 4, pp. 12–14.
15. Ryans, John K., Jr., "A Tiger in Every Tank?" *Columbia Journal of World Business,* March/April 1969, Vol. IV, No. 2, pp. 69–75.
16. Ryans, John K., Jr., and Fry, Claudia. "Some European Attitudes on the Advertising Transference Questions: A Research Note." *Journal of Advertising,* Vol. 5, No. 2, Spring 1976, pp. 11–13.

17. Ryans, John and Wills, James. *Consumerism's Impact on Advertising Regulation (Worldwide)*. New York: International Advertising Association, Inc., May 1979.

18. Schiffman, Leon G., Dillon, William R., and Ngumah, Festus E. "The Influence of Subcultural and Personality Factors on Consumer Acculturation." *Journal of International Business Studies*, Fall 1981, Vol. XII, No. 2, pp. 137–43.

19. Stratte-McClure, Joel. "Now Divided but United by Lifestyle." *Advertising Age's Focus*, January 1982, pp. 12, 13, 15.

20. "Toward the *Wired Society*." *World Business Weekly*, June 8, 1981, Vol. 4, No. 22, p. 33.

21. "The Eighties: An Era of Marketing Warfare." *Madison Avenue*, May 1980, Vol. 22, No. 5, pp. 35, 36, 38, 40.

22. *Transnational Satellite Broadcasting in Europe*. New York: Benton & Bowles, 1981. An in-house monograph.

23. Wind, Yoram and Douglas, Susan. "International Portfolio Analysis and Strategy: The Challenge of the Eighties." *Journal of International Business Studies*, Fall 1982, p. 72.

24. Yovovich, B. G. "Maintaining a Balance of Planning." *Advertising Age*, May 17, 1982, p. M–22.

7 MARKETING:
The Missing Link in Economic Development
S. Prakash Sethi and Hamid Etemad

Marketing as a Neglected Subject in Economic Development Process

An understanding of the role of marketing function and its contribution to economic development has been one of the most neglected subjects in the economic literature, both as a theoretical concept and as an area for empirical study. Economic planners and administrators have also ignored or severely downplayed its importance in the development process. This neglect can be attributed to a number of factors, for example:

1. The issue of economic development in less-developed countries (LDCs) starts with the assumption that there is too much demand and too little supply. Marketing function is associated, somewhat prejudicially, with advertising and demand creation. Since demand creation is not the problem in the development process, it is reasoned that marketing activity is not necessary.
2. Another assumption about the development process lies in the shortage of savings and investment capital to generate growth. Therefore, it is considered necessary to contain or reduce demand in order to free

resources from current consumption and divert them toward savings and investment. High level of consumption is presumed undesirable for its alleged adverse impact on savings and capital formation. Since marketing acts in stimulating demand, it should be actively discouraged.

3. Economic planners ignore marketing, as Holton suggests, because marketing practice is treated as a passive element which adapts itself to whatever economic conditions that prevail in an economy [Holton, 1953]. This view, however, seems to be myopic. Modern marketing can also act as a catalyst for economic growth, as opposed merely to being the aftereffect of economic development.

4. Development economists have traditionally failed to incorporate (or model) the complexities of selling and distribution in a world of imperfect competition and incomplete information. For example, as early as 1953, in an article, Professor Holton called this tendency a traditional economic bias. The same comment seems relevant even today [Holton, 1953; Galbraith and Holton, 1955]. As such, marketing still remains underdeveloped in LDCs.

5. Development economists and planners generally have failed to accept the notion that improvements in marketing practices can facilitate economic development, while existing inefficient marketing practices can hinder it [Shapiro, 1965, p. 421]. Hence, even an overhaul of existing marketing practices is not given serious priority.

6. In most LDCs, marketing function is also associated with the army of intermediaries and middlemen, who control the distribution process and raise the cost of goods to consumers through creating locational monopolies. They are viewed as parasites, who do not make any positive contribution to the development process. [Kindleberger, 1958, p. 106]

7. Commercial activities in general and marketing practices in particular— as characterized by intermediaries and traders—have not enjoyed high social and professional status. This has contributed to the neglect of marketing in LDCs.

8. A large part of the population in LDCs is engaged in or connected with some form of agriculture-related activities, where people share a universal hostility toward marketing middlemen. They believe that one person's gain must be at another's expense. This view has contributed to the lack of cooperation and coordination between agricultural sector and marketing intermediaries, and has led to massive inefficiencies in marketing and distribution of agricultural products.

9. Finally, marketing suffers from most economic planners' view that marketing and distribution expertise in one country is not applicable in another country and, above all, cannot be transferred.

Marketing's Role in Economic Development

Arguments against assigning a significant role to marketing in the development process suffer from three serious flaws:

1. Marketing is seen as an outcome rather than a process. It is assumed to create more demand and, therefore, is injurious to savings and investment. This argument has attracted a great deal of attention [Nurske, 1953, pp. 61–75; Shapiro, 1965, p. 416], but its validity, in view of its interaction with a host of other variables, remains as yet untested. It is equally possible that marketing practices that cause an increase in consumption can also be directed to promote savings and investments.
2. Where marketing is treated as an outcome, it is *a priori* assumed that such an outcome will be undesirable for the economic growth. Consumption, if it were to increase, does not occur in a vacuum. A desire for increased consumption could lead to a greater urge to earn the means that could be used to buy consumable goods. Thus, it may be reasoned that consumption and production are linked together and must grow simultaneously. Smithies argues in favor of putting more emphasis on stimulating individuals to make additional efforts and use greater ingenuity in financing their consumption. If increased consumer demand causes labor to become more productive or work harder, the forced savings to accumulate capital will be unnecessary. He discusses at length the conditions under which output of capital and consumer goods could increase simultaneously [Smithies, 1961, pp. 225–57].
3. Where marketing is treated as a process, its value is downgraded by assuming the then-existing level of performance as the optimun level. An inefficient distribution system does not obviate the need for a distribution system, but intensifies it. Middlemen in the existing system may indeed be performing poorly by extracting monopoly profits, but they can also be used to create time and place utilities thereby adding value to tangible products. In a study of marketing activities in Puerto Rico, Galbraith and Holton found that there were massive inefficiencies involved in the distribution system and that a redesigning of the system would lead to substantial savings. Furthermore, they pointed out that, depending on the variations in assumptions and design, the savings in the island's food bill alone could come to anywhere between 16% to 19% [Galbraith and Holton, 1955, pp. 177–98]. Higgins has suggested that the neglect of marketing has deterred growth of small-scale industries. Are such industries inherently and inevitably inefficient? Higgins asked, "Or are they just badly planned and badly managed? Is it simply that some essential aspect of the production process, such as marketing, is neglected?" [Higgins, 1959, p. 769].

Underdevelopment and Marketing in Perspective

To understand the role of marketing in economic development process, it is necessary that we analyze the antecedents, the resource factors, and the assumptions that underlie the growth process and evidence of development that characterizes different countries. Although different economists may define growth processes differently, they all emanate from certain common characteristics, such as lack of efficiency, undefined or poorly defined direction (or orientation), inadequate factor endowment, and poor organization.

It is the thesis of this paper that modern marketing practices can be a potent catalyst that organizes, augments, and accelerates economic development. This is not to refute or to deny the role of well-established factors in the development process. Instead, it is to advocate that marketing as a concept possesses enhancing characteristics that can augment and accelerate the development process regardless of a country's state of factor endowments.

In modern marketing, consumer needs and wants hold a supreme position. Maximal satisfaction of consumers' incipient, latent, or existing wants for goods and services is the primary objective of marketing [Keegan, 1980, p. 211; Kotler, 1967, pp. 90–100]. While realization of a profit remains as the main criteria, delivery of goods to the right market place, at the right time, and above all at a reasonable price, are the major tasks that are performed to generate those profits. When all efforts are directed at organizing economic activities such that quality goods and services are provided, at a reasonable cost, to the largest possible number, several phenomena occur simultaneously—waste, spoilage, and inefficiencies in the employment and allocation of resources are minimized; consumer satisfaction is increased; and, finally, the system generates an economic surplus.

Factors or Preconditions for Economic Development and Growth

For economic development to initiate, take off, and sustain the existence of several factors is considered important. These include: effective market size,[1] natural resource endowment,[2] favorable geographical location,[3] preferential ties to large industrial countries,[4] stable political and hospitable social environment,[5] literate and skilled population,[6] foreign aid,[7] and foreign direct investment.[8] A survey of literature shows that, with the exception of foreign direct investment:

1. There is no clear agreement or evidence as to the extent of the impact of these factors on development. Of equal importance, there is no consensus as to whether their presence is absolutely necessary and to what extent their absence can hinder the process of economic development.
2. The mechanics, in terms of a chain of dynamic effects emanating from these factors and leading to the subsequent stages of economic development, are not universally established.

These ambiguities have left the policy makers and development planners in a real quandary, i.e., how to define and provide a clear-cut direction for economic development. Foreign direct investment (FDI) stands in a different class. Market orientation of multinational enterprises (MNEs), which are responsible for the bulk of expertise, separate FDI from other factors. Indeed, there is strong evidence supporting the effectiveness of MNEs' managerial skills in general and their marketing skills in particular.

Organizing for Economic Development

One of the basic questions in economic theory is how to organize and prepare for economic development. It is beyond the scope of this chapter to do even a brief review of various economic theories or their critique. An excellent review is provided in a survey article by Hahn and Matthews [1964], and in Burmeister and Dobell [1970]. Robert Solow's book, *Growth Theory: An Exposition* [1970], also offers a solid treatment of the subject. Notwithstanding the substantial efforts at explaining the economic development process, Hirschman contends that economists have failed in constructing a complete theory of economic development. "Economists have not been able to construct, much less agree on, a single and unbroken chain of causes and effects that would neatly explain the transition from underdevelopment to development." [Hirschman, 1958, p. 50].

In his critique of the theory of balanced growth that stresses the need for different parts of a developing economy to remain in step to avoid supply bottlenecks [Lewis, 1955; Rosenstein-Rodan, 1943; Nurkse, 1953; Scitovsky, 1954]; plus the theory of big push, that advocates economic development through a few big projects [Scitovsky, 1959], Hirschman [1958] concludes that these theories fail as a true theory. He argues that a theory of development must clearly spell out "the process of *change* of one type of economy *into* some other more advanced type" [Hirschman, 1958, pp. 51–52]; and in that regard, most theories, including the above two, are deficient.

Most supply-oriented theories of economic development suffer from their own myopic view of market mechanism, mostly based on Says' Law,[9] [Harrod, 1948], in presuming that supply creates its own demand. Equally valid criticism applies to economic development theories that have concentrated solely on expanding aggregate demand[10] without paying sufficient attention to the actual composition of demand. In the absence of complete integration or coordination of supply and demand, there is no guarantee that the actual components of aggregate demand and that of aggregate supply will reach market equilibrium as the economy travels from one stage of development to another. Under conditions of perfect information,[11] producers are totally aware of market needs and produce goods in response to those needs—there is a greater probability for simultaneous meeting of market needs and clearing of producers' supplies. Under a system of imperfect information, however, the chance of this happening decreases dramatically. Where markets are disorganized or marketing is de-emphasized, marketing channels fail to generate demand-related market information, which is no longer available to play an organizing and integrating role. Thus, producers must decide independently, and somewhat in isolation, about what to produce. [Figure 7-1] In so doing, producers tend to become supply- or production-oriented and satisfy their own objectives independent of market needs. Table 7-1 compares and contrasts this orientation with that of demand and strategic orientation. A supply-oriented marketing and management system suffers from similar symptoms. These are reviewed in table 7-2.

Marketing, in contrast, concentrates on market *segments,* as opposed to markets. In contrast to aggregate consumption behavior, marketing studies a consumer's—an individual's—behavior (or a segment's behavior, when that segment is relatively homogenous) with respect to a single product (or a product class). In so doing, marketing is capable of studying and then satisfying an individual's needs to the extent of its commercial feasibility. The rapid developments in the area of consumer behavior should be taken as positive evidence for the success of these studies [see: Alderson, 1965; Engel, Kollat, and Blackwell, 1973; Howard and Sheth, 1969; Nicosia, 1966; Sheth and Sethi, 1977]. Indeed, marketing theories have developed frameworks of consumer behavior that capture individual characteristics and capitalize upon them. Societal structure and influences, social class, personality profiles, demographics, marketing environment, and institutions, communications, marketing inputs, and consumer feedback all play instrumental roles in theories of consumer behavior.

In Sheth and Sethi's model, for example, cultural and environmental aspects of a buyer's behavior are particularly emphasized. This feature of

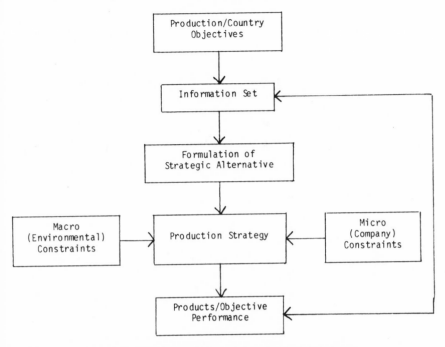

Figure 7–1.   A Schematic Presentation of Supply-Push Strategy.

Note: In a supply-oriented ED, information set leading to formulation of strategy and satisfying objectives may be independent of market's needs and wants. Thus, producers must decide in isolation and use a push strategy to move their goods and services through channels to markets.

the model allows and perhaps warrants economic development planners and marketers to take notice of cross-cultural differences as well. Another added benefit is the model's clear-cut implications for market segmentation based on cultural variables along with other characteristics [Sheth and Sethi, 1977, pp. 369–89].

In a demand-oriented system of information—whereby markets originate information and reflect market's (or individual's) needs and wants—production will respond to such information. It stands a greater chance of clearing supplies at a reasonable price, realizing profits, and, above all, satisfying market needs. Conversely, where supply-oriented producers have to push their products (push strategy), in a marketing-oriented economy, marketing intermediaries and marketing institutions pull the product from producer through the channels of distribution to appropriate markets. Thus, the possibility of mismatch, inventory buildups, spoilage, and pilferage are

Table 7–1. Comparison of Different Economic Development (ED) Orientations with Different Orientation in Marketing and Management's Evolutionary Path

Concept	ED with **Production/** Supply-Side *Orientation*	ED with **Marketing** *Orientation*	ED with **Strategic** *Orientation*
Focus/Emphasis	Increasing physical production capacity High return to capital investment	Social welfare -buyer satisfaction -marketing and distribution	Complete societal welfare
Ends/Objectives/ Criteria	Increased production Utilization of resources Higher *material* possession	Maximization of social or buyer satisfaction to lead to higher objective productivity Fair return to all productive factors	Maximized social welfare subject to global welfare constraints Fair return to all productive factors—local and foreign
Means for Accomplishing the Ends	Installing new production capacity by: -capital investment through increased savings, decreased consumption Protective tariff and	Strong marketing orientation by: -emphasizing comparative advantage -encouraging competition -increasing choice	Integrated, coordinated, strategic international decision-making Emphasis on comparative advantage Regionally or internationally

	non-tariff barriers Import substitution Foreign borrowings Inward orientation	-increasing discrimination possibilities -decreasing protective barriers Establishing incentive systems -subsidies to local producers -subsidies to exporters Open international market operation Selective outward orientation on goods with comparative advantage	integrated production-distribution system Complete environmental consciousness Social and global responsibility Fair international competition and trade Integrated inward-outward orientation
Prominent Issues Overriding Others	Supply-side issues -production, capacity	Marketing orientation Comparative advantage	Law of comparative advantage
Relatively Ignored or De-emphasized Issues	Social welfare Consumer satisfaction Marketing and distribution Demand-side issues Competition Benefits of trade Exports	Nationalism Local sourcing and local content requirements Across-the-board local production Import substitution Supply-side issues	Nationalism

Table 7-2. Evolutionary Path of Marketing and Management

Concept	Old Marketing/Management Concept	New Marketing/Management Concept	Emerging Strategic Marketing/Management Concept
Focus/Emphasis	*Objective* quality products (by production and engineering standard) Production economies Product improvement	Consumer satisfaction leading to *subjective* quality (by consumer standard) Total marketing Product, price, promotion, distribution and after-sales service Advertising/promotion	Integrated total societal satisfaction
Ends/Objectives/ Criteria	Returns to stockholders Profitability	High objective as well as subjective productivity	Fair return to all stakeholders: stockholders, consumers, employees, management, environment
Means for Accomplishing the Ends	Selling what is produced Large sale force Large distribution network New and improved products	Total marketing Market segmentation Large communication budgets/campaigns	Integrated and coordinated strategic decision-making; Integrated marketing-production

	Large product/production-oriented R&D Minimization of overall costs/maximization of material output	Extensive pomotion Extensive consumer research Extensive consumer-oriented R&D Product variety and choice Maximization of consumer satisfaction/minimization of cognitive dissonance	Environmental consciousness Societal responsibility Fair competition Fair trade
Prominent Issues Overriding Others	Objective quality Product Cost Supply-side issues	Consumer satisfaction Subjective quality Marketing in general Demand-side issues	Non (ultimately)
Relatively Ignored or De-emphasized Issues	Consumer satisfaction After-sales service Other marketing mix components: communication, pricing, convenience factor in distribution Demand-side issues Product choice and variety	Objective quality Supply-side issues Production economies	Non (ultimately)

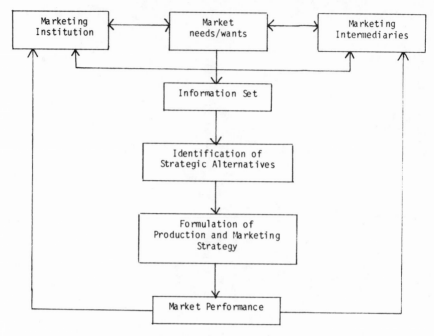

Figure 7–2.　A Schematic Presentation of Demand-Pull Strategy.

Note: In a marketing-oriented production or ED, information set leading to formulation of strategy reflects marketing needs and wants, and is reinforced by market performance which plays an organizing and integrating role. Thus, once producers respond to market needs and wants, markets, marketing intermediaries and institutions, pull such goods and services through channels and minimize waste, inventory build up and resource misallocation.

minimized. New marketing concepts and marketing-oriented management have a great deal in common with marketing-oriented economic development, and their main characteristics are reviewed in figure 7–2.

Marketing and Economic Development

Marketing can contribute in three important ways in the economic development of less developed countries: (1) increasing individual welfare, (2) maximizing social output, and (3) minimizing distribution costs.

Marketing Increases Individual Welfare

In industrialized countries, consumers have an abundance of products from which to choose to satisfy their needs. Manufacturers utilize the marketing concept to analyze consumer wants and preferences. The objective is to discern those wants and preferences that are not being currently served or served well. A marketer develops products and services that satisfy those unmet wants, thereby getting an edge on his or her competitors. The consumer derives greater satisfaction from such consumption, thereby increasing his or her utility. Marketing thus makes a contribution toward consumer welfare.

The same logic applies with greater validity in the case of LDCs, where a consumer has limited income and less discretion. The marginal utility of money is quite high. Under these circumstances, consumer satisfaction from product usage would be vastly greater if the limited number of goods available were to meet more closely the consumer's wants and preferences. According to Hans Thorelli, "No vehicle is more powerful than contemporary marketing philosophy in changing attitudes in a manner conducive to improving standard of living in a democratic society." [Thorelli, 1964]

Marketing Maximizes Social Output

By placing primary, if not the sole, emphasis on investment and production, development economists assume that the worker is a passive consumer, i.e., consumption as an incentive is not important. One has only to look at the black markets for imported goods or better quality domestically produced goods in the socialist paradises of the Soviet bloc and in most developing economies to realize the gratuitousness of such an assumption. Similarly, a disregard of consumer preferences causes vast production of goods and services that go begging for want of buyers. Newspapers are full of stories from planned economies where grandiose plans have gone astray and factories are making products that have to be sold at terrible losses. The enormous waste of scarce resources bears sad testimony to the preciousness of the planners' arguments that a primarily capital-goods-oriented economic growth model is the most desirable, if not the only feasible, approach for LDCs to follow.

Workers will most likley work harder and produce more, if they can see attractive possibilities with which to enjoy the fruits of their labor. Appeals to patriotism and affluence at some indefinite future, in the absence of direct rewards for one's efforts, are poor crutches to build a solid foundation for economic growth and a prosperous society.

Similarly, when a nation must restrict the amount of resources that can be devoted to the production of consumer goods, it becomes even more important that the goods produced are most appropriate for meeting consumer needs, thereby maximizing the return on the use of resources. In less-developed countries more so than in developed countries, consumers strive to gain maximum satisfaction from that use of their meager resources and limited purchasing power. A closer match between the demand for and supply of particular products enhances the value of consumers' existing purchasing power, leading to higher level of social satisfaction than in the previous case. It also reinforces the efficient producers by rewarding them handsomely while penalizing the inefficient ones. A higher level of satisfaction at the societal level, then, can be converted to higher motivational level [McClelland, 1961; McClelland & Winter, 1969], resulting in greater productivity of the labor force. The final result of this process is a gradual but substantive structural—as opposed to marginal—reorganization of the economy toward a more efficient, productive, and self-propelled system.

Marketing, therefore, maximizes social welfare by creating consumer goods that provide the most incentive to workers to be more productive, and rationalizes the use of scarce resources by mobilizing them in the most efficient manner.

Peter Drucker has best summarized the case of marketing in economic development:

> Marketing occupies a critical role in respect to development of such *growth* areas. Indeed, marketing is the most important *multiplier* of such development. It is, in itself, in every one of these areas, the least developed, the most backward part of economic system. Its development, above all others, makes possible economic integration and the fullest utilization of whatever assets and productive capacity an economy already possesses. It mobilizes latent economic energy. It contributes to the greatest needs: that for the rapid development of entrepreneurs and managers, and at the same time it may be the easiest area of managerial work to get going . . . It is the most systematized, and, therefore, the most learnable and the most teachable of all areas of business management and entrepreneurship [Drucker, 1958, p. 253].

Marketing Minimizes Distribution (Channel) Costs

Finally, marketing can provide enormous growth dividends by improving distribution economics in the less-developed countries. LDCs suffer dearly because of poor distribution, storage, and channel inefficiencies. This is largely due to two factors.

First, planners seldom do a good job in providing for storage and distribution facilities because they have poor understanding of these needs, being contemptuous of and deficient in grasping consumer needs and putting a low value on the consumer's conveniences. Stories about spoilage and wastage—because of poor storage—are legend in poor countries. For example, it is estimated that almost ten percent of farm production in India is lost to mice, rodents, and spillage, because of poor storage and transportation facilities. Poor and inadequate storage facilities also force farmers to sell their produce at the peak of harvest season, when abundant supplies create product glut and cause prices to decline. Thus, the farmer gets a lower total overall return for his or her output than would be otherwise possible. Minimization of waste and spoilage in distribution allows for further employment of those previously wasted resources in more productive endeavors, thereby increasing the overall capabilities.

Secondly, consumer satisfaction creates a massive pulling force, which causes a fast and efficient movement of goods and services throughout the channels of distribution—from the main producers to the final retailers—minimizing inventory costs, storage waste, and pilferage, and above all guaranteeing a continuous flow in the system. Economic planners put little value to space and time utilities created by efficient middlemen and distribution system, since they are intangible in character. This makes it possible for inefficient middlemen to create space and time monopolies and adds to the cost of products, reduces consumer surplus, and also lowers the share of revenues that goes to the producers, thereby reinforcing the suspicion and contempt of people in LDCs toward middlemen. Kindleberger, the noted international economist, recognized distribution's vital role in economic development by observing:

> Whether markets pull development or lag behind it, it is evident that much planning in the area of economic development today neglects distribution ... (and) ... storage facilities in particular tend to be neglected. Distribution is inescapable ... distribution takes resources. It cannot be overlooked. [Kindleberger, 1958, p. 107]

Integration of Marketing Function in Economic Development

Modern marketing concepts, as commonly understood and practiced in the industrialized economies of the West, must be adapted to the needs of less-developed countries, or they run the risk of being ineffective or even counterproductive. There are several reasons for such an approach.

First, in the industrially advanced countries, consumers' most basic needs have been largely met. Given an overabundance of goods and services, a major portion of marketing effort is directed at consumers to switch their loyalty among competing brands with only marginal differences among them. This is not wholly undesirable because, given a large discretionary income, the marginal utility of last dollar is low, and added psychological satisfaction is a highly positive factor. Also, since the differences between competing brands are minor, the disutility for not consuming existing brands is quite low, and consumer loss is minor even if the consumer makes a wrong choice in terms of switching to another brand.

These conditions, by and large, do not hold true in LDCs. Most new products are not introduced for brand-switching, but lead to shifts in consumption patterns themselves, thereby causing both significant increases in utility gains from new uses and also significant losses in utility from giving up existing consumption patterns. Similarly, given a very low level of discretionary spending power, the loss in net utility to the consumer is quite high, if he or she makes a wrong choice and expends scarce monetary resources.

Secondly the flexible and fluctuating social classes mean that consumers in industrialized societies do not suffer any adverse consequences from changes in their consumption patterns. This is generally not true in developing economies where class system is often quite rigid. Thus, a product use belonging to class A is unlikely to receive social support for adoption in class B, making such a product less useful as a system of incentives and also reducing its utility to the consumer.

Finally, rigid class and social structures in LDCs makes for a highly stable system of market segments. And yet, most less-developed countries have self-contained tribes, village communities, each one a microcosm or mirror image of other similar units. Most of these units are largely self-contained, both economically and socially. They depend on the outside world for a much smaller number of exchange transactions than is true in the case of industrialized countries. Although some of these barriers are coming down with the increase in urbanization, the proportion of total population and economic activity that remains in the self-contained economic and social units in LDCs is still very large. This condition is further aggravated from inadequate mass transportation and communication facilities and other elements that form the social infrastructure in a society.

This situation has three important consequences: (1) many of the mass merchandising techniques that create large markets and economies of scale are not feasible in less-developed countries; (2) some of the activities of middlemen, although inefficient when viewed from the perspective of industrialized countries, are nevertheless necessary and inevitable in LDCs; and (3) various actors in the marketing chain are not only tied through their economic roles, but also have strong social and cultural ties, which are not easily displaced. Thus, even inefficient middlemen are important because of their place in the social hierarchy. It should be stated here that this phenomenon is present to a greater or lesser degree in all societies where historical and cultural ties are important, e.g., Japan.

Marketing and Economic Development: a Plan for Action

A two-pronged action strategy is necessary for marketing to play an important role in the economic development process.

New Frameworks for Understanding Buyer Behavior

The first step in the successful use of marketing in economic development would call for a different model of consumer behavior, one that takes into account, to a greater extent, society-related exogenous variables in understanding individual consumer behavior than is considered necessary in developed societies.

One such approach has been suggested by Sheth and Sethi [1977, pp. 369–89]. These authors suggest that products should be classified as they are perceived by the buyers within their personality-culture structures. Thus, an important dimension has been added to our understanding of consumer behavior by incorporating socio-cultural variables in the buyer's decision-making framework. A brief summary of their three-class scheme is given below.

Consumption Substitution Innovation.   The buyer is familiar with the basic product and its uses, which have been stable over time and are socially acceptable. Purchase of a product implies that (1) the buyer seeks variety— he or she is tired of his or her present brand and simply wants to try something different; and (2) the buyer perceives the new product to be of better quality, however defined, than the one he or she is currently using.

New Want-Creating Innovations.   Three types of products fall in this category: (1) complementary products—the purchase is made to improve the use of an existing product or to increase the satisfaction currently derived from a product the buyer already possesses; (2) satisfying new contingencies—the purchase is made because a new need has arisen due to a change in the buyer's social situation; (3) availability of culturally neutral new products—these are products with which the buyer has no prior familiarity and no experiential-cultural framework for evaluating them.

To assess the probability of its adoption, one should look at not only the perceived satisfactions a buyer might derive from its purchase and use, but also the dissatisfaction that might accrue when the buyer has to forego the purchase and use of another product that is currently part of his or her cultural inventory.

Income-Adding Innovations.   This category includes all products that may have a positive effect on the buyer's income (e.g., purchase of fertilizer or a tractor by a farmer to increase the productivity of his or her farm). The buyer sees this product not in terms of how it would affect his or her income, but of how this income would affect his or her standing in his or her social milieu.

Consumption substitution types of purchases are the most common and constitute a major part of all purchases in industrially advanced societies, where change is a way of life. Discretionary income is relatively high, and the buyer has no fixed or stable socio-cultural milieu and is constantly looking for new products or new ways to satisfy his or her wants.

In the category of new want-creating innovations, the first two types, complementary products and products that satisfy new contingencies, fall on a continuum of perceived newness with the greatest degree of occurrence among the advanced societies. In traditional societies with stable social status, people with increased income first tend to buy more of what they currently use and what is already present in their social surroundings rather than something that would indicate a desire to move into a different socio-economic class.

The category of culturally neutral products is perhaps the most challenging in terms of innovation adoption. While the phenomenon is quite rare in industrially advanced countries, its occurrence is still quite common in traditional societies.

Income-adding innovations are by far the most critical for societies concerned with their far-reaching impact and for the MNCs in terms of the ambiguity and confusion surrounding the problems of diffusion and adoption.

The Concept of Strategic Marketing

The concept of strategic marketing implies that marketing should not be looked upon as a series of discrete functions, but as an integrative process where all stakeholders are given their proper roles to play. There is no single focus and no group is systematically ignored.

In contrast to the evolutionary path of marketing or management, economic development theories still are based on increasing supply and minimize marketing's positive role. Local production of goods and services are emphasized, and protective tariff and non-tariff barriers are recommended. Thus, customers end up paying higher prices for low quality products; producer surplus, as opposed to consumer surplus, is maximized, and capital is accumulated. It is not clear, however, whether this accumulated capital can indeed lead the country to the next stage of economic development.

A marketing-oriented economic development process would recommend a set of different policies. For example, rather than erecting protective barriers that bar competitors from entering the market, a system of incentives for local producers would be created. These incentives would aim at subsidizing local producers in their formative stages to become more competitive in those markets where strong demand exists or can be created. The emphasis would be in meeting competition as opposed to thwarting competition. Government activity would focus primarily in creating a politically and economically stable, and competitively energetic, environment where private entrepreneurs assume risks in accumulating capital and producing and marketing goods and services.

Notes

1. For detailed studies on the effect of market or country size, see for example: Balassa, 1980; Havrylyshyn, 1981; Kuznets, 1960; and Science Council of Canada, 1981.

2. A detailed exposition of natural resources' effect on economic development is given by Balassa, 1980; Chenery, 1968; Clague and Tanzi, 1972; and Kindleberger, 1958.

3. Advantages of geographical location can be clearly understood by studying countries at the crossroads of trade and commerce throughout history. A more modern version is captured by membership in a common market, for example, in the EEC. For detailed discussion of custom unions, see Jacob Viner, 1950.

4. Old colonial ties are examples of preferential alliances. Former British colonies still receive a preferential treatment as part of the British Commonwealth. Israel is also a recipient of U.S. preferential treatment. See: Bruno, 1962.

5. See Clark, 1957; and Deutsch, 1961.

6. A great deal is written on the positive long-term effects of education on economic development. See Clague and Tanzi, 1972; Clark, 1957; Hagen, 1957; Harbison and Myers, 1964 and 1965; Harbison, Maruhnic, and Resnick, 1970; Gutman, 1965; and Schultz, 1964.

7. There is a lot written on the effects of foreign aid on economic development. The evidence is mixed and inconclusive. For a sample, see: Adleman and Chenery, 1966; Chenery and Carter, 1963; Griffin and Enos, 1970; Hirschman and Bird, 1968; and Papanek, 1972.

8. Effects of foreign direct investment on economic development overlaps with the theory of FDI. For a discussion of FDI's effect, see: Papanek, 1972; Pearson, 1969; and Weisskopf, 1972.

9. For a discussion of supply-oriented theories of economic development see Harrod, R. F., *Toward a Dynamic Economics* (London: Macmillan, 1948), pp. 60–70.

10. The work of Keynes must be viewed as a formal beginning of economics of aggregate demand. This has led to further development of demand-oriented theories of economic development. Most of these theories are known as neo-Keynesian theories.

11. Perfect information is one of the prerequisites of perfect competition. Perfect competition has greatly influenced economic thoughts and development.

References

1. Adelman, I., and Chenery, H. B. "Foreign Aid and Economic Development: The Case of Greece." *Review of Economics and Statistics* (February, 1966), pp. 1–19.

2. Alderson, W. *Dynamic Marketing Behaviour* (Homewood, Illinois: Irwin, 1965).

3. Balassa, Bela. "The Process of Industrial Development and Alternatives Development Strategies." *Essay in International Finance* No. 141, (Princeton, N.J.: Princeton University Press, 1980), p. 1.

4. Bauer, P. T. *West African Trade* (Cambridge: Cambridge University Press, 1954).

5. Bauer, P. T. and Yamey, Basil. *The Economics of Underdeveloped Countries* (Chicago, Ill.: University of Chicago Press, 1957).

6. Burmeister, E. and Dobell, A. R. *Mathematical Theories of Economic Growth* (New York: Macmillan, 1970).

7. Chenery, H. B. "Land: The Effect of Resources on Economic Growth." In: K. Berril (ed.), *Economic Development with Special Reference to East Asia* (New York: St. Martin's Publishing Co., 1968).

8. Chenery, H. B., and Carter, N. G. "Foreign Assistance and Development Performance." *American Economic Review* (May, 1963), pp. 459–68.

9. Claque, C. and Tanzi, V. "Human Capital, Natural Resources and the Purchasing Power Parity Doctorine: Some Empirical Results." *Economica Internationale* (February, 1972), pp. 3–17.

10. Clark, C. *The Condition of Economic Progress* (London: Macmillan, 1957).

11. Deutsch, K. W. "Social Mobilization and Political Development." *American Economic Review* (September, 1961), pp. 493–514.

12. Drucker, Peter F. "Marketing and Economic Development." *Journal of Marketing* (January, 1958), pp. 252–59.

13. Engel, J. F., Kollat, D. T., and Blackwell, R. D. *Consumer Behavior*. Second Edition (New York: Holt, Rinehart and Winston, 1973).

14. Etemad, H. "World Product Mandating in Perspective." *Proceedings of ASAC-International Business* (Ottawa, Canada: May, 1982).

15. Galbraith, John K. and Holton, R. H. *Marketing Efficiency in Puerto Rico* (Cambridge, Mass.: Harvard University Press, 1955).

16. Griffin, K. B., and Enos, J. L. "Foreign Assistance: Objective and Consequences." *Economic Development and Cultural Change* (April, 1979), pp. 313–27.

17. Gutmann, P. "The Anatomy of Economic Growth." In: P. Gutmann (ed.), *Economic Growth* (Englewood Cliffs, N.J.: Prentice-Hall, 1965), pp. 27–29.
18. Hagen, Everett. "The Process of Economic Development." *Economic Development and Cultural Change* (April, 1957), pp. 202–204.
19. Hahn, F. H. and Matthews, R. C. O. "The Theory of Economic Growth." *Economic Journal* (December, 1964).
20. Harbison, F. H., Maruhnic, J., and Resnick, J. *Quantitative Analysis of Modernization and Development* (Princeton, N.J.: Princeton University Press, 1970), pp. 58–73.
21. Harbison, F. H. and Myers, C. *Education, Manpower, and Economic Growth* (New York: McGraw Hill, 1964).
22. Harbison, F. H. and Myers, C. *Education: Country Studies in Economic Development* (New York: McGraw Hill, 1965).
23. Harrod, R. F. *Towards a Dynamic Economics* (London: Macmillan, 1948).
24. Havrylyshyn, Oli. "Trade Among Developing Countries: Theory Policy Issues, and Principal Trends." *World Bank Staff Working Paper* No. 479 (Washington, D.C.: World Bank, 1981), pp. 18–20.
25. Higgins, Benjamin. *Economic Development* (New York: W. W. Norton and Co., 1959).
26. Hirschman, Albert O. *The Strategy of Economic Development* (New Haven, Conn.: Yale University Press, 1958).
27. Hirschman, A. O., and Bird, R. M. "Foreign Aid—A Critique and Proposal." *Essays in International Finance* No. 69 (Princeton, N.J.: Princeton University Press, July, 1968).
28. Holton, Richard H. "Marketing Structure and Economic Development." *Quarterly Journal of Economics* (August, 1953), pp. 344–61.
29. Houthakker, H. S. "On Some Determinants of Savings in Developed and Underdeveloped Countries." In: Robinson, E. A. G. (ed.), *Problems of Economic Development* (London: Macmillan, 1965).
30. Houthakker, H. S. "An International Comparison of Personal Saving." *Proceeding of International Statistical Institute* 32nd Session, Part 2, (Tokyo: 1961), pp. 56–59.
31. Howard, J. A. and Sheth, J. N. *The Theory of Buyer Behavior* (New York: Wiley, 1969).
32. Keegan, W. J. *Multinational Marketing Management* (Englewood Cliffs, N.J.: Prentice Hall, 1980).
33. Keynes, John Maynard. *The General Theory of Employment, Interest, and Money* (New York: Harcourt, Brace & World, 1964).
34. Kindleberger, C. P. *Economic Development* (New York: McGraw Hill, 1958), pp. 106–108.
35. Kotler, Philip. *Marketing Management: Analysis, Planning and Control* (Englewood Cliffs, N.J.: Prentice Hall, 1967).
36. Kuznets, S. "Economic Growth and Small Nations." In: Robinson, E. A. G., (ed.), *Economic Consequences of the Size of Nations* (London: Macmillan, 1960).

37. Landau, L. "Saving Function in Latin America." In: H. B. Chenery (ed.), *Studies in Development Planning* (Cambridge, Mass.: Harvard University Press, 1971).

38. Lewis, W. A. *The Theory of Economic Growth* (London: Allen and Unwin, 1955), pp. 274–83.

39. Lluch, C. and Powell, A. *International Comparison of Expenditure and Saving Patterns*. IBRD Development Research Center (1973).

40. McClelland, David C. *The Achieving Society* (New York: Free Press, 1961).

41. McClelland, D. C., and Winter, David G. *Motivating Economic Achievement* (New York: Free Press, 1969), pp. 390–397.

42. Mikesel, R. F. "Public Foreign Capital For Private Enterprise in Developing Countries." *Essays in International Finance* No. 52 (Princeton, N.J.: Princeton University Press, 1966).

43. Mikesel, R. F. and Zinser, J. E. "The Nature of Savings Function in Developing Countries: A Survey of Theoretical and Empirical Literature." *Journal of Economic Literature* (March, 1973), pp. 1–26.

44. Nicosia, F. M. *Consumer Decision Process* (Englewood Cliffs, N.J.: Prentice Hall, 1966).

45. Nurske, Ragnar. *Problems of Capital Formation in Underdeveloped Countries* (New York: Oxford University Press, 1953), pp. 61–75.

46. Papanek, Gustav F. "The Effect of Aid and Other Resources Transfers on Savings and Growth in Less Developed Countries." *Economic Journal* (September, 1972), pp. 934–50.

47. Papanek, Gustav F. "The Development of Entrepreneurship." *American Economic Review*, Vol. LII, No. 2 (1962), p. 54.

48. Pearson, L. B. *Partners in Development* (New York: Praeger, 1969), pp. 99–123.

49. Robinson, E. A. G. (ed.) *Economic Consequences of the Size of Nations* (London: Macmillan, 1960).

50. Robinson, E. A. G. (ed.) *Problems of Economic Development* (London, England: Macmillan, 1965).

51. Rosenstein-Rodan, P. N. "Problems of Industrialization of Eastern and South Eastern Europe." *Economic Journal*, 53 (June/September, 1943).

52. Schultz, T. "Investment in Human Capital." In: P. Gutmann (ed.), *Economic Growth* (Englewood Cliffs, N.J.: Prentice Hall, 1964), pp. 125–42.

53. Science Council of Canada. "Multinationals and Industrial Strategy: The Role of World Product Mandates." In: Dhawan, Etemad, and Wright (eds.), *International Business: A Canadian Perspective* (Don Mills, Ontario, Canada: Addison-Wesley, 1981), pp. 582–87.

54. Scitovsky, T. "Growth—Balanced or Unbalanced?" In: Abramovitz, M. (ed.), *Allocation of Economic Resources* (Stanford, Calif.: Stanford University Press, 1959).

55. Shapiro, S. J. "Comparative Marketing and Economic Development." In: G. Schwartz (ed.), *Science in Marketing* (New York: John Wiley and Sons Inc., 1965), pp. 398–429.

56. Sheth, J. N. and Sethi, S. P. "A Theory of Cross-Cultural Buyer Behavior." In: A. G. Woodside, J. N. Sheth, and P. D. Bennett (eds.), *Consumer and Industrial Buying Behavior* (New York: North Holland, 1977), pp. 369–89.

57. Singer, Hans. "Social Development—Key Growth Sector." *International Development Review* (March, 1965).

58. Smithies, A. "Rising Expectation and Economic Development." *The Economic Journal* (June, 1961).

59. Solow, R. M. *Growth Theory: An Exposition* (New York: Oxford University Press, 1970).

60. Thorelli, H. B. "Political Science and Marketing." In: R. Cox, W. Alderson, and S. J. Shapiro (eds.), *Theory in Marketing: Second Series* (Homewood, Ill.: Richard D. Irwin, 1964).

61. Viner, Jacob. *The Custom Union Issue* (Endowment for International Peace: New York, 1950).

62. Weisskopf, T. E. "The Impact of Foreign Capital Inflow on Domestic Savings in Underdeveloped Countries." *Journal of International Economics* (February, 1972) pp. 25–38.

8 THE FOREIGN ORIENTATION OF MANAGEMENT AS A CENTRAL CONSTRUCT IN EXPORT-CENTERED DECISION-MAKING PROCESSES

Erwin Dichtl, M. Leibold, H.-G. Köglmayr,
and S. Müller

The Problem Statement

The Federal Republic of Germany currently has an average export ratio of 33 percent and occupies the position as the second-largest trading nation in the world. In the past, this success apparently led many academicians in Western Germany to regard commitment to the field of international business and international marketing as superfluous. However, this perspective seems now to be changing. As in other industrial nations, the unfavorable development in the balance of payments as well as zero growth in the economy have caused increasing interest on the part of university economists in these questions. In conjunction with this development, and in deviation from the hitherto dominating concern with the multinational firm, increasing attention is being cast upon the export-related decision-making

This contribution has originated from Sonderforschungsbereich 24, Sozialwissenschaftliche Entscheidungsforschung, University of Mannheim, through funds made available by the Deutsche Forschungsgemeinschaft and with support of the State of Baden-Württemberg.

processes of small firms. [See Olson & Wiedersheim-Paul, 1978; Rabino, 1980; Steinmann et al., 1977, 1981]

The underlying motivation for both the discussion of the overall topic and the concentration on smaller firms is the intention to activate export potential in order to make a contribution toward diminishing the current account deficits and to facilitate economic growth. The focus on this particular type of enterprise, which in Germany is labeled "Mittelstand,"[1] is based upon the assumption that these firms have a substantial export potential which, because of their high degree of flexibility, can quickly be activated. However, problems often arise with the supply and utilization of information, and, consequently, have an adverse effect on the systematic assessment of market opportunities.

The following analysis serves as a basis for development of a research concept which carries the conviction that, as first priority, the fear threshold of those non-exporting firms, which according to objective criteria dispose of unutilized export potential, should be overcome. The reasoning is that if the first step has been taken—the overall decision to go international—then the ensuing questions regarding the decision to favor a certain internationalization concept (characterized by the parameters market, product, and strategy) pose no fundamental problems. Consequently, we concentrate on the overall decision to go international and explore, among others, the question regarding which export stimuli, whether internal or external to the firm and whether of an objective or subjective nature, are in the final instance determinative of the decision to commence activities in foreign markets.

The Export Decision in Economic Literature[2]

The literature concerning the fundamental decision by small firms to go international can be divided into three categories: (1) sources limited to the enumeration of motives for exporting; (2) efforts which strive to attain a particular structuring of the subject matter, in which the typical attribute profile of exporting firms is revealed; and finally (3) contributions which portray the elements and structure of the export decision in the form of complex decision-making models, but which lack the explicit decision-theoretical framework. A large number of the published works limit themselves to a description of the field in the form of motive lists. Characteristic of these studies are efforts to list possible export incentives and so-called determinants of export success (e.g., information behavior; perception of export impediments; competitive situation; size; technological level; and similarity of the markets; export promotion programs; company philosophy; political risks; and consumer behavior). The provision of such lists of factors in the overall context of export decisions is unquestionably important. However, they do not succeed in the identification of the determinative attributes, i.e., the distinctive characteristics which allow a differential diagnosis of those firms, which in all probability would also be able to survive in foreign markets. On the other hand, it should be acknowledged that these hypotheses-free and frequently casuistical approaches [see, e.g., Berekoven, 1978; Business International Corporation, 1974] establish, in a more or less modified form, building blocks for advanced profile and modeling procedures.

Four contributions, properly identified as profile analyses, have attempted to estimate the export potential of firms with a view toward improving the efficacy of export promotional measures. According to Tesar [1975], e.g., the typical profile of the exporting firm comprises the following factors: management has very favorable expectations regarding the effect of exporting on the firm's growth; plans for developing its markets; has favorable expectations regarding the impact of exporting on the firm's market development, and the company has annual sales of $1 million or more.

Work done in this area by Snavely et al. [1964], Simpson & Kujawa [1974][3], Tesar [1975] and Cavusgil & Nevin [1981], however, suffers from serious drawbacks. First, it is difficult to actually compare the profiles. Secondly, they lack the proper theoretical foundation, which manifests itself in the application of pragmatical structuring tools such as AID. Especially the definition of certain variables as independent ones by Tesar [1975] and Cavusgil & Nevin [1981] seems to be problematical. Of a total of 18 independent variables which had been considered by Cavusgil & Nevin [1981, p. 114], two out of four groups, namely "expectations of management about the effects of exporting on firm's growth" and "level of firm's commitment to export marketing" (market planning, fixed policy toward export, systematic exploration of the possibility of exporting) were found to determine the profile of exporting firms. Because the dependent variable divides the objects of investigation into exporting and non-exporting firms, the stated findings are, in our opinion, tautological. Knowledge derived from consistency-theory, that in the post-decision-phase re-evaluation takes place in order to avoid or decrease cognitive dissonance, leads to no other conclusion than that managers who have already decided in favor of exporting and actually do so, associate higher expectations with foreign activities. They also conduct more export marketing planning than managers of non-exporting firms who have probably for the first time been confronted, within the framework of an export decision investigation, with the question of commencement of export activities.

Leaving aside all theoretical considerations, profile analysis should at least demonstrate that firms with a typical exporter-resembling profile in fact develop into exporters, if one only establishes contacts with foreign inquirers. Yet from such a pragmatic point of view, the profile method does not serve its purpose well. There is empirical evidence that firms with large export potential, i.e., non-exporting firms with a typical exporter profile, do not turn into exporters easily. This is even so if they are brought into contact with foreign inquirers [Weiner & Krok, 1967]. However, it is fair to concede that this must not only be attributed to the inadequacy of the profile method. Interviews conducted by Simpson & Kujawa [1974] with decisionmakers of 120 manufacturing firms revealed that an external stimulus, like an unsolicited order from a foreign customer, is a significant but not sufficient condition for initation of exports. Only in conjunction with certain opinions and attitudes of the managers concerned does this latent incentive become effective. Those who had received unsolicited orders and really developed into exporters assess their chances of success on export markets relative to local markets higher than non-exporters. They also display a higher education level, less fear of the risks involved, lower cost estimates of export activities, and less fear of communication difficulties than their colleagues concentrating on the local market.

In view of the shortcomings associated with motive lists and profile analysis, devising export decision-making models remains as the most exacting descriptive method. However, the multifaceted nature of the subject matter to be investigated prevents the researcher from aspiring to an all-encompassing export decision-making model. To test this empirically would be difficult, if not impossible. Thus, it is not surprising that the models presented so far represent only parts of this utopic global model [e.g., Cavusgil, 1976; Bilkey & Tesar, 1977; Lee & Brasch, 1978; Reid, 1981].

In spite of a number of serious objections, we consider the export-propensity model of Olson & Wiedersheim-Paul [1978], which is based on concepts developed by Welch & Wiedersheim-Paul [1977] and Wiedersheim-Paul et al. [1978], as the best founded concept available. Their model suggests that the different kinds of stimuli which are latent in the firm's internal (e.g., product characteristics, expansion objectives) and external environment (e.g., market opportunities, government stimulation) are interesting only to the extent that they are perceived by the decisionmaker. Managerial characteristics which moderate the strength of the impact of export stimuli are the cognitive style and the degree of international orientation of the decisionmaker. However, the inadequate theoretical basis and the complete lack of an indication as to how to operationalize these central components of the model need to be overcome. As long as the relevance of a factor, such as the cognitive style of the decisionmaker in the perception of export incentives, is simply postulated but not tested, such a model remains vague and can only aspire to the function of a conceptual approach.

A Proposal for a New Research Approach: A Model for Foreign Market Orientation

In the final analysis, existing research in the area of export decision-making has found the obvious, and postulated incomplete insights. It appears this is due both to a lack of a theoretical and terminological consensus in this field of research, and to the discrepancy between the complexity of the suggested models and the simplicity of the attempts at empirical validation.

In light of the necessity of a precise (qualitative) definition of the enterprise type to be investigated (small- and medium-sized firms), the establishment of a catalog of relevant descriptive dimensions (which would allow comparisons of the various studies to be made), and the improvement of the research design, we regard the following procedure as essential to overcome the stagnation in this field of research:

It is imperative to limit the research approaches to empirically verifiable parts of the relevant decision-making process;

A fundamental precondition for verification of theoretical assertions is the operationalization of the constructs involved;

As the operationalization of the construct of foreign orientation of management, which is viewed by us as a central element in the export-related decision process, indicates a task of large endeavor, the reduction to a single construct is unavoidable;

If one is interested in indicating how and why non-exporting firms become exporters, then the analysis must be initiated before the first export takes place. The recollections of export-experienced managers concerning the precedences, attitudes, backgrounds, etc., which in their firms at the time had led to an export decision, seem unsuitable, not only on memory-psychological but also on dissonance-theoretical grounds.

The Constructs and Levels of Measurement

The foreign orientation of managers is, like all constructs, not amenable to direct observation and, therefore, has to be determined through a series of indicators which can be regarded as a reflection of foreign orientation. The operationalization of a construct is to ascertain open, evident behavior and statements which seem appropriate to represent the not directly observable characteristics or hypothetical processes, structures, etc. The basic idea of this extensive procedure is to arrange the research concept [Cattell, 1964] in a theoretical-empirical reference system—the nomological network. The placement of the construct in this structure of theoretical and empirical assertions illuminates its significance.

At the outset of establishing of a construct, i.e., of sucessive approxima-tins of the test procedure to the empirical reality, usually stands a purely theoretical elucidation. Immediately thereupon follows the phase of empiri-cism which starts a continuous revision of the verbal concept and the procedure of measurement. Herein all evaluatory approaches may be applied—logical, correlation-statistical, as well as experimental ones. [See Cronbach & Meehl, 1955]

The first phase, the establishment of the construct on the conceptual level in form of its factorial structure, is portrayed in figure 8–1. Accordingly, the multidimensional construct is unlocked on four levels of measurement. It is through a psychophysical, projective, psychometric, and demographic measurement that the desired nomological network emerges. Our theoretical considerations are reflected briefly by the hypothesis that managers displaying the following characteristics display little foreign market orientation:

They witness foreign markets in greater-than-average degree as strange or odd in nature (psychic distance),

They are rigid, resistant to change, and risk averse, as well as expecting negative consequences of lengthy stays abroad on their careers (subjective managerial characteristics),

They do not master foreign languages to any extent, seldom pay a visit to a foreign country, and display a limited education level (objective managerial characteristics),

They do not consider export as a company strategy, or, if so, only half-heartedly (attitude toward export).

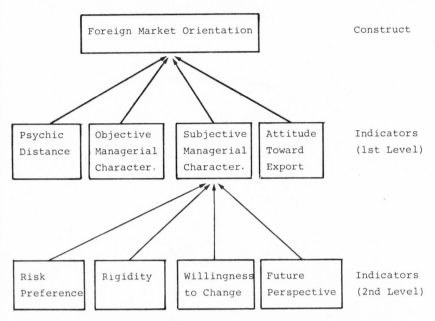

Figure 8–1. The Factorial Structure Model of Foreign Market Orientation

If, on the other hand, the majority of the criteria above display positive manifestations, we rank the respondent as being foreign-market orientated.

The Psychic Distance. The concept of psychic distance comprises all those factors which, in the instance of greater-than-average distance, weaken the existing export incentives and, in case of a particularly small distance, lead to their accentuation.[4] The foreign nature of markets, as displayed by differences in language, culture, industrial development, business practices, etc., is measured through positioning by the respondents of the symbols of foreign markets[5] in a given space in such a way that the respective distances to the center point portray the subjectively experienced foreignness (see figure 8–2). The provision of a reference stimulus (Netherlands) leads to a standardization of the answers. The sum of all distances (in cm) is employed as a measure of the psychic distance of the respondent to foreign markets.

Beyond that, this procedure may be seen as an intuitive application of facet theory [e.g., Guttman, 1959], which reveals the subjectively ex-

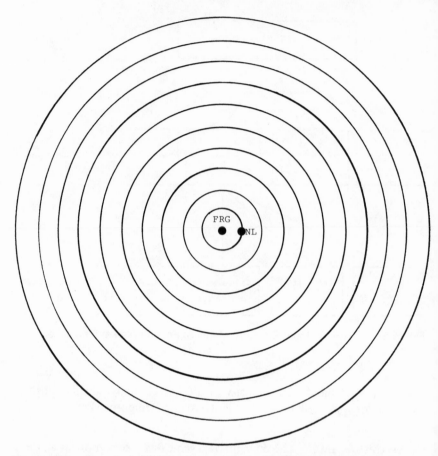

Figure 8–2. The Operationalization of the Psychic Distance of Managers to Foreign Markets.

perienced similarities between markets. This is the case when respondents are instructed to consider the distances between all markets under investigation.

Objective Managerial Characteristics.   The socio-demographic data chosen have proven themselves in earlier studies as either limiting or promoting the fundamental export decision. [For a summary, see Reid, 1981, pp. 104–105]

1. Which age group do you belong to?	25–39 years	( )
	40–50 years	( )
	51 years and older	( )
2. Which level of education or training did you attain?	Elementary School	( )
	High School	( )
	College	( )
	University	( )
	Apprenticeship	( )
	Traineeship	( )
	. . . .	
3. Which foreign language(s) do you master to an extent, that—after some time— would render it possible to you to work in the respective country (countries)?	English	( )
	French	( )
	Italian	( )
	Russian	( )
	Spanish	( )
	. . . .	( )
	. . . .	( )
4. Do you pass your vacation frequently	. . . in German speaking countries?	( )
	. . . in other European countries?	( )
	. . . overseas?	( )
5. Were you born in a foreign country?	yes	( )
	no	( )
6. Did you ever live in a foreign country for a lengthy period of time?	yes	( )
	no	( )
7. Are you a citizen of a foreign country?	yes	( )
	no	( )

The idea behind these questions is that young, highly educated, and polyglot managers display a stronger foreign market orientation as compared with others.

Subjective Managerial Characteristics. The structure of this indicator of foreign market orientation is given by four second-level-indicators. [See Figure 8–1] They are the personality traits of rigidity and risk perference, the value dimension of willingness to change, and the *lebensraum-*dimension, future perspective. This distinction may appear artificial; however, it reflects the fact that these concepts originate from distinctive theoretical backgrounds (personality psychology, sociology, social psychology).

The measurement proposal for the personality trait of rigidity is based upon a corresponding scale of Wesley [1953]. We assume that the tendency of rigid persons to harden in their ways of behaving, which in earlier situations had been appropriate but do not appear adequate to achieve current goals or solve contemporary problems, obstructs the launching of boundary-transcending (company) activities. There are ten items to which the respondents may or may not agree:

	Tendency	
	... to agree	... not to agree
1. I am often the last one to give up trying to do a thing.	☒	☐
2. There is usually only one best way to solve a problem.	☒	☐
3. I would like to have a position which requires frequent changes from one task to another.	☐	☒
4. I usually stick to my opinion even though many other people may have a different point of view.	☒	☐
5. I prefer to stop and think before I act, even on trifling matters.	☐	☒
6. My interests tend to change quickly.	☐	☒

	Tendency	
	... to agree	... not to agree

7. I usually find that my own way of attacking a problem is best even if it doesn't seem to work in the beginning. ☒ ☐

8. I think it is usually wise to do things in a conventional way. ☒ ☐

9. I have taken a good many courses on the spur of the moment. ☐ ☒

10. I prefer to do things according to a routine which I plan myself. ☒ ☐

The crosses inserted denote rigidity—and in the final instance a low foreign orientation. Whether this form of operationalization proves to be adequate will be seen in the course of the criterion validation. The chances are that the scales will have to be reformulated.

In the literature on international business, different forms of risk [e.g., the transfer risk; see, e.g., Stahr, 1981] play a prominent role. The problem of assessment of risk as perceived by the individual has been treated intensively in social science. [See Otway, 1977] But in our opinion, measurement proposals put forward to date are not adequate to assess managerial risk perception. Therefore, following an approach adopted by Cantril [1965], we have developed a simple operationalization in the form of a self-anchoring-scale. (See figure 8–3) Suppose, the number 100 on the scale stands for a managerial decision which is really irresponsible and therefore terribly risky. Correspondingly, zero implies no risk whatsoever. According to your personal view, what degree of risk should be accepted or should not be exceeded in certain managerial decisions, considering the present economic situation. Please specify where you would place market research, distribution management, price policy, product development, advertising, and personnel management on the scale.

Furthermore, we hold that managers who experience change as something negative will tend to show little inclination to react upon export incentives or to seek information on possibilities for conducting boundary-transcending company activities. The approach to measure the willingness

A terribly risky, even irresponsible decision

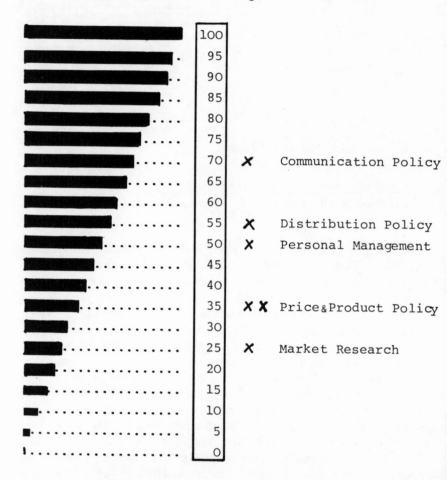

A decision entirely free of risk

Figure 8–3.   A Self-Anchoring Scale to Gauge the Proneness to Risk.
Note: In this example, an average value of 45 for the risk perference would result.

to change (value) is based upon preliminary work by Shartle et al. [1964], as well as Gabele [1981]. It also comprises ten items.

		Tendency	
		. . . to agree	. . . not to agree
1.	Chances should be taken, even if this means taking large risks.	☐	☒
2.	Firms should try to operate in foreign countries.	☐	☒
3.	In companies, innovations should be realized as quickly as possible.	☐	☒
4.	Companies should not aspire to solving international problems.	☒	☐
5.	Companies should actively support the development of the economies of other countries.	☐	☒
6.	A procedure or policy of a firm should never be changed until a better one has proved successful.	☒	☐
7.	Companies experiencing a crisis should avoid taking the risk of a fundamental organizational change.	☒	☐
8.	Managers should strive systematically for changes and innovations in the companies they represent.	☐	☒
9.	Companies should always be very cautious in making changes.	☒	☐
10.	In the future, even for small- and medium-sized companies, it will no longer suffice to take an interest in the home market only.	☐	☒

Finally, we suggest that managers who fear that a lengthy stay abroad will hamper their careers (future perspective) will demonstrate less willingness to internationalize. The operationalization of this lebensraum-dimension [see Lewin, 1948] is based on a survey by von Landsberg & Wölke [1982].

	Tendency	
	... to agree	... not to agree
1. If one has been sent abroad for some time by his company, the old job will no longer be available.	☒	☐
2. The difficulties associated with a lengthy stay abroad are balanced by the opportunity to see a new part of the world and pick up a foreign language.	☐	☒
3. Expectations related to a transfer abroad frequently are not matched by reality.	☒	☐
4. More than 50% of top managers owe their present position at least in part to having served abroad for a number of years.	☐	☒
5. The awkward side of a transfer abroad is the necessity to accommodate to a new way of life.	☒	☐
6. The gains accruing from living abroad for a while with regard to meeting people, making friends, and becoming more mature are often underestimated.	☐	☒
7. Lengthy stays abroad frequently cause problems with one's spouse and children.	☒	☐
8. Additional hardships and expenses emanating from having to live abroad are usually covered by the expatriate allowance one is entitled to.	☐	☒

	Tendency	
	... to agree	... not to agree

9. Even very able employees often succumb to the difficulties arising from having to adjust themselves to new surroundings. As a result, they find it extremely hard to reintegrate at home after having spent a number of years abroad.   ☒   ☐

10. Due to the increasing internationalization of firms, experience gathered abroad is getting more and more indispensable in everyday business.   ☐   ☒

The Attitude Toward Export. The measurement of attitudes toward exporting as a company strategy should be conducted in such a way that the measurement effect [reactivity of measurement, see Campbell & Stanley, 1963] is weakened, if not competely eliminated. With most of the classical measuring techniques (e.g., the semantic differential or the Likert scale), the respondents are generally aware of the fact that their attitudes regarding a particular subject of opinion are being measured. This often leads to biased response sets, e.g., the attempt to provide socially desirable answers [see Cronbach, 1961]. Thus, the measuring procedure changes the object to be measured. With the aid of indirect, non-reactive procedures [see Webb, Campbell, Schwartz, & Sechrest, 1966], which do not enable the respondents to recognize that their attitudes are being measured, this effect can be eliminated.

Within the framework of our operationalization proposal, we attempt to overcome this problem through implementation of the principle of projection. In this context, projection means striving to ascribe one's own feeling, thoughts, or attitudes [see Murray, 1951] to another person. The attitudes of respondents regarding the export option will therefore not be surveyed directly. Whether export is fundamentally seen as rather positive or negative, or, as Simpson [1973] and Bilkey & Tesar [1977] suggested, whether the diffuse impression exists that an export activity is *per se* desirable irrespective of the consideration of what contribution it makes to the attainment of the firm's goals, should be ascertained as follows:

The respondents are exposed to unspecific stimuli (economic situation, company situation, action alternatives) and to concrete decisions without being forced into a rigid system of true or false replies. The situations described are relatively unstructured and ambiguous, i.e., they do not prejudice answers in the sense of export as the only appropriate alternative. Due to the presentation of various forms of action, the respondents do not recognize that their attitudes toward export are of interest and that the additional facets provide only the background for a comparatively realistic decision situation. The fundamental assumption is that in such ambiguous situations the respondents project their attitudes to the targets (here: fictitional managers who in the situation described made particular decisions). If one is, so to speak, able to put his or her own opinions or secret prejudices in others' mouths, without having to account for it, one feels released from the obligation to provide rational, unprejudiced answers. In this manner, the respondents unconsciously open themselves to the intention of the measurement and dispense with the rationalization of their answers.

This central element of the questionnaire, according to our view, repairs the existing neglect of the decision-making connection and, through its comparatively reality-close problem statement, provides the economic side of the study with respectability, without neglecting the social-scientific implications.

Instruction

For this task you should evaluate three hypothetical managers according to the criteria provided. Against the background of a particular economic and company situation, as well as seven concrete decision alternatives, these managers have chosen different solutions.

Economic Situation

The years 1980 and 1981 were for German firms of the most severe of the post-war period. Energy crisis, mass unemployment, and environmental protection are some of the rousing words of the recent past. The real income of private households stagnated. Rising prices, unstable cyclical tendencies, high interest levels, a strongly oscillating dollar exchange rate, and a substantial balance of payments deficit provided the framework for the economy.

Company Situation

The Electro Ltd., a small firm with 250 employees in earlier years, experienced considerable expansion but lately has been suffering from high competitive pressure, stagnating turnover, and a noticeable regression of orders, which are not typical of the industry.

Its production facilities are antiquated and thereby sometimes overstrained. Apart from this, new products could, due to a shortage of qualified labor, only be developed to a limited extent. The equity capital is relatively small, and the distribution organization does not offer any appreciable improvement possibilities. It is to be feared that the turnover situation would further deteriorate in the immediate future, if decisive strategy measures were not taken. In these circumstances, the following courses of action are deemed feasible by the management:

Alternative A: Modernizing production facilities employing outside (dept) capital.

Alternative B: Increasing one's own research efforts and development of personnel.

Alternative C: Appointing management consultants who are qualified to indicate a solution of the problems at hand.

Alternative D: Cooperating with a firm of equal strength which disposes over considerable product know-how.

Alternative E: Gaining access to foreign markets.

Alternative F: Searching for a partner with excess funds and persuading him or her to cooperate.

Alternative G: Adjusting the number of personnel to present needs of the company.

In order to overcome the present state of affairs, three managers proposed various combinations of feasible alternatives. For the sake of brevity, however, only the core element of one of these propositions is given here.

Manager III Chooses Alternative E

How would you characterize a manager who decides, in view of the overall and company situation described, to seek access to foreign markets? Please indicate, by way of crosses, at each of the following pairs of statements the expression which best fits manager III.

Manager III . . .

1. . . . aims at risk reduction through market diversification. $\boxtimes$

... engages in the incalculable risk of foreign markets. $\square$

2. . . . submits to a certain trend to engage in foreign market activities. $\square$

... has recognized that the development of foreign markets presents a real alternative. $\boxtimes$

3. . . . makes a contribution to narrowing the gap in the balance of payments and, in the final instance, to the improvement of the welfare of his or her country. $\boxtimes$

... adds to the political and economic risks of the already heavy export-laden German economy. $\square$

4. . . . uses foreign market activities as a pretense to satisfy his or her desire for traveling abroad. $\square$

... does not let himself or herself be restrained by the exertions of foreign traveling in the tying of new business contacts. $\boxtimes$

5. . . . in the final instance secures local job positions. $\boxtimes$

... takes the first step toward displacement of production to foreign countries and thereby endangers employment at home. $\square$

The dimensions depicted above are phrased in such a way that their manifestations signal a positive and a negative foreign market orientation, respectively. The number of positive assessments $\boxtimes$ is indicative of the degree of positive attitudes regarding export as a feasible strategy and therewith the degree of foreign market orientation of the respondent.

From the Indicators to the Construct: Some Comments on the Pilot Study, Sample, Validation, and Molding of the Indicators into an Index

The first step in testing the measurement instruments is to discuss them with a group of managers. This step relies less on the concrete measurements but much more on the acceptance of the measuring instruments. The question is whether real managers regard the question provided or tasks given as reasonable (say: too personal?, too long-winded?) and whether they view these instruments as appropriate in delineating foreign market orientation. If the pilot study shows "face validity" then a large sample will be taken.

The actual survey will be done in cooperation with the Chamber of Industry and Commerce, Mannheim, which hopefully will help to diminish the non-response. In accordance with the aim of our study, emphasis lies with about 150 small firms from the Rhine-Neckar area which are presently not active internationally. The additional inclusion of 50 exporting firms, which should be structurally comparable with non-exporters as far as possible, in this stage enables us to find out whether the measured foreign market orientation allows a distinction to be made between export-experienced and export-unexperienced managers (known-group validation).

In this phase of the longitudinal/cross-sectional study which we have projected [see figure 8–4], it is sufficient to affix simple cut-off values to the various measuring levels which, in the case of psychic distance, are stipulated according to the shape of the distribution of the measuring values. As to the remaining indicators, their cut-off values are defined on the basis of either their medians or logical consideratins. Everytime a cut-off value is exceeded, this counts as one point. The sum of such points, which under these conditions could vary between zero and four, would then form the index value for the construct to be measured.

More significant at this point of the study, however, is the testing of the factorial validity of the construct which, similar to known-group validation, is part of the construct validation. Is the four-dimensional structure of the chosen construct, as hypothesized, reflected in the values measured?[6] If the scales employed were interval scales, this could be established with the aid of factory analysis. As this is not the case (with the exception of the measuring of psychic distance and risk preference), it must be clarified with the aid of configuration frequency analysis [Krauth & Lienert, 1973]. This will show whether the empirical values organize according to a latent pattern or rather independent of each other. This technique enables us to determine whether all respondents who on one dimension generated a specific answering pattern, also reacted similarly on all other dimensions, which would then speak for a single-factorial construct structure. However, if the reactions on one level of measuring do not prejudice the answers to the others, then the multidimensionality hypothesis must not be rejected.

After a period of two to three months, another round of questioning will have to be initiated in order to assess the (retest) reliability of the measuring instrument.

The criterion validation should then be tackled after about a further 18 months, both regarding the relevance of every single item as well as the

STAGE OF STUDY	SAMPLE	METHOD	MAIN OBJECTIVE
PILOT STUDY	CONVENIENCE SAMPLE	SEMI-STRUCTURED INTERVIEW	FACE VALIDITY
MAIN SURVEY	MANAGERS OF - 150 SMALL NON-EXPORTING FIRMS - 50 SMALL EX-PORTING FIRMS	QUESTIONNAIRE	CONSTRUCT VALIDITY - KNOWN-GROUP VALIDATION - FACTORIAL VALIDITY
RETEST			RELIABILITY
TREATMENT	150 SMALL NON-EX-PORTING FIRMS	DISSEMINATING INFORMATION	ACTIVATION OF EXPORT POTENTIAL
FINAL ASSESSMENT	150 SMALL NON-EX-PORTING FIRMS	QUESTIONNAIRE	CRITERION VALIDITY - ITEM ANALYSIS - ALLOCATING WEIGHTS TO SUBTESTS

Figure 8–4. The Design of a Mixed Longitudinal/Cross-Sectional Study to Validate the Measuring Approach to the Concept of Foreign Orientation of Managers

weights to be allocated to the four subtests with a view to determining the overall score. In the final test form, there should remain only such questions which engender an adequate variation of the answers and consistently co-vary with the criteria (dependent variables: different levels of preparation for, or commencement of, export-activities). In order to ascertain the relative importance of the various measuring levels, it is necessary to proceed analogous to the specification of the beta weights in multiple regression analysis.

There are still at least two problems not completely resolved at this stage of the research study. How can one vouch that the non-exporting firms in the sample dispose over an export-potential? (Here we rely on an assessment by experts of the local Chamber of Industry and Commerce). Can the chances that in the foreseen time period a relevant number of firms actually commence with foreign activities or make according preparations, be increased through purposeful provision of information and export counseling (treatment)?

Summary

The authors' critical review of studies on export-related decision-making processes of small- and medium-sized firms results in the conclusion that the current stagnation in this field can only be overcome if attempts to set up global models of the export decision are replaced by investigatory approaches of a smaller scope. Their proposal for a new research approach focuses on the operationalization of a model for foreign market orientation. This model is built-up on four levels: psychic distance, objective managerial characteristics, subjective managerial characteristics (risk preference, rigidity, willingness to change, future perspective), and attitude toward export. A design of a mixed longitudinal/cross-sectional study to validate the construct is also proposed.

Notes

1. In the discussion on economic policy, the term "Mittelstand" comprises self-employed and especially small- and medium-sized commercial firms. However, any quantitative definition, based for example on criteria such as number of employees or sales volume, is inadequate to reflect the specific meaning of this term. The statement made by the Federal Government of Western Germany that "the existence of small- and medium-sized business is the best guarantee for the continuation of a liberal economic system and thus essential for a free and democratic society" gives some insight in the economic and social implications of this type of firm and the need for a qualitative definition. Management by the proprietors, who also bear the commercial risk, is the most important qualitative criterion pertaining to small- and medium-sized firms. [See Dichtl et al., 1981]

2. The literature related to export-decisions is reviewed more extensively by Dichtl et al. [1982].

3. Due to insufficient details, this study is neither classifiable as profile approach nor modeling approach. Contemplation of its content points to an integration in this regard.

4. Simmonds & Smith [1968] define this distance as a measure of international outlook (to what extent a decision-maker perceives and considers what is happening outside his or her own country as interesting), whilst Johanson & Vahlne [1977] see it as the sum of factors preventing the flow of information from and to the market. However, like Wiedersheim-Paul [1972] and Carlson [1974] they content themselves with paraphrasing this concept.

5. The selection of these countries is based upon the clustering of 163 world markets by Sethi [1971] in eight groups, with one country taken from each of these.

6. Analogous considerations are to be taken with regard to the testing of the subjective managerial characteristics as an indicator.

Bibliography

Berekoven, L. *Internationales Marketing.* Wiesbaden 1978.

Bilkey, W. & Tesar, G. "The Export Behavior of Smaller-Sized Wisconsin Manufacturing Firms." *Journal of International Business Studies,* 1977, 8(1), p. 93–98.

Business International Corporation (ed.). *Decision Making in International Operations.* New York 1974.

Campbell, D. T. & Stanley, J. C. "Experimental and Quasi-experimental Designs for Research on Teaching." In: Gage, N. L. (ed.), *Handbook of Research on Teaching,* Chicago 1963, p. 171–246.

Cantril, H. *The Pattern of Human Concerns.* New Brunswick, N.J., 1965.

Cattell, D. T. "Beyond Validity and Reliability: Some Further Concepts and Coefficients for Evaluating Tests." *Journal of Educational Measurement,* 1964, 33 (2), p. 133–43.

Cavusgil, S. T. "Organizational Determinants of Firm's Export Behavior: An Empirical Analysis." Ph.D. Dissertation, University of Wisconsin 1976.

Cavusgil, S. T. & Nevin, J. R. "Internal Determinants of Export Marketing Behavior: An Empirical Investigation." *Journal of Marketing Research,* 1981, 28 (1), p. 114–19.

Cronbach, L. J. *Essentials of Psychological Testing.* New York 1961 (2nd ed.).

Cronbach, L. J. & Meehl, P. E. "Construct Validity in Psychological Tests." *Psychological Bulletin,* 1955, 52 (4), p. 281–302.

Dichtl, E., Raffée, H. & Wellenreuther, H. "Public Policy Towards Small- and Medium-sized Retail Businesses in the Federal Republic of Germany." Arbeitspapier Nr. 9 des Instituts für Marketing, Mannheim 1981.

Dichtl, E., Leibold, M., Köglmayr, H.-G., Müller, S. & Potucek, V. "The Decision to Go International—With the Focus on Small- and Medium-sized Firms." In: *Journal of International Business Studies* (forthcoming).

Gabele, E. *Values in Small- and Medium-sized Firms.* Bamberg 1981.

Guttman, L. "Introduction to Facet Design and Analysis." In: *Proceedings of the 15th International Congress of Psychology Brussels 1957,* Amsterdam 1959.

Krauth, J. & Lienert, G. A. *Die Konfigurations-Frequenz-Analyse und ihre Anwendung in Psychologie and Medizin.* Freiburg 1973.

Landsberg, G. von & Wölke, G. *Auslandsmüde Deutsche? Auslandserfahrung im Urteil der Wirtschaft.* Institut der deutschen Wirtschaft: Beiträge zur Gesellschafts- and Bildungspolitik (74), Köln 1982.

Lee, W. Y. & Brasch, J. J. "The Adoption of Export as an Innovative Strategy." *Journal of International Business Studies,* 1978, 9 (1), p. 85–93.

Lewin, K. "Time Perspective and Morale." In: Lewin, K. (ed.), *Resolving Social Conflicts,* New York, 1948, p. 103–124.

Lienert, G. A. *Testaufbau und Testanalyse.* Weinheim 1967 (2nd ed.).

Murray, H. A. "Foreword." In: Anderson, H. M. & Anderson, G. L. (eds.), *An Introduction to Projective Techniques,* Englewood Cliffs, N.J., 1951, p. 11–14.

Olson, H. C. & Wiedersheim-Paul, F. "Factors Affecting the Pre-Export Behavior of Non-Exporting Firms." In: Ghertman, M. & Leontiades, J. (eds.), *European Research in International Business,* New York 1978, p. 283–305.

Otway, H. J. "The Status of Risk Assessment." Paper Presented at the Tenth International TNO Conference on Risk Analysis, Rotterdam 1977.

Rabino, S. "An Examination of Barriers to Exporting Encountered by Small Manufacturing Companies." *Management International Review,* 1980, 20 (1), p. 67–73.

Reid, R. S. "The Decision Maker and Export Entry and Expansion." *Journal of International Business Studies,* 1981, 12 (2), p. 101–112.

Shartle, C. L., Brumback, G. B. & Rizzo, J. R. "An Approach to Dimensions of Value." *Journal of Psychology,* 1964, 57 (1), p. 101–111.

Simpson, C. L. "The Export Decision: An Interview Study of the Decision Process in Tennessee Manufacturing Firms." Ph.D. Dissertation, Georgia State University, Atlanta, Georgia, 1973.

Simpson, C. L. & Kujawa, D. "The Export Decision Process: An Empirical Inquiry." *Journal of International Business Studies,* 1974, 5 (1), p. 107–117.

Snavely, W. P., Weiner, P., Ulbrich, H. H. & Enright, E. J. *Export Survey of the Greater Hartford Area.* Vols. 1 & 2, University of Connecticut, Storrs, Connecticut 1964.

Stahr, G. "Risiken im Auslandsgeschäft und Maßnahmen zu ihrer Absicherung." *Das Wirtschaftsstudium* 1981, 10 (3), 115–18, und 1981, 10 (4), 167–71.

Steinmann, H., Kumar, B. & Wasner, A. "Internationalisierung von Mittelbetrieben. Eine empirische Untersuchung in Mittelfranken." In: *Zeitschriftenreihe der ZfB,* Vol. 6, Wiesbaden 1977.

Steinmann, H., Kumar, B. & Wasner, A. "Der Internationalisierungsprozes von Mittelbetrieben—Überlegungen zum Entwurf eines Forschungskonzepts." In: Pausenberger, E. (ed.), *Internationales Management,* Stuttgart 1981, 107–127.

Tesar, G. "Empirical Study of Export Operations Among Small- and Medium-Sized Manufacturing Firms." Ph.D. Dissertation, University of Wisconsin, Madison, Wisconsin 1975.

Webb, E. J., Campbell, D. T., Schwartz, R. D. & Sechrest, L. *Unobtrusive Measures: Nonreactive Research in the Social Sciences,* Chicago 1966.

Weiner, P. & Krok, M. *A Study of the Attempts and Results of Directly Stimulating Exporting.* Research Report of the Federal Reserve Bank of Boston, No. 38, March 1967.

Welch, L. S. & Wiedersheim-Paul, F. *Extra-Regional Expansion—Internationalization within the Domestic Market.* Center of International Business Studies, Department of Business Administration, University of Uppsala, Sweden, January 1977.

Wesley, E. "Perseverative Behavior, Manifest Anxiety, and Rigidity." *Journal of Abnormal and Social Psychology,* 1953, 48 (1), p. 129–34.

Wiedersheim-Paul, F., Olson, H. C. & Welch, L. A. "Pre-Export Activity: The First Steps in Internationalization." *Journal of International Business Studies,* 1978, 9 (1), p. 47–58.

\

9 INTERNATIONAL MARKETING PLANNING: An Iconoclastic View

Malcolm H. B. McDonald

Marketing planning in an international context remains one of the most baffling subjects both for academics and practitioners alike. This chapter, however, has a deadly serious intention and is not concerned with logically deduced theories based on ungrounded assumptions, which is often what happens when an academic sets out to assail cherished beliefs [Glaser & Strauss [1] refer to this as exampling]. My polemic is with those who completely miss the point when writing about marketing planning, and the purpose of this chapter is to remove some of the myths which surround this very complex area of marketing management.

This chapter is based on my PhD dissertation, which during a four year period examined the way British industrial goods companies trading internationally carry out their marketing planning. Four hundred directors were interviewed in 200 companies broadly representative of the complete spectrum of type and size of industrial company. A number of papers and monographs have already been published describing the major findings [2; 3; 4]. This chapter will focus only on those issues which the writer thinks will be of interest to delegates at this conference.

Let me start by telling you a little about Cranfield. Cranfield is a remarkable university because it is pledged to the total integration of engineering and

143

technology with marketing. At Cranfield we quite simply believe that without the closest and mutually respectful relationship between these two creative elements in any business, there is little or no future worth contemplating. That is why at Cranfield the marketers are direct colleagues, for instance, with aerospace, biotechnology, and robotics specialists.

Marketing's contribution to business success in manufacturing, distribution, or merchanting activities lies in its commitment to detailed analysis of future opportunities to meet customer needs and a wholly professional approach to selling to well-defined market segments those products or services that deliver the sought-after benefits. Whilst prices and discounts are important, as are advertising and promotion, the link with engineering through the product is paramount. Such a commitment and activities must not be mistaken for budgets and forecasts. Those, of course, we need and we have already got. Our accounting colleagues have long since seen to that. Put quite bluntly, the process of marketing planning is concerned with identifying what and to whom sales are going to be made in the longer term to give revenue budgets and sales forecasts any chance of achievement. Furthermore, chances of achievement are a function of how good our intelligence services are; and how well suited our strategies are; and how well we are led.

My engineering colleagues at Cranfield are most demanding of their marketers. They want to know how marketing planning can add anything much in a market where an organization has a well-established position and knows everybody worth selling to; and where success thus far has not been based on any particularly rigorous approach to marketing planning. Our answer is that all leadership positions are transitory. No industry based in the United Kingdom needs reminding of that today. Our competitive position in engineering and marketing worldwide today is an insult to the founding fathers of British industry, like Abraham Darby, or the motor industry barons or even more recently to Sir Denis Gabor, who did so much of the pioneering work in Britain on holography. It seemed to me, then, that it would be a good idea to carry out a detailed exploration of how British industrial goods companies planned the way in which they relate to their customers and markets around the world.

What is Marketing Planning?

Let me begin by defining most carefully what marketing planning is. It is a logical sequence and a series of activities leading to the setting of marketing objectives and the formulation of plans for achieving them. Conceptually, the process is very simple, and, in summary, comprises the following steps:

Gathering information on both the external environment and the company internally (the marketing audit);

Identifying major strengths, weaknesses, opportunities, and threats (SWOT analysis);

Formulating basic assumptions;

Deciding on the marketing objectives of the business, based on the information gathered; the SWOT analysis; and the assumptions made;

Laying down strategies for achieving the objectives;

Formulating programs for implementing the strategies, to include timing, responsibilities, and costs;

Measuring progress towards achievement of the objectives; reviewing and amending the plan as necessary.

I found this process to be universally agreed by the experts. Formalized marketing planning by means of a planning system is, *per se,* little more than a structured way of identifying a range of options for the company, of making them explicit in writing, of formulating marketing objectives which are consistent with the company's overall objectives, and of scheduling and costing-out the specific activities most likely to bring about the achievement of the objectives. It is the systemization of this process which is distinctive and was found to lie at the heart of the theory of marketing planning. Figures 9–1, 9–2, 9–3, and 9–4 detail out precisely what elements are found in a typical system.

Naiveté about Marketing Planning

I have just rehearsed with you the notions that any textbook would offer should you care to re-read it. We have long been bemused at Cranfield, however, by the fact that many meticulous marketing planning companies fare badly whilst the sloppy or inarticulate in marketing terms do well. Was there any real relationship between marketing planning and commercial success? And, if so, how did that relationship work its way through?

There are, of course, many studies, such as those of Thompson, Kollatt, Ansoff, Thune and House, Leighton, Boyd and Massey, and Camillus [5; 6; 7; 8; 9; 10; 11], which are based on empirical work and which identify a number of benefits to be obtained from marketing planning. But there is little explanation for the commercial success of those companies that do not engage in formalized planning. Nor is there much exploration of the

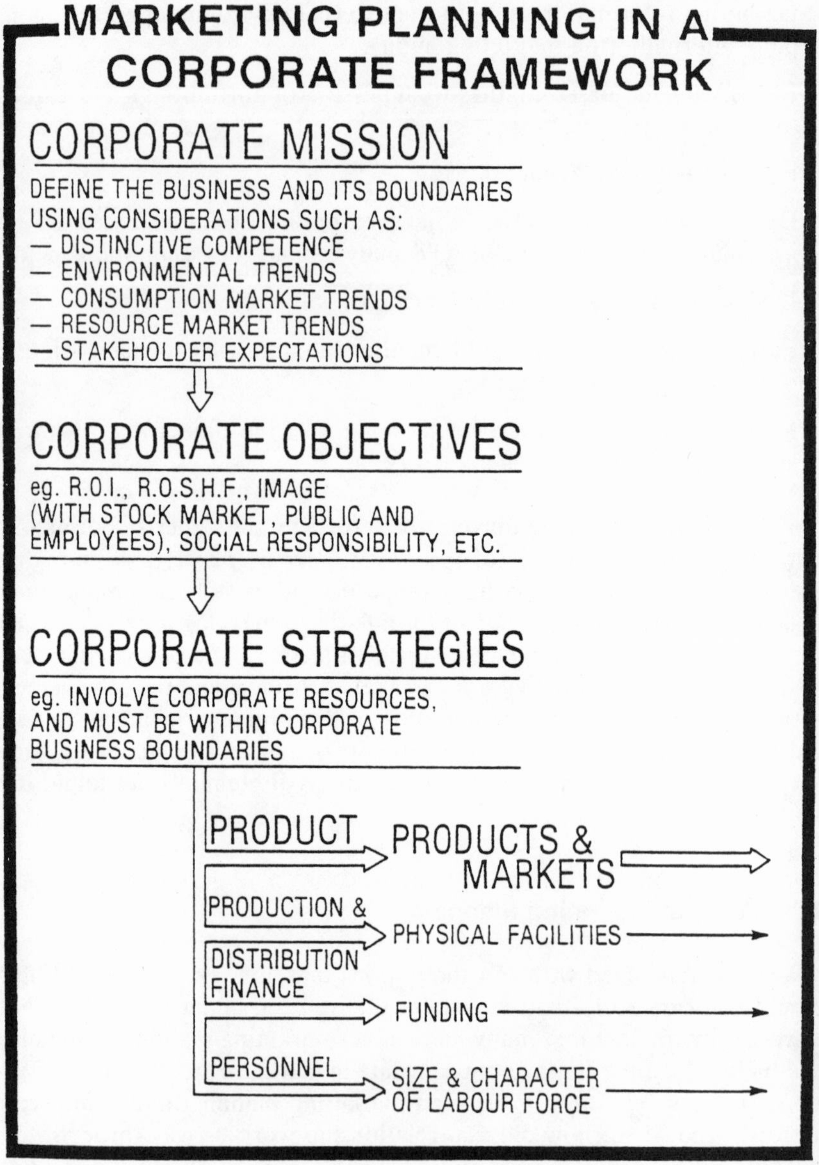

MARKETING PLANNING IN A CORPORATE FRAMEWORK

CORPORATE MISSION

DEFINE THE BUSINESS AND ITS BOUNDARIES
USING CONSIDERATIONS SUCH AS:
— DISTINCTIVE COMPETENCE
— ENVIRONMENTAL TRENDS
— CONSUMPTION MARKET TRENDS
— RESOURCE MARKET TRENDS
— STAKEHOLDER EXPECTATIONS

⇩

CORPORATE OBJECTIVES

eg. R.O.I., R.O.S.H.F., IMAGE
(WITH STOCK MARKET, PUBLIC AND
EMPLOYEES), SOCIAL RESPONSIBILITY, ETC.

⇩

CORPORATE STRATEGIES

eg. INVOLVE CORPORATE RESOURCES,
AND MUST BE WITHIN CORPORATE
BUSINESS BOUNDARIES

PRODUCT ⟶ PRODUCTS & MARKETS ⟹

PRODUCTION & DISTRIBUTION ⟶ PHYSICAL FACILITIES ⟶

FINANCE ⟶ FUNDING ⟶

PERSONNEL ⟶ SIZE & CHARACTER OF LABOUR FORCE ⟶

Figure 9–1. Marketing Planning in a Corporate Framework

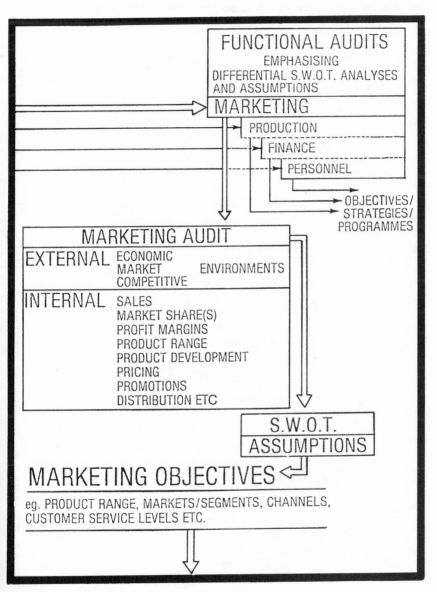

Figure 9-2. Marketing Planning in a Corporate Framework

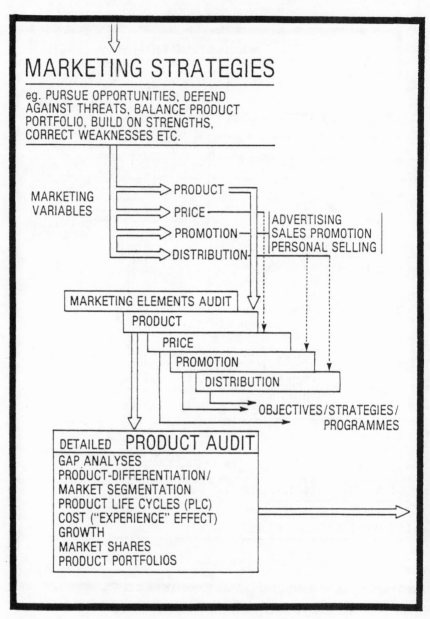

MARKETING STRATEGIES

eg. PURSUE OPPORTUNITIES, DEFEND
AGAINST THREATS, BALANCE PRODUCT
PORTFOLIO, BUILD ON STRENGTHS,
CORRECT WEAKNESSES ETC.

MARKETING
VARIABLES

PRODUCT
PRICE
PROMOTION
DISTRIBUTION

ADVERTISING
SALES PROMOTION
PERSONAL SELLING

MARKETING ELEMENTS AUDIT
PRODUCT
PRICE
PROMOTION
DISTRIBUTION

OBJECTIVES/STRATEGIES/
PROGRAMMES

DETAILED **PRODUCT AUDIT**

GAP ANALYSES
PRODUCT-DIFFERENTIATION/
MARKET SEGMENTATION
PRODUCT LIFE CYCLES (PLC)
COST ("EXPERIENCE" EFFECT)
GROWTH
MARKET SHARES
PRODUCT PORTFOLIOS

Figure 9–3. Marketing Planning in a Corporate Framework

$\Longrightarrow$ # PRODUCT OBJECTIVES

eg. INCREASE RANGE, MARKET SHARE, AND PROFITABILITY: MAINTAIN OR IMPROVE DESIGN AND QUALITY ETC. NEW PRODUCT DEVELOPMENT: PACKAGING:

$\Downarrow$

PRODUCT STRATEGIES

eg. BUILD SHARE, HOLD SHARE, HARVEST, OR WITHDRAW product(s) DEPENDING UPON PRESENT MARKET & COST POSITION, PLC STAGE (GROWTH RATE), FIRM'S RESOURCE'S VIS A VIS COMPETITORS, LIKELY ACTIONS AND REACTIONS ETC.

Figure 9–4. Marketing Planning in a Corporate Framework

circumstances of those commercially unsuccessful companies that also have formalized marketing planning systems; and, where the dysfunctional consequences are recognized, there is a failure to link this back to any kind of theory. Success is, of course, influenced by many factors apart from just planning procedures, for example:

1. Financial performance at any one point in time is not necessarily a reflection of the adequacy or otherwise of planning procedures (c.f., the hotel industry, location, tourism etc.).
2. Some companies just happen to be in the right place at the right time(s) [12].
3. Companies have many and varied objectives; such as, for example, stylistic objectives [13].
4. There is a proven relationship between management style and commercial success [14; 15].

In other words, marketing planning procedures alone are not enough for success. Thus, the research study was multifaceted and was concerned with the total system, and effectiveness was considered to be a qualitative assessment of how a company coped with its environment. The output was theory that attempted to describe what was actually going on in the area under investigation and that accounted for much of the relevant behavior observed.

I have said that the process of marketing planning is conceptually very simple and universally applicable. However, it is this very simplicity and universality that makes it extremely complex once a number of contextual issues are added such as (1) company size; (2) degree of internationalization; (3) management style; (4) degree of business environmental turbulence and competitive hostility; (5) market growth rate; (6) market share; (7) technological changes, and so forth. It is very clear that the simplistic theories do not adequately address such contextual issues in relation to marketing planning, which may well account for the fact that so few companies actually do it.

In fact, 90 percent of international industrial goods companies did not, by their own admission, produce anything approximating to an integrated, coordinated and internally consistent plan for their marketing activities. This included a substantial number of companies in the simple frame that had highly formalized procedures for marketing planning. Certainly, few of these companies enjoyed the claimed benefits of formalized marketing planning, which in summary are as follows: (1) coordination of the activities of many individuals whose actions are interrelated over time; (2) identification of expected developments; (3) preparedness to meet changes when they occur; (4) minimization of non-rational responses to the unexpected; (5) better communication among executives; and (6) minimization of conflicts among individuals which would result in a subordination of the goals of the company to those of the individual.

The important fact which emerged was that many of the companies examined which had many of the trappings of sophisticated marketing planning systems suffered as many dysfunctional consequences as those companies that had only forecasting and budgeting systems.

It is clear that for any marketing planning system to be effective, certain conditions have to be satisfied. I shall deal with these conditions in detail shortly. However, there are some other findings which are worth mentioning.

Firstly, it is possible to state that it is by no means essential for any company not suffereing from hostile and unstable competitive and environmental conditions to have a complete marketing planning system. However, without exception, all those companies which did not have a complete marketing planning system and which were profitable were also operating in buoyant or high-growth markets. Such companies, however, were less successful than comparable companies with complete marketing planning systems. Success was considered to be not only a company's financial performance over a number of years, but also the way it coped with its environment.

What this means is that, apart from profitability, a company with a complete marketing planning system is likely to have: widely understood objectives; highly motivated employees; high levels of actionable market information; greater interfunctional coordination; minimum waste and duplication of resources; acceptance of the need for continuous change and a clear understanding of priorities, and greater control over the business and less vulnerability from the unexpected.

In the case of companies without complete marketing planning systems, whilst it is possible to be profitable over a number of years—especially in high growth markets—such companies will tend to be less profitable over time and to suffer problems which are the very opposite of the benefits referred to above. Furthermore, companies without complete marketing planning systems tend to suffer more serious commercial organization consequences when environmental and competitive conditions become hostile and unstable.

None of these findings are new, however, in the sense that most of these benefits and problems are discernable to the careful observer. They are, however, actionable propositions for marketers.

**Planning System Completeness and Requisite
Marketing Planning**

Many companies currently under siege have recognized the need for a more structured approach to planning their marketing and had opted for the kind of standardized, formalized procedures written about so much in textbooks. These rarely brought the claimed benefits and often brought marketing planning itself into disrepute. It is quite clear that any attempt at the introduction of formalized marketing planning systems has serious organizational and behavioral implications for an international company, as it requires a change in its approach to managing its business. It is also clear that unless a company recognizes these implications and plans to seek ways of coping with them, formalized marketing planning will be ineffective. My research showed that the implications are principally as follows:

1. Any closed loop marketing planning system (but especially one that is essentially a forecasting and budgeting system) will lead to entropy of marketing and creativity. Therefore, there has to be some mechanism for preventing inertia from setting in through the over-bureaucratization of the system.
2. Marketing planning undertaken at the functional level of marketing, in the absence of a means of integration with other functional areas of the business at general management level, will be largely ineffective.
3. The separation of responsibility for operational and strategic marketing planning will lead to a divergence of the short-term thrust of a business at the operational level from the long-term objectives of the enterprise as a whole. This will encourage a preoccupation with short-term results at operational level, which normally makes the firm less effective in the long term.
4. Unless the chief executive understands and takes an active role in marketing planning, it will never be a complete system and will, therefore, certainly be ineffective.
5. A period of up to three years is necessary (especially in large firms), for the introduction of a complete marketing planning system.

I can now return usefully to explore what is meant by the term requisite marketing planning, mentioned earlier.

Some indication of the potential complexity of marketing planning can be seen in figure 9–5. Even in a generalized model such as this, it can be seen that in a large diversified group operating in many foreign markets, a

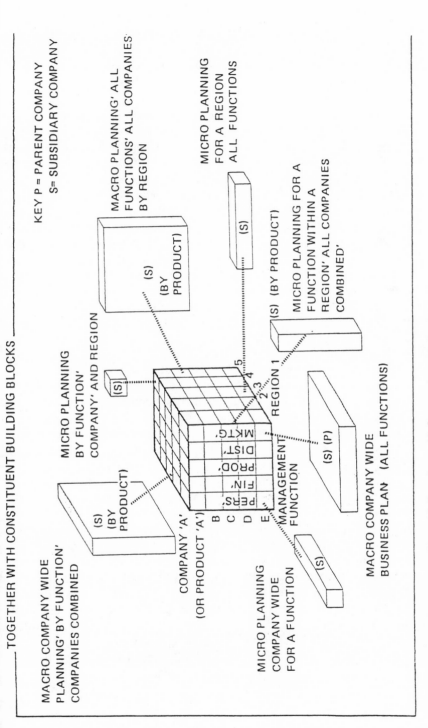

TOGETHER WITH CONSTITUENT BUILDING BLOCKS

KEY P = PARENT COMPANY
S= SUBSIDIARY COMPANY

MACRO PLANNING' ALL
FUNCTIONS' ALL COMPANIES'
BY REGION

MICRO PLANNING
FOR A REGION
ALL FUNCTIONS

(S)
(BY PRODUCT)

MICRO PLANNING
BY FUNCTION'
COMPANY' AND REGION

(S)

(S)

(S) (BY PRODUCT)

MICRO PLANNING FOR A
FUNCTION WITHIN A
REGION' ALL COMPANIES
COMBINED'

REGION 1

MACRO COMPANY WIDE
PLANNING' BY FUNCTION'
COMPANIES COMBINED

(S)
(BY PRODUCT)

COMPANY 'A'
(OR PRODUCT 'A')

B
C
D
E

PERS'
FIN'
PROD'
DIST'
MKTG'

MANAGEMENT
FUNCTION

(S) (P)

MACRO COMPANY WIDE
BUSINESS PLAN (ALL FUNCTIONS)

MICRO PLANNING
COMPANY WIDE
FOR A FUNCTION

(S)

Figure 9–5. Macro Business Plan, All Functions, All Companies, All Regions

complex combination of product, market, and functional plans is possible. For example, what is required at regional level will be different from what is required at headquarters level, whilst it is clear that the total corporate plan has to be built from the individual building blocks. Furthermore, the function of marketing itself may be further functionalized for the purpose of planning, such as marketing research, advertising, selling, distribution, promotion, and so forth, whilst different customer groups may need to have separate plans drawn up.

Let me be dogmatic about requisite planning levels. Firstly, in a large, diversified group, irrespective of such organizational issues, anything other than a systematic approach approximating to a formalized marketing planning system is unlikely to enable the necessary control to be exercised over the corporate identity. Secondly, unnecessary planning, or overplanning, could easily result from an inadequate or indiscriminate consideration of the real planning needs at the different levels in the hierarchical chain. Thirdly, as size and diversity grow, so the degree of formalization of the marketing planning process must also increase.

This can be simplified in the form of a matrix. [figure 9–6] The degree of formalization must increase with the evolving size and diversity of operations. However, whilst the degree of formalization will change, the need for a complete marketing planning system does not. The problems that companies suffer, then, are a function of either the degree to which they have a complete marketing planning system or the degree to which the formalization of their system grows with the situational complexities attendant upon the size and diversity of operations. Figure 9–7 explores four key outcomes that marketing planning can evoke.

It can be seen that systems I, III, and IV, i.e., where the individual is totally subordinate to a formalized system or where individuals are allowed to do what they want without any system or where there is neither system nor creativity, are less successful than system II, in which the individual is allowed to be entrepreneurial within a total system. System II, then, will be a complete marketing planning system, but one in which the degree of formalization will be a function of company size and diversity.

Creativity cannot flourish in a closed-loop formalized system. There would be little disagreement that in today's abrasive, turbulent, and highly competitive environment that those firms which succeed in extracting entrepreneurial ideas and creative marketing programs from systems that are necessarily yet acceptably formalized will succeed in the long run. Much innovative flair can so easily get stifled by systems.

Certainly there was ample evidence of international companies with

COMPANY SIZE

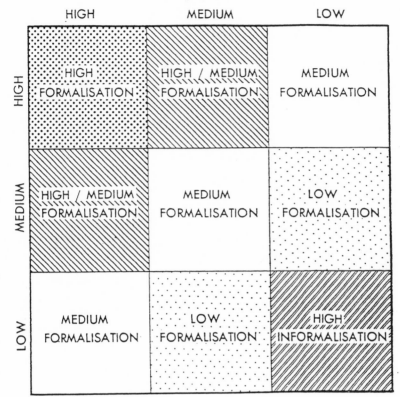

Figure 9–6.   Degree of Formalization

highly formalized systems that produced stale and repetitive plans, with little changed from year-to-year, and that failed to point up the really key strategic issues as a result. The scandalous waste this implies is largely due to a lack of personal intervention by key managers during the early stages of the planning cycle. There is clearly a need, therefore, to find a way of perpetually renewing the planning life cycle each time around. Inertia must never set in. Without some such valve or means of opening up the loop, inertia quickly produces decay.

Such a valve has to be inserted early in the planning cycle during the audit, or situation review, stage. In companies with complete marketing

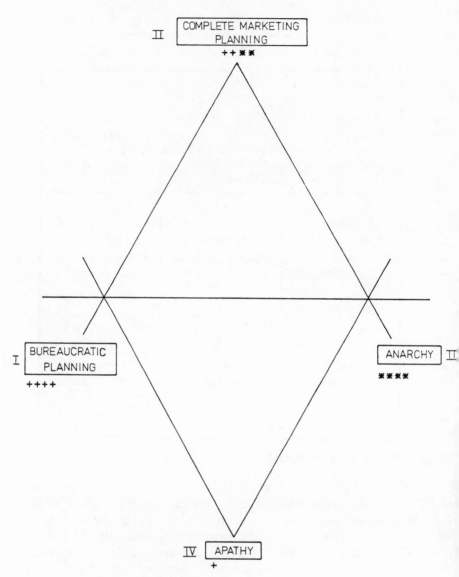

Figure 9–7. Key Outcomes of Marketing Planning

planning systems, whether such systems were formalized or informal, the critical intervention of senior managers, from the chief executive down through the hierarchical chain, comes at the audit stage. Essentially what takes place is a personalized presentation of audit findings, together with proposed marketing objectives and strategies and outline budgets for the strategic planning period. These are discussed, amended where necessary, and agreed in various synthesized formats at the hierarchical levels in the organization *before* any detailed operational planning takes place. It is at such meetings that managers are called upon to justify their views, which tend to force them to be more bold and creative than they would have been had they allowed merely to send in their proposals.

Obviously, however, even here much depends on the degree to which managers take a critical stance, which is much greater when the chief executive himself takes an active part in the process. Every hour of time devoted at this stage by the chief executive has a multiplier effect throughout the remainder of the process. And let it be remembered we are not, repeat not, talking about budgets at this juncture in anything other than outline form.

Until recently it was envisaged that there may well be fundamental differences in marketing planning approaches, depending on factors such as the type of industrial goods and markets involved, company size, the degree of dependence on overseas sales, and the methods used to market goods abroad. In particular, the much-debated role of headquarters management in the marketing planning process was envisaged as being a potential cause of great difficulty.

One of the most encouraging findings to emerge from my work at Cranfield is that the theory of marketing planning is universally applicable and that such issues are largely irrelevant. Whilst the planning task is less complicated in small, undiversified companies and there is less need for formalized procedures than in large, diversified companies, the fact is that exactly the same framework should be used in all circumstances and that this approach brings similar benefits to all.

In a multinational conglomerate, headquarters management is able to assess major trends in products and markets around the world and is thus able to develop strategies for investment, expansion, diversification, and divestment on a global basis. For their part, subsidiary management can develop appropriate strategies with a sense of locomotion towards the achievement of coherent overall goals. This is achieved by means of synthesized information flows from the bottom upwards, which facilitates useful comparison of performances around the world and the diffusion of valuable information, skills, experiences, and systems from the top downwards. The particular benefits which accrue to companies using such systems can be classified under the major headings of the marketing mix elements as follows:

Marketing information: there is a transfer of knowledge, a sharing of expertise, and an optimization of effort around the world.

Product: control is exercised over the product range. Maximum effectiveness is gained by concentrating on certain products in certain markets, based on experience gained throughout the world.

Price: pricing policies are sufficiently flexible to enable local management to trade effectively, whilst the damaging effects of interaction are considerably mitigated.

Place: substantial gains are made by rationalization of the logistics function.

Promotion: duplication of effort and a multitude of different platforms/company images are ameliorated. Efforts in one part of the world reinforce those in another.

The procedures which facilitate the provision of such information and knowledge transfers also encourage operational management to think strategically about their own areas of responsibility, instead of managing only for the short term.

It is abundantly clear that it is through a marketing planning system and planning skills that such benefits are achieved, and that discussions such as those about the standardization of marketing strategies in the absence of some form of standardized *process* are largely irrelevant. Any standardization that may be possible will become clear only if a company can successfully develop a system for identifying the needs of each market and each segment in which it operates and for organizing resources to satisfy those needs in such a way that best resource utilization results worldwide. This very same conclusion was reached very recently by Shuptrine and Toyne. [16]

Checklists

There are many checklists of things you have to do to go through the motions of marketing planning. But pages of figures and marketing prose, well typed, elegantly bound, and retrievably filed, do not make much difference. It makes some difference because the requirements of writing a plan demand deep thought. However, it is vital that companies must always search for the requisite level of marketing planning, just as in engineering one will often seek the requisite level of variety in product or services offered.

There is also a second aspect of requisiteness to be considered. It concerns the requisite location of the marketing planning activity in a company. The answer is simple to give. Marketing planning should take place as near to the marketplace as possible in the first instance, but such plans should then move up within an organization to see what issues have been overlooked, because it is sometimes too close to the market. Figure 9–8, 9–9, and 9–10 illustrate the principles by which the marketing planning process should be implemented in any company, irrespective of whether it is a small exporting company or a major multinational. In essence, these exhibits show a hierarchy of audits, SWOT analyses, objectives, strategies, and programs.

In Conclusion

The problem we have in most British international companies today is not that the philosophy of marketing is not believed, but that most industrial goods companies just cannot make it work. This is largely because of ignorance about the process of planning their marketing activities, and it is a sad reflection on all of us that little help is given them in the extant body of literature, which basically falls into three categories: (1) textbooks which provide guidance on the management of the marketing function, but not on the actual process of marketing planning itself; (2) papers which treat marketing planning in a very generalized way, telling about the need to carry out situation reviews, set objectives and strategies, and so on, without providing any real guidance of operational significance; and (3) papers which discuss various aspects of marketing planning, such as top down/bottom up processes.

It is abundantly clear that it is only through a requisite marketing planning system and the systematic development of planning skills that any benefits as a result of standardization of marketing strategies will become a reality. Any standardization that may be possible will become clear only if a company can successfully develop a system for identifying the needs of each market in which it operates and for organizing resources to satisfy those needs in such a way that optimization of resource utilization results worldwide. Such a system as that described in my thesis and summarized

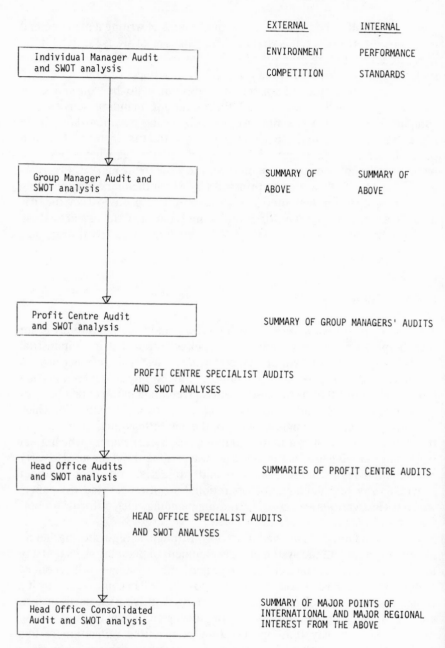

EXTERNAL   INTERNAL

| Individual Manager Audit and SWOT analysis | ENVIRONMENT | PERFORMANCE |
| | COMPETITION | STANDARDS |

| Group Manager Audit and SWOT analysis | SUMMARY OF | SUMMARY OF |
| | ABOVE | ABOVE |

Profit Centre Audit and SWOT analysis

SUMMARY OF GROUP MANAGERS' AUDITS

PROFIT CENTRE SPECIALIST AUDITS
AND SWOT ANALYSES

Head Office Audits and SWOT analysis

SUMMARIES OF PROFIT CENTRE AUDITS

HEAD OFFICE SPECIALIST AUDITS
AND SWOT ANALYSES

Head Office Consolidated Audit and SWOT analysis

SUMMARY OF MAJOR POINTS OF
INTERNATIONAL AND MAJOR REGIONAL
INTEREST FROM THE ABOVE

Figure 9–8. Hierarchy of Audits

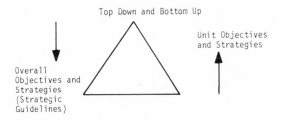

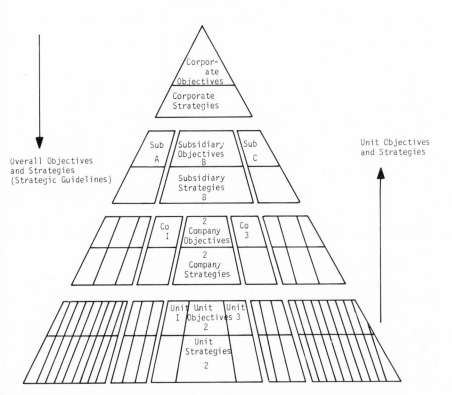

Figure 9-9.   Strategic and Operational Planning.
Source: M. H. B. McDonald, Ph.D., 1981.

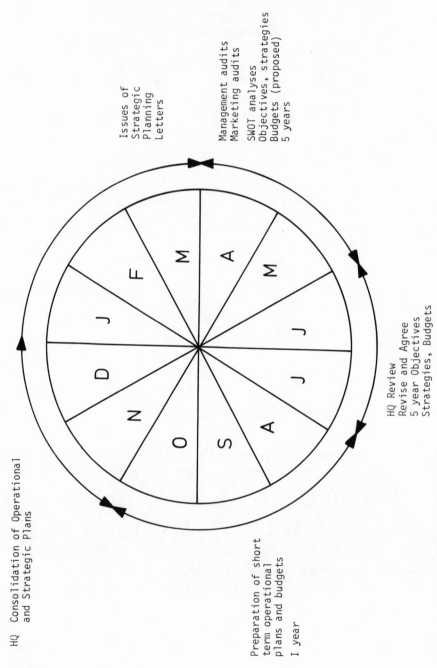

HQ Consolidation of Operational
    and Strategic Plans

Issues of
Strategic
Planning
Letters

Management audits
Marketing audits

SWOT analyses
Objectives, strategies
Budgets (proposed)
5 years

HQ Review
Revise and Agree
5 year Objectives
Strategies, Budgets

Preparation of short
term operational
plans and budgets

I year

Figure 9-10   Strategic and Operational Planning

briefly here will enable a company to take account both of similarities and differences between countries and operations, so that the key determinants of international success are controlled at the appropriate level, allowing for local deviations where necessary. In order to achieve this balance, a complete marketing planning system is necessary. The smaller the degree of control which it is possible to exercise over a marketing program, as for example, when operating through agents and distributors, the greater is the reason to find a way of controlling what happens.

It is very important to stress that the degree to which any company can succeed in developing an integrated and internally-consistent view of their marketing in the form of a plan clearly depends on a deep understanding of the marketing planning process itself. Such an understanding comes only from the hard experience of actually trying to develop a workable system within a company and from an endless willingness to adapt the resulting systems and procedures to the particular personality and organizational peculiarities of the company.

References

1. Glaser, B. G. and Strauss, A. C. *The Discovery of Grounded Theory: Strategies for Qualitative Research.* Aldine Publishing Company, New York, 1967.
2. McDonald, M. H. B. "International Marketing Planning: Some New Insights (1)." *Journal of International Marketing,* Winter 1981.
3. McDonald, M. H. B. "International Marketing Planning: Some New Insights (2)." *Journal of International Marketing,* Spring 1982.
4. Mcdonald, M. H. B. *International Marketing Planning.* MCB Monograph, 1982.
5. Thompson, S. "How Companies Plan." A.M.A. Research Study, No. 54. A.M.A.
6. Kollatt, D. T., Blackwell, R. D., and Robeson, J. F. *Strategic Marketing.* Holt, Rinehart and Winston, Inc., 1972
7. Ansoff, H. I. "The State of Practice of Planning Systems." *Sloan Management Review,* Vol. 18, No. 2, Winter 1977.
8. Thune, S. and House, R. "Where Long Range Planning Pays Off." *Business Horizons,* Vol. VII, No. 4, August 1970.
9. Leighton, D. S. R. *International Marketing—Text and Cases.* McGraw Hill, New York, 1966.
10. Boyd, H. and Massey, W. *Marketing Management.* 1972.
11. Camillus, J. C. "Evaluating the Benefits of Formal Planning Systems." *Long Range Planning,* June 1975.

12. Kotler, P. "Corporate Models, Better Marketing Plans." *Harvard Business Review,* July 1970.
13. Ackoff, R. *A Concept of Corporate Planning.* Interscience, Wiley, New York, 1970.
14. Likert, R. "Human Resource Accounting." *Personnel (NY),* Vol. 50, 1973.
15. Wilson, A. *The Marketing of Industrial Products.* Hutchinson, London, 1965.
16. Shuptrine F. K. and Toyne, B. "International Marketing Planning: A Standardised Process." *Journal of International Marketing,* Winter 1981.

10 EXPORT MARKETING CHANNELS:
Some Theoretical Considerations
Matthew Meulenberg

Introduction

In this article, export marketing channels are discussed from a theoretical point of view. There are many studies on export marketing channels, both empirically and theoretically oriented [Bakker, 1980]. It seems to us, however, that their link with general theory of marketing channels is weak [e.g., Stern & El Ansary, 1982]. International marketing, as a subdiscipline of general marketing, might possibly enlarge its understanding of marketing channels by relating general marketing theory to specific features of international marketing.

In applying general marketing theory to export marketing, it will be necessary to establish which features are characteristic for export marketing. The process of international marketing involves the transport of products

The author is indebted to Dr. Cecil Smith for comments and suggestions.

over international boundaries. Some marketing attributes are characteristic of export marketing but not of domestic marketing. A major attribute relates to exchange rates between various currencies and their conversion into acceptable currency for the exporter. Specific and detailed documents, often involving customs brokers and other agents, are required for export marketing. Additional related requirements may pertain to product identification, not required in domestic marketing, on product packages or shipping containers. Often international marketing requires the payment of import duties, thereby raising the effective price to the buyer (or lowering it to the seller, depending on relative bargaining power), and on occasion by quotas and trade regulations, which effectively limit the amount of a commodity that may be sold in a market during a specific time interval. Many international trade transactions involve the financing by a shipper, a bank, or a governmental agency, of the product traded and sometimes the cost of transporting it. In a survey of 122 Dutch food industries in 1980 on exporting to West Germany, 21% of the companies interviewed had export problems with the German Food and Drug Act, 17% with formalities at the border, 16% with transport regulations, 11% with competition, 9% with a different mentality, and 6% with an importing company [NIAM, 1980a]. These results illustrate that it is hard to determine specific variables for export marketing. Nevertheless, such variables are needed if one is to apply the principles of general marketing theory to export marketing. Obviously geographic distance to market is a specific characteristic of an export market. Let us summarize differences between domestic and export market in norms, values, life-style, customs, and laws as the variable cultural distance.

So, the influence of distance to market on export marketing channels will be analyzed. In this paper only, a partial analysis is offered, since the influence on marketing channels of features specific to export marketing is examined. In fact, general marketing characteristics like product type may be ultimately decisive in determining export marketing channels.

The plan of the paper is first to analyze the influence of distance on distribution decisions. This is discussed within the framework of the Dorfman-Steiner model. Afterwards, a more specific qualitative analysis is given of the impact of distance to market on marketing channels. Some major marketing theories on channel formation are reviewed, so that the influence of distance to markets can be viewed in the light of these theories. Finally inferences are drawn that might contribute to our understanding of export marketing channels.

Impact of Distance to Market on Distribution Decisions: A General Treatment

A general model for marketing decision-making with the objective of maximizing profits is the Dorfman-Steiner model [Dorfman & Steiner, 1954]:

$$S = f(P, D, A, Q) \text{ where: } S = \text{amount sold} \qquad (10.1)$$
$$P = \text{price}$$
$$C = g(S, Q) \qquad\qquad D = \text{distribution expenditure} \qquad (10.2)$$
$$R = S \cdot P - S \cdot C - D - A = \text{max!} \qquad (10.3)$$
$$A = \text{advertising expenditure}$$
$$Q = \text{quality of product}$$
$$C = \text{production costs per unit}$$
$$R = \text{profit}$$

from which the following profit-maximizing conditions are derived:

$$\epsilon_p = \mu_D = \mu_A = \epsilon_Q \cdot \frac{P}{C} \qquad (10.4)$$

$$\text{for } \epsilon_p = \frac{\partial S}{\partial P} \cdot \frac{P}{S}; \ \mu_D = -\frac{\partial S}{\partial D} \cdot P; \ \mu_A = -\frac{\partial S}{\partial A} \cdot P; \ \epsilon_Q = -\frac{\partial S/\partial Q}{\partial C/\partial Q} \cdot \frac{C}{S}$$

Distance to market was proposed as characteristic of export markets. Distance, L, is introduced as an additional variable. In this section, no distinction between cultural and geographic distance is made:

$$S = f(P, D, A, Q, L) \qquad (10.5)$$

$$C = g(S, Q) \qquad (10.6)$$

Distance to market could influence sales indirectly by impact on distribution effort, D, and advertising, A. Given a specific distance $L = L_0$, profit-maximizing conditions (equation 10.4) remain valid, but their value depends on the specific value L_0. If distance affects the influence of distribution and advertising on sales, an increase of L_0 to L_1 will affect marketing expenditures according to the values of

$$\frac{\partial^2 S}{\partial D \partial L} \text{ and } \frac{\partial^2 S}{\partial A \partial L}.$$

For instance, if

$$\frac{\partial^2 S}{\partial D \partial L} < 0 \text{ and } \frac{\partial^2 S}{\partial A \partial L} = 0$$

and if a firm aims to maximize profits, this firm will increase advertising expenditure relative to distribution expenditure in a market at distance L_1 as compared with the profit-maximizing expenditures at L_0, provided that $L_1 > L_0$ and the sales and cost functions remain the same.

In order to be more specific about the effect of distance, let us specify the sales function in more detail. Some alternative specifications will be considered.

Specification 1

$$S = \alpha P^\beta D^{(\gamma + \delta/L)} A^\eta Q^\zeta \tag{10.7}$$

for parameters:

$$\alpha, \gamma, \delta, \eta, \zeta > 0 \text{ and } \beta < 0; \; L \geq 1$$

$$C = f(S, Q) \tag{10.8}$$

This specification implies that distribution elasticity of sales decreases from $\gamma + \delta$ to γ with increasing distance, L, to the market. The marginal decrease in sales with an increase in L levels off with the square of the distance since

$$\frac{\partial S}{\partial L} = -(\delta/L^2)S \cdot \ln D, \text{ given } P, D, A, \text{ and } Q.$$

Profit-maximizing conditions for market 0, $L = L_0$, are, analogously to equation 10.4, equal to

$$\beta = -\left(\gamma + \frac{\delta}{L_0}\right) \cdot \frac{SP}{D}, \; \beta = -\eta \frac{SP}{A} \tag{10.9}$$

Assume now another export Market 1 at distance L_1, $L_1 > L_0$, having the same sales functions as Market 0. On the basis of equations 10.9,

$$\frac{A_i}{D_i} = \frac{\eta}{\gamma + (\delta/L_i)} \text{ for } i = 0, 1 \tag{10.10}$$

under profit maximization.

Consequently, the ratio of A to D will be larger in Market 1 than in 0 if $L_1 > L_0$ and α, β, γ, δ, η, and ζ are the same in both markets. This is in agreement with the fact that distribution functions are spun-off to middlemen, agents, or export houses when distance to market increases. Equation 10.9 also indicates that a producer might try to maximize profit in Market 1 by a decrease of price, P, relative to the profit-maximizing price on Market 0. Obviously the latter strategy makes sense only if $\beta < -1$.

So, under the objective of profit maximization, there will be a tendency to increase advertising expenditure and to decrease price in markets if they are otherwise the same, at greater distance. The conclusion of a price decrease is valid only if demand is elastic in price. Similar specifications, implying a more flexible influence of distance on sales, are, for instance, the same multiplicative sales function having an exponent of the variable D equal to

$$(\gamma + \delta e^{\theta L}) \text{ or } (\gamma + \delta e^{\theta L})/(1 + \lambda e^{\mu L}),$$

$$\text{for } \theta, \mu < 0, \text{ and } \gamma, \delta, \lambda > 0.$$

Such specifications imply that the distribution elasticity varies between $(\gamma + \delta)$ and γ, respectively, and between $(\gamma + \delta)/(1 + \lambda)$ and γ, for L varying between 0 and ∞.

Specification 2

Another specification of the sales function is that distance influences sales through distribution and advertising expenditure:

$$S = \alpha P^\beta \cdot D^{(\gamma + \delta/L)} \cdot A^{(\eta + \zeta/L)} \cdot Q^\theta \qquad (10.11)$$

for: α, γ, δ, η, ζ, $\theta > 0$; $\beta < 0$

For $L = L_0$, profit-maximizing conditions, equation 10.4, become

$$\beta = -\left(\gamma + \frac{\delta}{L_0}\right) \cdot \frac{SP}{D} = -\left(\eta + \frac{\zeta}{L_0}\right) \cdot \frac{SP}{A} \qquad (10.12)$$

So the ratio of distribution expenditure to advertising expenditure under profit maximization is

$$\frac{D}{A} = \frac{\gamma + \delta/L_0}{\eta + \zeta/L_0} = \frac{\gamma L_0 + \delta}{\eta L_0 + \zeta} = \frac{\gamma}{\eta} + \frac{\delta/\zeta - \gamma/\eta}{(\eta/\zeta) \cdot L_0 + 1} \qquad (10.13)$$

With larger values of L, *ceteris paribus,* the profit-maximizing ratio D/A will decrease if $\delta/\zeta > \gamma/\eta$, in other words, if the ratio of the marginal change of the exponents of distribution, D, and advertising, A, with respect to market distance, L, is larger than the ratio of the asymptotic values, $L \to \infty$, of these exponents.

The inferences about the impact of distance to market on distribution policy by using the Dorfman-Steiner model are of a general nature. However, our model specification does not offer a precise picture of distribution policy. The following section analyzes export marketing channels by combining general theory on marketing channels with distance of supplier to market, which is considered the specific variable of export marketing.

General Theories of Marketing Channels

To improve our understanding of export marketing channels, let us review some major theories on marketing channels and later apply them to export marketing. According to Mallen [1977], the following decision areas have to be considered about marketing channels: number of functions and type of middlemen, number of levels, number of middlemen at each level, number of channels, and degree of cooperation. Most theories on marketing channels take one or a subset of these decision areas into consideration. Mallen's classification provides a framework to review various theories on marketing channels.

The significance of these decision areas for marketing channels differs with the distribution objectives of a company. Distribution goals might be classified into optimum access to market, minimum distribution costs, and maximum bargaining power. Mallen [1977] distinguishes the objectives of maximizing sales, minimizing costs, maximizing channel goodwill, and maximizing channel control. These objectives will be considered insofar as they have been used explicitly in various theories on marketing channels.

The number of functions (type of middlemen) to be performed is crucial for the structure of marketing channels. The functions are summarized in various ways. Kotler (1980) distinguishes functions dealing with consummating transactions and functions facilitating transactions. Differences in marketing policy, in particular in the type of product, require differences in type and in number of distributive functions. For instance, distributive functions vary with intensive, selective, or exclusive distribution.

Theories or authoritative statements on the relationship between distribution policy and number of functions are scarce. The number of functions and consequently the type of middleman will depend on whether producers spin off distribution functions. Following Stigler, Mallen [1977] suggests that the cost curve for each function will determine whether a function will be spun-off. Dommermuth & Anderson [1969] classify efficiency improvement in distribution as intrafunctional, ".... lowering the cost of performing a particular function while holding output constant," and interfunctional, ".... total expenditure for performance of one function results in a more than offsetting decrease in the total cost of another function." Such improvements in efficiency may be achieved either by the firm itself (intrafirm) or by arrangement with another firm (interfirm). This spin-off of functions also has relevance for the number of levels in a marketing channel. Mallen [1977] argues that full-service middlemen are more compatible with the objective of minimizing costs or maximizing channel goodwill than limited-function middlemen, while the reverse is true with respect to the objective of maximizing channel control. Aspinwall [1962] related product characteristics to the functions to be performed by a marketing channel; for instance, red goods, with a high replacement rate, low gross margin, low adjustment, short time of consumption, and short searching time, will have intensive distribution. Theories on the evolution of retailing, like the "wheel of retailing" of McNair (1958) and the "simplex, multiplex, omniplex" theory of Regan (1964), stress the evolution of the number of functions during the life cycle of a particular retail institution.

The number of levels in a marketing channel has raised a substantial amount of marketing channel theory. Mallen's spin-off concept is relevant for the number of levels: if it is profitable for a producer to spin-off a marketing function, the number of levels in the marketing channel may increase. Mallen [1977] argues also that direct channels are more compatible with the objectives of maximizing sales and channel goodwill, or channel control, whereas the objective minimizing costs is more compatible with an indirect channel.

A specific theory on the number of levels in the marketing channel is the minimum-transaction criterion of Alderson [1954]: a middleman will arise between producers and customers, if the number of transactions decreases. Bucklin [1965] argues that delivery time in relation to postponement and speculation governs the choice of indirect or direct channels. With short delivery time, indirect channels give lower distribution costs per unit than direct ones. With long delivery time, the reverse situation holds. Aspinwall [1962] argues that red goods, as defined above, will be preferably distributed through indirect channels. Jackson et al. [1982] observed that the length of marketing channels for industrial products increased when the number of capable middlemen and the number of customers increased, and that this length decreased when the significance of purchase, the customer volume, the geographic concentration of the market, and the industrial concentration of the market increased.

The number of middlemen at each level of the marketing channel as a decision area of marketing channels has not evoked much marketing theory. Relevant is the distinction between intensive, selective, and exclusive distribution of products, which has obvious consequences for the number of selling points. Mallen [1977] states that the objective of maximizing sales is more compatible with intensive distribution; whereas the objectives of minimizing costs, maximizing channel goodwill and maximizing channel control are more compatible with exclusive distribution. Stern & El Ansary [1982] suggest as a law of marketing: "... the more intensive a product's distribution, the greater the sales that product will achieve in the short run." Mallen [1977] argues that the number of middlemen at a specific level in a marketing channel is related to the ratio of market size and optimum scale of operations of a company.

The number of channels a producer may choose has been discussed in various ways. Quantitative procedures have been proposed to assess the optimum use of marketing channels on the basis of demand and cost functions. For instance, Corstjens & Doyle [1979] used a geometric programming approach. Mallen [1977] asserted that the objectives to minimize costs, maximize channel goodwill, and maximize channel control were more compatible with a single channel; whereas the objective to maximize sales was more compatible with multiple channels. Qualitative contentions about the pros and cons of one or more marketing channels are numerous. Preston & Schramm [1965] mention additional markets and market segmentation on the positive side and loss of markets on the negative side. Potential retaliation and loss of motivation by members of the traditional channels when a producer is expanding the number of channels are other topics that have often been discussed.

A well-established subject in degree of cooperation in marketing channels is the concept of vertical marketing systems, which stresses cooperation between companies at different levels along the marketing channels. According to Mallen [1977], maximum cooperation in a marketing channel is more compatible with the objectives of maximum sales, maximum channel goodwill, and maximum channel control; whereas minimum cooperation is associated more with minimum costs. Stern & El Ansary [1982] have developed a theoretical framework for analyzing power and cooperation in marketing channels. This also seems relevant to cooperation in marketing channels. Another valuable contribution on that matter is the distinction made by Little [1970] between position power ("... involves from the placement of a firm function or activity in a given structure") and economic power (". . . is ultimately manifest in concentration of capital resources") in the marketing channel.

Our survey of some major contributions to the general theory of marketing channels demonstrates that there are a few partial theories. Nevertheless, it seems useful to evaluate their meaning for export marketing channels, which will be attempted further in this chapter.

Export Marketing and Marketing Channels

There are many studies on marketing channels in international marketing. For instance, Bakker [1980] reviews studies, especially on channel decisions in relation to entry strategy. Many books on international marketing, like that of Cateora & Hess [1979] have developed classifications of middlemen involved in international trade. Many classifications are based on the extent of control of the marketing channel by the producer, as, for example, is the following:

1. merchant wholesaler in exporting country;
2. merchant wholesaler in importing country;
3. sales agent in exporting country;
4. sales agent in importing country;
5. company sales branch in importing country;
6. direct exports to customers in importing country; and
7. production plant in importing country.

Marketing channels become shorter in the order one to seven. Various authors have formulated criteria for decisions on direct or indirect marketing strategies when entering an export market. They are related to marketing objectives, marketing environment, marketing strategy, and marketing information. Checklists have been developed on the basis of these criteria. Authoritative statements on the structure and development of export marketing channels are scarce. One example is that in which Bakker [1980] contends that a direct entry strategy is more attractive in export marketing than an indirect strategy, in view of marketing objectives, marketing strategy, marketing information, and marketing risk; whereas an indirect strategy is more attractive in view of product assortment and marketing costs. The literature asserts, too, that with increasing sales a company sales branch will become more attractive than a sales agent, if the former has smaller marginal costs than the latter.

A dynamic element of export marketing channels is that the optimum structure changes with the export life cycle. A selling agent might be preferable in the entry period because of lack of market knowledge and because of small amount exported; whereas a company sales branch might be preferable during growth and maturity. Joint distribution programs of exporting companies are institutionalized in various ways, like piggyback, licensing, joint selling, and export combinations. Strong and weak points of these types of cooperation are discussed in textbooks on international marketing. In conclusion, the literature on export marketing channels is pragmatic. General theories on marketing channels have not inspired international marketing a great deal. Are general theories on marketing channels relevant to export marketing? This question will be tackled later in this chapter.

Specific Features of Export Marketing Channels

A specific feature of the environment in export marketing is the great distance to the market, both geographically and culturally. The cultural distance refers to differences in consumer behavior, life-style, norms, and values, and consequently in laws and other regulations, which may hamper the marketing mix as programmed for the domestic market. It is probably also associated with differences in the distributive and competitive structure of the market. Let us confine ourselves to the relationship between distance to market and marketing channel structure in the light of general marketing theory, dealing first with choice of channel in entry strategy and second with the additional factors of order size and order frequency.

Impact of Distance on Export Marketing Channels in the Entry Stage

Number of Functions/Type of Middlemen. For the number of functions and type of middlemen in an export marketing channel, a distinction is needed between cultural distance and geographic distance. The performance of consummating functions will be related in particular to cultural distance and the performance of facilitating functions to geographic distance. Since cultural and geographic distances are not always strongly correlated, let us analyze the following four alternatives:

1. Short cultural distance and short geographic distance;
2. Long cultural distance and short geographic distance;

3.   Short cultural distance and long geographic distance;
4.   Long cultural distance and long geographic distance.

Clearly, the distinction for short and long distance is not precise. Empirical measurements will not be considered. Non-metric multidimensional scaling might be used for that purpose.

Situation 1.   There is not much difference between distribution functions in the domestic market and the export market. So there is no need for a specific export marketing channel, except possibly because of general market characteristics which are not specific for an export market.

Situation 2.   Because of the long cultural distance to market, the performance of consummating functions will differ in the export market from that in the domestic market. So, the exporter will have to rely upon special market knowledge. Whether the exporter incorporates this special market knowledge in his or her company or whether he or she relies on a middleman is essentially a matter of costs and of the desired extent of control. For limited amounts exported, the distribution costs per unit and the extent of control will increase in the sequence: exporting wholesaler, importing wholesaler, sales agent, company sales branch. The short geographic distance of producer to market does not cause special problems with facilitating functions. So, if the amount to be exported is small, as an entry strategy an exporter might use a sales agent.

Situation 3.   The combination of long geographic distance and small cultural distance calls for special attention to facilitating functions in the channel. Consequently, considerations of cost will determine to what extent export marketing channels will differ from domestic channels. Some physical distribution functions can be spun-off to companies specialized in transport or storage. So the exporter will be inclined to use direct selling, and a sales agent as next best, and to spin-off physical distribution functions to specialized companies.

Situation 4.   Long cultural distance and long geographic distance to export markets demand additional capacities in both consummating and facilitating functions. So, they favor the use of specialized wholesalers or export agents for the entry strategy.
   Mallen [1977] concluded a special relationship between the number of functions and the marketing objectives of minimizing costs, maximizing goodwill, and maximizing channel control. Long cultural distance to market makes maximization of goodwill and of channel control crucial for profita-

bility. The former objective would, according to Mallen, favor a full-service middleman, the latter a limited-function middleman; increasing cultural distance would have a dual influence on the structure of export marketing channels. A long geographic distance makes the objective of cost minimization crucial in decision making. This objective is, according to Mallen, more compatible with a limited-function middleman. An exporter would spin-off a limited number of functions to middlemen specialized on physical distribution or to a broker.

Number of Levels. The relevance of theories on the number of levels, examined earlier, will be discussed now in relation to marketing channels. Long distance to market advances, *ceteris paribus*, a narrow product assortment by exporters. In distant markets, a company will sell especially those products in which it is well-versed or which well suit the particular needs of those markets. Consequently, selling through middlemen would presumably decrease the number of transactions in comparison with direct marketing by exporters. A middleman can combine the imported product with related products from other exporters or domestic suppliers. In this situation, an alternative is selling by an export combination. So, according to the minimum transaction criterion, longer distance to the market might stimulate indirect marketing channels.

Bucklin's postponement-speculation theory asserts that shorter delivery time stimulates indirect marketing and vice versa. Since a longer distance to market will, *ceteris paribus*, increase the actual delivery time, it will also foster the use of indirect channels.

Long cultural distance to market brings the objectives of maximizing sales and goodwill and creating channel control more to the fore. Large geographic distance will do this for the objective of minimizing costs. Since that latter objective is, according to Mallen, more compatible with indirect channels and the former objectives with direct channels, a long geographic distance to market might foster indirect channels and a long cultural distance a direct one.

On the basis of Aspinwall's theory on product characteristics and marketing channels, it is not clear how distance to the market might influence export marketing channels. For potential customers in a market with a long cultural distance, the characteristic search time might increase, particularly during entry. This would, according to Aspinwall's theory, favor direct marketing.

Our conclusions on the number of levels in export marketing channels, as derived from general marketing theories, are limited. In particular, an opposite working on channel structure of cultural distance and geographic distance stresses the advantage of a functional approach to analyze the number of levels in export marketing channels.

Number of Middlemen at Each Level. There seems no strong relationship between distance to market and number of middlemen at each level. For instance, intensive, selective, or exclusive distribution seem fundamental to a marketing policy for a product, irrespective of the distance to the market.

A long cultural distance to the market may give the export product features of a shopping good or a specialty good, and a large geographic distance may go along with small market shares. Both elements will, at least during entry, stimulate selective distribution.

Cooperation in the Marketing Channel. A long cultural distance to the export market during entry weakens acquaintance with the goodwill of exporters. Consequently, sources of channel power, like identification and legitimacy, will be small. Neither will coercion be an attractive source of power in an entry strategy. Expertise and reward are the most appropriate ones. Also, the feasibility of contracts as a basis of coercive power depends on the reward and expertise that a foreign customer expects from an exporter.

Number of Channels. Choice between single and multiple channels seems fundamental to a marketing policy, and as such it will be made, irrespective of distance to market. Other factors, like type of customer, type of product, and stage of export marketing life cycle will be decisive. If a long distance to export market limits the amount exported, it encourages selective distribution and restricts the number of channels.

Conclusion. The analysis suggests that a long distance to market limits the number of marketing channels, which are preferably indirect, which have a limited number of middlemen at each level, and in which the supplier derives his or her channel power primarily from reward to the importing customer. General marketing theories increase our understanding of export marketing channels to a limited extent only.

Impact of Distance on Marketing Channels: Influence of Order Size and Order Frequency

The preceding section was concerned with a strategy for the marketing channel structure during entry. However, after entering an export market, a company will gradually increase its sales and its knowledge of the export market. The increase will depend on the choice of channel at entry, too. Therefore, decisions about channels should consider planned sales over the total export life cycle.

Order size and order frequency in total sales will change over the export life cycle. The expected joint effect of distance, order size, and order frequency on the structure of marketing channels is presented in figure 10–1. The impact of long distance to market may be offset by large and frequent orders. So a long distance to the export market will not consistently lead to indirect channels, as has been suggested in the preceding section. In particular, frequent orders will compensate lack of knowledge about the export market. The differentiation in spin-off between consummating and facilitating functions refines the evaluation in figure 10–1 as well.

One may extend the evaluation in figure 10–1 by combining long cultural distance with short geographic distance and vice versa. An additional suggestion on the basis of this extension is that indirect marketing channels are stimulated more by long cultural distance than by long geographic distance. So cultural distance is more fundamental to marketing channel than geographic distance.

Evidence from Dutch Food-Exporting Companies

The discussion of export marketing channels has been theoretical. However, it is interesting to provide some empirical evidence form the Dutch food industry as illustration. A survey in a sample of 102 companies in 1969 showed that indirect marketing channels were of increasing importance with greater distance to the market [NIAM, 1969], in agreement with the conclusions in the two preceding sections.

Table 10–1. Export Marketing Channels of 102 Dutch Food Companies in Various Regions of the World in 1969

Country of Export	Frequency in Sample	Direct to Customers	Frequency of Type of Marketing Channel in that Country (%)		
			Company Branch in Importing Country	Sales Agent in Importing Country	Trading Company in Exporting Country
West Germany	71	65	21	39	—
Scandinavia	40	55	5	53	—
North America	35	34	9	66	23
South America	39	28	15	62	23
Asia	40	25	3	48	38

Note: Values add up to more than 100% because of dual distribution by some companies.
Source: NIAM (1969).

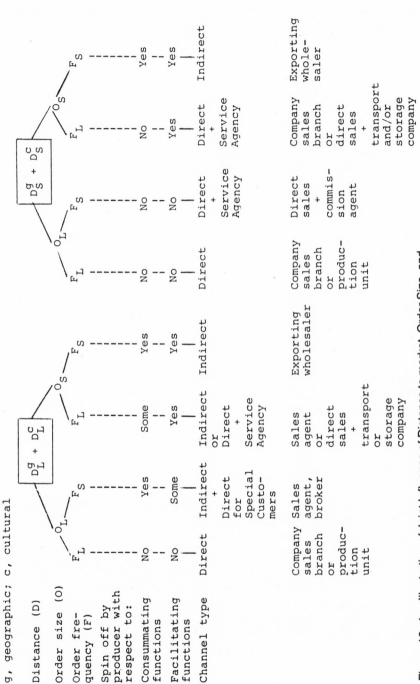

Figure 10—1. Illustration of Joint Influence of Distance to market, Order Size, and Order Frequency on Export Marketing Channels: Qualitative Evaluation

Table 10–2. Frequency (%) of Dominant or Exclusive Marketing Channel for 121 Dutch Food Companies to West Germany in 1980

	Turnover of Company				
Marketing Channel	<10 Million Guilders n = 18	10– <25 Million Guilders n = 19	25– <50 Million Guilders n = 24	50– <100 Million Guilders n = 17	≧100 Million Guilders n = 43
Direct direct to customer company branch	45	37	46	47	59
Indirect wholesaler importer agent	56	52	50	42	39
Others	—	10	4	12	2

Source: NIAM (1980*b*).

Another survey of 121 Dutch companies in 1980 demonstrated that direct marketing channels in food exports to West Germany increased with the turnover of the company, in agreement with the conclusions in the last section.

Summary and Conclusions

Export marketing channels have been examined on the basis of concepts and theories about marketing channels. The analysis was restricted to the impact of the variable, distance to market, both culturally and geographically. With various assumptions about the impact of distance to the market, the profit-maximizing conditions of the Dorfman-Steiner model provided some conclusions about the trade-off between distribution and advertising efforts. Some major theories on marketing channels and some results of research on international marketing channels were reviewed. Research on international marketing channels seems more empirical than conceptual. General marketing theory indicates that a long distance to market would stimulate indirect marketing channels as an entry strategy. Size and frequency of orders may level off this move towards indirect marketing.

Distance to market needs to be differentiated into cultural and geographic distance. The former seems more crucial to the structure of export marketing channels. It influences in particular consummating functions of the distribution process. Geographic distance influences facilitating functions. Marketing theory offers only crude insights into the structure of export marketing channels. International marketing will have to elaborate further theory by generalization from empirical studies.

References

Alderson, W. 1954, "Factors Governing the Development of Marketing Channels." In: Clewett, R. M. (ed.), 1954, *Marketing Channels for Manufactured Products,* R. D. Irwin Inc., Homewood (Ill.), pp. 5–22.

Aspinwall, L. V. 1962, "The Characteristics of Goods Theory." In: Lazer, W. and Kelley, E. G. (eds.), 1962, *Managerial Marketing Perspectives and Viewpoints,* R. D. Irwin Inc., Homewood (Ill.).

Bakker, B. A. 1980, *Export en Marketing.* Sansom, Alphen aan de Rijn.

Bucklin, L. P. 1965, "Postponement, Speculation, and the Structure of Distribution Channels." *Journal of Marketing Research,* 2, (1), pp. 26–31.

Cateora, P. and Hess, J. M. 1979, *International Marketing.* 4th ed., R. D. Irwin Inc., Homewood (Ill.).

Corstjens, M. and Doyle, P. 1979, "Channel Optimization in Complex Marketing Systems." *Management Science,* 25, October, pp. 1014–25.

Dommermuth, W. P. and Andersen, P. C. 1969, "Distribution Systems—Firms, Functions, and Efficiencies." *MSU Business Topics,* Spring 1969, pp. 51–56. Also in Moller, W. G. and Wilemon, D. L. (eds.), 1971, *Marketing Channels, A Systems Viewpoint,* R. D. Irwin Inc., Homewood (Ill.).

Dorfman, R. and Steiner, P. O. 1954, "Optimal Advertising and Optimal Quality." *American Economic Review,* XLIV (5), pp. 826–45.

Jackson, D. M., Krampf, R. F. and Konopa, L. J. 1982, "Factors that Influence the Length of Industrial Channels." *Industrial Marketing Management,* 11, pp. 263–68.

Kotler, P. 1980, *Marketing Management, Analysis, Planning, and Control.* 4th ed., Prentice Hall, Englewood Cliffs.

Little, R. W. 1970, "The Marketing Channel: Who Should Lead this Extracorporate Organization?" *Journal of Marketing,* 34 (1), pp. 31–38.

Mallen, B. 1977, *Principles of Marketing Channel Management.* Lexington Books, Lexington (Mass.).

McNair, M. P. 1958, "Significant Trends and Developments in the Postwar Period." In: Smith, A. B., (ed.), 1958, *Competitive Distribution in a Free, High-Level Economy and Its Implications for the University,* University of Pittsburgh Press, Pittsburgh, pp. 1–25.

Nederlands Instituut voor Agrarisch Marktonderzoek (NIAM). 1969, *Rapport betreffende een onderzoek naar de instelling van bedrijven in de agrarische sector ten opzichte van exportbevordering.* juni, 's-Gravenhage, Intern Rapport.

Nederlands Instituut voor Agrarisch Marktonderzoek (NIAM). 1980a, *Moeilijkheden en mogelijkheden i.v.m. export naar West-Duitsland.* oktober, 's-Gravenhage, Intern Rapport.

Nederlands Instituut voor Agrarisch Marktonderzoek (NIAM). 1980b, *Moeilijkheden en mogelijkheden i.v.m. export naar West-Duitsland.* mei, 's-Gravenhage, Intern Rapport.

Preston, L. E. and Schramm, A. E., Jr. 1965, "Dual Distribution and Its Impact on Marketing Organization." *California Management Review,* 8 (2), pp. 59–69.

Regan, W. J. 1964, "The Stages of Retail Development." In: Cox, R. S., Alderson, W. and Shapiro, S. (eds.), 1964, *Theory in Marketing,* 2nd series, R. D. Irwin Inc., Homewood (Ill.).

Stern, L. W. and El-Ansary, A. I. 1982, *Marketing Channels.* 2nd ed., Prentice Hall, Englewood Cliffs (N.J.).

11 GLOBAL STRATEGY AND THE CONTROL OF MARKET SUBSIDIARIES

Kenneth Simmonds

Most multinational corporations adopt an organization and control pattern in which primary responsibility for performance is placed upon units allocated a geographical market segment. Primary responsibility refers here to responsibility for performance measured at its lowest level of aggregation—the lowest level at which the control system operates to measure and report business performance to the multinational center. This level is usually the country level. In some cases, the primary units may represent smaller market areas than a full country, such as a district or a sales territory. In others, a much larger market area, such as sales throughout Latin America, will be a primary unit. In almost all cases, however, the primary units within multinationals have a geographical attribute as an essential element of their definition.

Not only are the primary units separated on a geographical basis, but successive levels of responsibility and control are also normally based on geographical aggregation. Thus, in one multinational the primary units may be responsible for performance in marketing a specified product range within a district. Performance of these units may then be aggregated in successive steps to show performance of this product range for a country, regional performance of the product division, worldwide divisional performance, and finally corporate performance. In another firm, the primary units may be subsidiaries responsible for all the firm's sales within a country and these, then, are aggregated on a geographical basis into regional or international division performance and finally worldwide corporate performance.

These two phenomena of geographically-defined primary units and geographical aggregation appear to exist no matter what the overall organization structure of the multinational. The extensive research attention devoted to the organizational structure of multinationals has traditionally examined and classified structures according to the attribute on which responsibility is disaggregated immediately below the chief executive [Stopford & Wells, 1972; Duerr & Roach, 1973; Business International, 1981]. Hence multinational organizational structures are described variously as:

1. national subsidiary structures;
2. international division structures;
3. functional structures;
4. regional structures;
5. product division structures;
6. matrix structures;
7. combination structures.

The apparent dissimilarity of organizational structures classified this way, however, tends to obscure the strong common element of primary organization and control by geographical market units—however that market is defined on other attributes.

The geographical market characteristic of these primary units, which will be called market units throughout this chapter, brings with it a range of problems in aligning the motivational power of the control system with the demands of multinational competition that cuts across geographical boundaries. Control of market units in multinationals has typically been based on conventional measures of sales volume, market share, profit, and return on investment. Market units aware that their performance will be recorded in terms of achievement of such measures within their own geographical area are not likely to work strongly for achievement that will show against other units. The goals of action become direct unit achievement—as though global competitive performance were the direct sum of performance in a series of unconnected local competitions. Such motivation is not very appropriate for a complex multinational struggle.

The Cross-Unit Requirements of Global Competition

The system of control and the way in which it motivates large numbers of relatively small primary market units and successive levels of aggregation, should be of major concern to multinationals faced with increasingly sophisticated competition on a global scale. More and more firms are seeing their worldwide profits determined not predominantly by the growth, size, or stability of individual markets in which they operate, nor by the degree of government constraints placed upon their operations, but more by the firm's competitive position relative to other firms worldwide [Porter, 1980, chapter 13]. The firm managing to achieve advantages over competition can translate these into higher relative profits or use them to build even further advantage. Conversely, the firm with disadvantages will either record lower profits or fall further behind in the global competitive race. At the extreme, the firm with the greatest disadvantage may see its accounting profits disappear completely as others use their advantage to lower their prices or otherwise increase value to the customer, and force the weakest to the wall.

Multinationals that see their aggregate global performance as ultimately determined by competitive position in this way need to search the global scene continually for opportunities to unlock competitive advantages or remove competitive disadvantages. There will, of course, be many opportunities for achievement through changing competitive positioning within single geographical markets. That is why primary market units are chosen in the first place. The customers for those units differ, and a different mix of competitive actions is appropriate [Duerr & Roach, 1973, p. 23]. But global achievement is very unlikely to be maximized without actions that cut across market unit boundaries. Such cross-unit actions can be divided into three main types: (1) relocating activities, from research through to merchandising, into different market units; (2) changing the relative emphasis placed upon achievement in different market units; or (3) taking offensive or defensive action in market units that will show up either in the performance of other units or in decreased competitor performance.

The first type of cross-unit action, relocation, can involve a search for lower cost sites or for scale economies, or both. Not only may market units themselves not see these possibilities because of their small size and narrow geographical focus, but they may actually lose performance as a result of relocation and common accounting practices. It is quite possible, for example, that a unit previously supplying itself and others may find itself faced with a higher cost as a unit, following relocation of the supply to the site with the lowest cost for the multinational as a whole. Tariff, transport, and handling rates do not have to be high to offset lower unit costs into a market that previously produced locally and charged itself at average cost.

Changes in the relative emphasis placed upon market units can also require decreased profit performance from some units in order for the system to gain more. Examples would be a switch in sales effort to higher growth or higher profit markets, or to earlier participation in new market areas in which customer brand recognition can be built up less expensively ahead of competition. It would be unreasonable to expect small market units, measured by their direct unit performance, to waive their demands for resources and crimp their performance voluntarily simply because some other units might do better.

The third type of cross-unit action involves direct offense or defense by a market unit for which results will show in the performance of other units or in overall decreased performance of a competitor. Offensive action to lower the price level in a market and remove a competitor's source of cash for global expansion elsewhere would fall into this category. So too would a defensive action to hold a competitor from expanding in a market at an expense that could never be justified for that market but which would discourage or delay pressure on other markets. Actions such as these run directly counter to control measures of direct unit achievement.

Few multinationals today can expect to build competitive advantage or remove disadvantage without cross-unit actions. A firm that attempted to advance through a summation of direct unit performance could find itself easy prey to more flexible competition. A clever competitor might attack by building on economies obtained from a secure market base, or at little cost to itself by lowering the market prices in those markets in which the defending firm leads and generally obtains its cash resources. Only actions which would have a cross-unit payoff could impose a discouraging penalty on such a competitor. Penalizing actions would have to be taken where the competitor in turn was making high contributions and was vulnerable to retaliation, such as a lowering of price level.

The Conflict Between Global Competition and Unit Control

When competition has escalated to a global level, the need for flexible cross-unit reactions requires a pliable control system for planning and evaluating the achievement of market units. The systems used in many multinationals, however, are not at all pliable. At their worst, the systems completely obscure the need for, and any contribution that is made to, cross-unit actions. Even relatively flexible systems, however, can set up a continual stress between the demands of a strategist endeavoring to fight a global battle and the demands for unit performance implicit in the measurements that make up the control system. With a rigid control system, it can be very difficult to initiate moves or react to competitor attacks if the action involved requires actual reduction in the performance of even one market unit involved.

The rigidity starts with the planning and budgeting process. Many multinationals emphasize the geographical independence of market units in setting their plans:

> Each of our companies overseas is a profit center and develops its own plans. Guidelines, based on corporate or regional strategy, are provided as a framework for each company's short- and long-range plans and objectives. Because of corporate fiscal responsibilities, each company's financial plans—individually and totally—must meet specific corporate objectives. When we feel that these are not being developed properly, specific suggestions for changes are recommended for implementation. [Duerr & Roach, 1973, p. 22]

When a global plan is built up from plans and budgets made independently by separate market units in this way, it is unlikely that it will contain many provisions for cross-unit actions. Furthermore, added barriers to carefully orchestrated global competition are often imposed by aggregation into regional or non-domestic divisions. It can be very hard to build such a strategy when market unit plans will have already been agreed and incorporated into regional plans before the global picture is looked at:

> Some companies seek to minimize the number of budgets passing through headquarters, in order to spend more time on reviewing and evaluating key expenditures. To accomplish this, the regional offices are given a considerable degree of authority in monitoring, assisting, and compiling the budgets of all those corporate entities within their respective regions. [Business International, 1976, pp. 134–35]

Within multinationals, budgets and the review of subsequent achievement have been widely elevated to a position of considerable importance:

> For the majority of international firms, the annual budget is the key marketing control mechanism and performance measure. While a few enterprises are more concerned with profitability or growth, most of those interviewed feel that the budget tells headquarters more about how well a subsidiary is actually doing than any other indicator. [Business International, 1976, p. 134]

> ... budgeting is even more important in international operations than in domestic operations. One reason is that the budgeting process gives managers the opportunity to state how well they think they should do and so provides

performance standards. These standards (if correctly determined) are all the more important in the international environment where top management is not as familiar with what can be done and what the standards should be. [Scott, 1979, p. 158]

The very importance placed upon budgets within multinationals further reduces the pliability of market units in the face of changing competitor actions. Budgets become sacrosanct—something to be achieved at all costs. Effective reaction to an international competitor's attack will almost inevitably require the reallocation of international effort. But reallocation will be difficult to achieve if all market units fight to retain resources and performance that have been enshrined in their budgets. In the majority of multinationals, the market units' reluctance to change is further supported by accounting control practices of refusal to adjust budgets to allow for significant changes:

> There seems to be a conflicting view over whether or not to permit subsidiaries to change their budgets in midstream to reflect changed or unexpected situations. Most companies do not allow this, requiring subsidiaries to carry on according to their agreed-upon budgets, explaining any variances both as they arise and at the end of the budget period. [Business International, 1976, p. 135]

The Bias of Financial Control

The inflexibility introduced by the emphasis on budgets and their achievement by individual market units is further accentuated by three failings that glorify financial performance at the expense of competitive performance. First, few firms bother to evaluate market units in terms of their contribution to the overall global system. Secondly, there is a marked tendency to allow financial figures to dominate market figures. Lastly, a general practice of separating budget and performance figures from verbal descriptions of the strategy involved as the figures progress up the organizational hierarchy makes it clear that figures have to stand alone. Market unit managers in many multinationals can be fairly certain that they are evaluated on the direct financial performance of their unit. It is not surprising that they behave accordingly. [Otley, 1978, p. 122]

Multinational accounting texts point out that foreign subsidiaries should not be evaluated as independent profit centers when they are really strategic components of a multinational system [Choi and Mueller, 1978, p. 271]. Yet, as Robbins and Stobaugh point out, this precept tends to be honored by its breach:

MNE managements establish and operate their overseas ventures as strategic systems; however they tend to forget this fact when subsequently evaluating their foreign subsidiaries' performance. The system in all its interrelationships is liable to be hidden under an account book when the moment arrives to add up the score and judge the performance of individual foreign units. [Robbins & Stobaugh, 1973, p. 81]

The second failing is to allow financial figures to dominate market figures. Over and over in accounting studies there are mentions that top executives in multinationals fall back on return on sales, return on investment, and direct operating profit for evaluating subsidiaries [Schoenfeld, 1981, p. 93; Morscicato & Radebaugh, 1979; Robbins & Stobaugh, 1973, p. 83; Leksell, 1981, p. 218].

It is significant to note how often market achievement and other indicators of relative competitive position are referred to as supporting or secondary goals:

While a subsidiary manager might be evaluated as a primary goal of annual profit, he should also be judged on such secondary criteria as market share, introduction of new products, strength of brand franchise, gross margin, manufacturing costs, man-hours per unit of production, overhead costs, and various balance sheet items. [Robbins & Stobaugh 1973, p. 83]

But few multinationals seem to bother with this so-called secondary data as regularly as they report financial figures. It would appear that market share data is often not reported and when it is then only once a year [Leksell 1981, p. 214]. Many firms apparently have no fixed rules for calculating market share, and accuracy is doubted. Comparison of performance from market to market, which is essential for monitoring international competition, is consequently unreliable.

The most startling findings about attitudes toward market share, however, are that even at the center some multinationals place a value on maintaining short-term profitability that absolutely dominates market share:

In terms of the value placed on market share as a measure, most businesses consider it less important than profitability, and say that they do not sacrifice profitability to increase market share. A few state that they will opt for building market share over profitability *temporarily,* but not as a long-term practice.

When market share performance is viewed as secondary, market unit managers are unlikely to place great emphasis on achieving it. They will be even less likely to emphasize relative market share compared to leading competitors, which will be an important objective for many global strategists. Market unit managers will be more likely to aim for accounting profits, even if it means sacrificing competitive position in the short-term to obtain them.

The overall message that comes through is of financial control systems that are designed and used to support very strongly a global strategy of achievement through profit improvement in each market unit. So strong is this support that the systems may be actively discouraging to global strategies of flexible offense and defense that would build long-term profit through improved competitive position.

Relative Cost, Volume, and Profit

The battle for global competitive position and consequent ability to make higher profits can be regarded in many cases as a competition to achieve lower costs. Such an orientation is particularly appropriate for relatively mature products sold at standard prices. The emphasis changes from volume and profit achievement to an emphasis on relative cost, and attention turns towards the unlocking of cost economies and perhaps opportunities to create fluctuations in competitor sales that effectively raise their costs. Such cost effects can be particularly severe for competitors with steep short-term cost functions. For example, a competitor who has just opened a large capital-intensive plant designed to cope with increased global sales targets, is likely to be especially vulnerable to price cutting and lower sales volume at that point in time. The decreased contribution on sales, along with the outflow of capital and higher overheads, could bring cash flow problems and force the competitor to back away from expansion aims.

Again, the control systems used in multinationals seem to be designed to motivate market unit managers away from the most appropriate actions for cost competition. Production or services supplied from other market units are usually transferred at standard transfer prices. Moreover, these prices are usually set at a fairly high level and seldom at marginal cost [Burns, 1980]. As a result, market unit managers tend to take market actions that do not reflect marginal cost. In pricing so as to maximize their individual market unit profits, they would set a higher-than-optimal price to give a less-than-optimal volume for the system as a whole. A single competitor facing such units but making centralized decisions, however, could benefit by gaining volume and consequent cost economies at less price reduction than would otherwise have been needed.

Not only do high, fixed transfer prices to market units discourage volume achievement, but they also hide the effect of lower volume aims in allowing higher volume, and consequently lower costs, to competitors.

Control through Global Strategy Participation and Feedback

Control systems in multinationals have evolved from the systems originally used in the parents' domestic operations [Choi & Mueller, 1978, pp. 269–72]. These systems were not designed from the beginning to motivate and control firms organized with market units as primary building blocks yet facing global competition. Furthermore, the evolution of control systems has lagged seriously behind the needs of the multinational systems and sometimes has not changed at all [Leksell, 1981, p. 217; McInnes, 1971]. What then can be done to overcome the basic weaknesses of these systems?

The obvious answer is not to make minor amendments in the control systems by adding relative market share data or changing internal transfer prices. Nor is it to change the organization to avoid the geographic market units, because these units represent the firm in the different areas in which the competition takes different shapes. The answer, instead, is to build market unit budgets at the outset in terms of their contribution to the firm's global strategy.

To achieve market unit budgets that are globally strategic, market units would need a flow of information on the firm's overall global strategy and its achievement against worldwide competition. Control would become much more of a circular feedback and adjustment system than the one-way flow of data and evaluation it is at the moment in many multinationals. The international product or market manager responsible for the preparation and monitoring of a global strategy [Business International, 1973, pp. 109–115] would be, in one sense, reporting to market unit managers.

The process could be taken a step further with participation by market unit managers in the ongoing formation and adaptation of a global strategy. More meetings would be needed, but they would be participative planning sessions rather than standard budget presentations and reviews. The pressure for performance as a global unit would still apply—but where this performance could be supported by a market unit carrying out a role that would jeopardize its own performance in conventional financial terms, the need for adapting its budget accordingly would be much more clearly established.

There is considerable evidence for the belief that feedback and participation would produce a positive effect on market unit actions. Hedlund [1980] found that foreign subsidiaries often feel alienated from the strategy formulation process in multinationals and lack direction as to their strategic role. Leksell found, too, that most subsidiaries investigated requested "more specific and timely headquarters opinions and expectations about performance levels, etc." [1981, p. 221]. Control through participation and feedback rests very simply on a belief that market unit managers working as a team will be motivated to achieve team performance. It is quite straightforward, and, furthermore, directly opposed to the complex manipulation proposed by recent writers, such as Prahalad & Doz [1981] who advocate manipulation of data, management, and conflict resolution to achieve an end desired by head office.

Even if conventional financial controls were to be retained, feedback on global competitive performance should encourage more cross-unit cooperation. The motivation to increase performance through cost reduction, for instance, is very strong under conventional financial assessment. Feedback on cost performance relative to worldwide competition simply adds the direct incentive to obtain cost reduction known to have been achieved by others.

It would be preferable, however, for the reporting and evaluation emphasis for an individual market unit to be recouched in terms of the principle strategic objectives set for it. Uniform control measures would be dispensed with at levels below global product division level, and controllers would be faced with the need to change control measurements each time the planned strategic task changed significantly. Flexible control measurements are not impossible to operate. The priority indicators can be determined as part of the annual planning process.

Bibliography

Burns, Jane O. "Transfer Pricing Decisions in U.S. Multinational Corporations." *Journal of International Business Studies,* Fall 1980, pp. 23–39.

Business International. *New Directions in Multinationals Corporate Organization.* (New York: Business International Corp., 1981).

Business International. *Managing Global Marketing: A Headquarters Perspective.* (New York: Business International Corp., 1976).

Choi, Frederick D. S. and Mueller, Gerhard G. *An Introduction to Multinational Accounting.* (Englewood Cliffs, New Jersey: Prentice-Hall, Inc., 1978).

Duerr, Michael G. and Roach, John M. *Organization and Control of International Operations.* (New York: The Conference Board, Inc., 1973).

Hedlund, G. "The Role of Foreign Subsidiaries in Strategic Decision Making In Swedish Multinational Corporations." *Journal of Strategic Management,* Vol. 1, 1980, pp. 23–36.

Leksell, Laurent. "The Design and Function of the Financial Reporting System In Multinational Companies." In: Lars Otterbeck (ed.), *The Management of Headquarters-Subsidiary Relationships in Multinational Companies.* (Aldershot, Hampshire: Gower Publishing Co. Ltd., 1981), pp. 205–232.

McInnes, J. M. "Financial Control Systems for Multinational Operations: An Empirical Investigation." *Journal of International Business Studies*, Fall 1971, pp. 11–28.

Morscicato, H. G. and Radebaugh, L. H. "Internal Performance Evaluation of Multinational Operations." *Journal of International Accounting*, Fall 1979, pp. 77–94.

Otley, David T. "Budget Use and Managerial Performance." *Journal of Accounting Research*, Vol. 16, 1978, p. 122.

Porter, Michael E. *Competitive Strategy*. (New York: The Free Press, 1980).

Prahalad, C. K. and Doz, Yves L. "An Approach to Strategic Control In MNCs." *Sloan Management Review*, Summer 1981, 22, No. 4, pp. 5–13.

Robbins, S. M. and Stobaugh, R. D. "The Bent Measuring Stick for Foreign Subsidiaries." *Harvard Business Review*, September/October 1973, pp. 80–88.

Schoenfeld, Hanns-Martin W. "International Accounting: Development, Issues, and Future Directions." *Journal of International Business Studies*, Fall 1981, pp. 83–100.

Scott, George M. "Planning, Control, and Performance Evaluation." In: Frederick D. S. Choi and Gerhard G. Mueller (eds.), *Essentials of Multinational Accounting: An Anthology*, (Ann Arbor, Michigan: University Microfilms International, 1979), pp. 154–59.

Stopford, John M. and Wells, Louis T., Jr. *Managing the Multinational Enterprise*, (New York: Basic Books, 1972).

12 INTERNATIONAL MARKETING IN THE 1980s AND BEYOND: Research Frontiers

Gerald M. Hampton and Aart P. van Gent

Introduction

Marketing is one discipline often perceived to be broad and general in scope [17]. It is practiced not only in business firms, but also in nonprofit and public sector organizations, such as schools, hospitals, and government agencies. While some criticize this broadening of the discipline, most agree that the central tasks of marketing, including target market definition, marketing mix formulation, and marketing research support, have worldwide application [19]. Therefore, the extension of marketing to the international arena is quite natural. As a result, one would expect to find a substantial international orientation in the field, especially in academic circles.

Yet, reviewing international marketing literature and business school curriculum, one reaches the inevitable conclusion that international marketing is perceived as an area of relatively low interest. The purpose of this chapter is to explore the reasons for this low interest level and to develop a series of international marketing research proposals. An examination of these reasons and the development of research priorities is seen as an important step in increasing the international orientation of the field. Before discussing the methodology and results, we will briefly review why international marketing can be perceived as an area of low interest.

International Marketing as an Area of Low Interest

The assessment of the internationalization of marketing can be done in at least two ways. The first is to examine international marketing research efforts as published in academic journals. The second is to evaluate marketing curriculum surveys that report the number of schools offering international marketing courses, as well as trends in curriculum development. This seems to be a reasonable approach, for the major journals and curriculum surveys would reflect the influence of internationalization efforts.

In examining international marketing research efforts, there appears to be a decline in the number of studies done in this area. This is dramatically demonstrated in figure 12–1, the result of a content analysis of the *Journal of Marketing* (*JM*) over a 40-year period. It shows that about 5% of *JM* articles in the early period were concerned with international marketing,

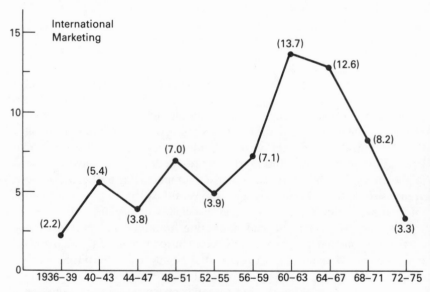

Figure 12–1.   Content Analysis of the *Journal of Marketing*.

Source: E. T. Grether, "The First Forty Years," *Journal of Marketing*, 40 (July, 1976), p. 66, published by The American Marketing Association.

they peaked at 13.7% in the 1960–1963 period, and declined abruptly since then [11].

In a more recent content analysis study of the *Journal of Marketing, Journal of Marketing Research,* and *Journal of Consumer Research* from 1970 through 1980, Professors Ghymn and White found that international content as a percentage of total articles was 6.5%, 1.2%, and 1% respectively [8]. An article was considered international if it contained a cross-cultural or international aspect. While *JM's* international orientation had modest improvement from a low of 3.3% in the earlier study by Grether, there clearly is a lack of published research here in an area of such importance.

The recent work by Myers, Massy, and Greyser, *Marketing Research and Knowledge Development: An Assessment for Marketing Management,* also supports the notion that international marketing is an area of low interest for most marketing scholars. It was probably such a background that led the editors of *JM* in the Summer 1980 publication to issue the following call:

> In stark contrast to the importance and growth of international marketing is the lack of high quality research in this area. This is clearly reflected by the manuscripts *JM* receives. During 1979, only 9% of the manuscripts submitted had an international focus; of these, only 10% were of adequate quality to be accepted, and 27% are still in various stages of revision. Even more disturbing is the lack of attention by most "domestically" oriented papers to the international dimension. While increased attention to international marketing sometimes requires special inquiry into international markets *per se,* specialists in all areas of marketing might consider the international implications of their work so that most material published in *JM* could have an international dimension. [7]

Not only is there lack of research in the international marketing area, the current published research has received severe criticism. In an article reviewing over 250 publications, Professors Cavusgil and Nevin acknowledge that international marketing is in the state of becoming a respected subdiscipline, but lags behind in its development [4]. They criticize the quality of much of the current efforts and conclude that in too many studies there is an absence of conceptual and theoretical frameworks, as well as hypothesis, to guide research. In addition, they indicate that researchers tend to ignore previous studies and that there is a general lack of concern for methodology.

Another indicator of the international orientation of marketing is the number of schools offering international or comparative marketing courses, the number of courses offered, and trends in this area. Comparing the results of the 1974 and 1980 AIB International Business Curriculum Surveys reveals that there was an increase of 4% during the six-year period—from 152 schools to 158 schools offering international marketing courses [5; 12]. However, only 43% of those schools in the survey offered courses in international marketing. Yet there was an increase in the number of courses offered.

In the 1980 Murphy and Laczniak survey of marketing education in America, they found that international marketing courses are offered by 48% of the responding schools—108 out of 225 [21]. The course is required by only 7% of the schools, offered at least once a year by 79% of the schools, but less than once a year by 14% of them. In total, only 7% offer an international marketing course more than once a year.

In an international curriculum survey of U.S. accredited and nonaccredited business schools and foreign institutions, Stem and Lamb found that 31% of U.S. undergraduate schools offered one or more international marketing courses, while only 5.1% offered two or more [26]. For U.S. graduate schools, the percentages were 14.9% and 3.2% respectively. Accredited U.S. schools offered a higher percentage of international marketing courses, which would be expected, given the AACSB's requirements. For example, at U.S. accredited undergraduate schools, 50% offered international marketing courses while only 28% of nonaccredited schools did so.

In the foreign schools, 26.4% of the undergraduate institutions offered one or more international marketing courses, while only 5.3% offered two or more. At the graduate level in foreign schools, the percentages were 15.8% and 0% respectively. It is interesting to note in terms of the total marketing courses offered, international marketing was the fifth most offered course in foreign schools, but ranked ninth in U.S. schools [26].

Another perspective on the international orientation in marketing is what trends department chairpersons felt were developing in marketing education. In one survey, the most important trend was a more practical approach (39 percent of U.S. chairpersons checked this response), followed by interdisciplinary, quantitative, and behavioral trends [26]. The chairpersons in U.S. schools chose international trends in 6.9% of the responses, while foreign chairpersons chose international in 11% of the responses.

In a study to determine the relevance of marketing concepts taught, 60.6% of the students responded that international marketing was of little or no benefit to their careers [18]. In this study, international was rated the lowest of fourteen concepts in terms of career benefit. In a study of attitudes of managers and educators toward the graduate marketing curriculum, Bernhardt and Bellenger found that only 13% of educators and 16% of managers thought an international marketing course should be required [2].

In terms of percentage rank, the international course was ranked twelfth by educators and twenty-third by managers out of a total of 28 courses.

Finally, one marketer did an international content analysis of marketing and marketing management textbooks [8]. Thirty-six of the leading textbooks were reviewed. Most books included one chapter on international marketing, with little if any integration of the international material throughout the texts. The space devoted to the topic was also extremely low. In the basic marketing texts, only 2.4% of the space was of an international orientation and only 1.5% of marketing management texts was allocated to this topic.

This background does seem to indicate that international marketing is an area of relatively low interest to many marketing educators and managers. This state of affairs appears to exist not only in marketing, but in many functional areas of business education. The efforts to internationalize the business curriculum, the business faculty, and their research have been of increasing concern for not only the American Assembly of Collegiate Schools of Business (AACSB), but also for the European Foundation of Management Development (EFMD). At the June 1980 AACSB/EFMD international conference in Paris, this was a major topic of discussion. At the EFMD follow-up meetings in Nijenrode, The Netherlands in January 1981 and in Athens in May 1981, workshops were held on how best to approach the problem of internationalization. Therefore, while international marketing is presently considered an area of low interest, it appears to permeate all business schools.

Methodology

Use of the Delphi Technique

The data presented here are part of a study whose main purpose was to determine desirable future directions for international marketing research and to access the future international environment. To accomplish these objectives, a form of the Delphi method was used. The Delphi method is a research technique that was developed by the Rand Corporation [10; 13; 14]. It attempts to bring the knowledge and intuition of a group of qualified individuals to bear on the possibilities in a given situation, subject area, or problem. While it has been used most often in forecasting future technologies, it can be used to test and develop group response to contemporary issues of almost any nature.

A Delphi study is conducted in such a way that the opinions formulated or expressed by a group of experts are not influenced by the inevitable pressures in face-to-face group discussions. The technique, therefore, replaces group discussions with a series of sequential questionings that uses information for feedback derived from the preceding round of questioning. The original Delphi study recommended four rounds of questioning, but some studies used as many as thirteen. It appears that three rounds are sufficient when the participants are the best in the field under study [20]. The technique is an excellent method to generate and evaluate ideas, like proposals for future research [23; 30]. It is also felt that the predictions of recognized experts in a field will be considered with more respect and are likely to be accepted and acted upon [16].

Questioning Procedure

In the initial round of questioning, each respondent was presented a brief discussion outlining why international marketing might be perceived as an area of low interest. To the question, "Do you feel it justified that international marketing is considered an area of low interest?", opinions were expressed on a five-point scale ranging from strongly unjustified to strongly justified. Following this task, each participant was asked to give his or her reasons why international marketing might be considered an area of low interest. In Part two of the initial round, the respondents were asked to prepare a list of topics or areas of international marketing that they considered to be in greatest need of research. It was suggested that the topics be limited to no more than five and that each topic contain a brief statement of the research problem, a short discussion of the research methodology, and a brief statement on the topic's importance (see Appendix A).

The second round contained the responses of panel members from round I. In part one of this round, respondents were asked to evaluate the low interest question in light of round I results and to respond again on the five-point scale. The reasons given in the initial round concerning why international marketing is perceived to be an area of low interest were reduced, eliminating duplication, and consolidated into a list of twelve. In this round, each respondent was asked to rate each reason statement on a five-point agreement scale (strongly agree to strongly disagree) and a five-point importance scale (very unimportant to very important). For part two of round II, 47 projects were formulated and returned to each respondent with the following instructions:

1. Please spend some time studying the proposed projects and look for interesting combinations. Also look for projects that are interesting but

that could be broadened or made more complete by applying appropriate techniques.

2. We are hoping through this process to end up with a relatively small number of research proposals that will require a team approach and that also can be broken down into portions that could be used by individual researchers such as doctoral students.

3. Consequently, more detailed attention to research methodology will be particularly important.

4. We request that you attempt to submit four such reconstructed and elaborated proposals.

In round III, part one repeated the procedure used in round II with, of course, the ratings and selected comments of round II as part of the feedback information. In part two, after duplications were eliminated from topics presented in round II, 50 projects remained; these are given in appendix B. As part of this round, these 50 projects were sent to each member of the panel with the instructions to review, judge, and select ten projects which they felt are the most important (for more details, see appendix B).

Panel of Experts

A panel of 28 international marketing experts was chosen to participate in the study [31]. The marketing scholars, selected on the basis of past research and interest in international marketing, were from The Netherlands, Canada, United States, West Germany, Spain, England, Poland, and Switzerland. Twenty-three out of 28 participants responded to round I. The response rate was the same for rounds II and III. All correspondence with respondents was conducted in English. In addition, 150 international marketing practitioners were randomly selected from the membership rosters of the American Marketing Association (100) and the European Society for Opinion and Marketing Research Association (50). Each was mailed part two of round III. The instructions for these business people were the same as for the panel of academics. Unfortunately, only 16 business people responded. However, their responses and comments are useful for comparisons.

Results and Implications

This section is divided into two parts. Part one contains the results of the Delphi study on why international marketing is perceived to be an area of low interest. Part two concerns the research topics generated from the panel of scholars.

Part One—International Market: An Area of Low Interest

The response to the first question, "Considering the entire field of marketing, do you feel it justified that international marketing is considered an area of low interest?" was no surprise given that most panel members were international marketers. Ninety percent responded unjustified (14% strongly unjustified and 76% unjustified), 5% uncertain, and 5% justified. Some of the comments by panel members reflect their feelings toward this perceived low interest level in international marketing. One said, "There is not enough evidence to justify such opinion. Probably some American markets might accept that statement, but certainly not European ones." Another European was not quite as adamant, saying, "I appreciate the different opinions held regarding the subject as I would have answered differently myself if I had not taken some interest in the subject recently." Another said, "Everything is important—you would get the same result from a question about trademarks, closing techniques, on most questionnaires." Overall and as would be expected, most marketers with a strong interest in the international area see a low interest level here as unjustified.

However, the evidence points in this direction, and the reasons these scholars cite for this state of affairs might help increase the international orientation in marketing, as well as other functional areas in business. The 12 reasons cited here have been divided into four groups. They are in figures 12–2 to 12–5 and are related to the content of the discipline, research difficulty, business perspective, and the interest in the marketing area.

The Discipline Content. There are four reasons in this group, as shown in figure 12–2. In two of these, a consensus emerged in terms of both the agreement and importance dimensions and, consequently, are deemed the most significant. Ninety-two percent agree that international marketing has failed to develop a specific body of knowledge, and 79% view it as an important reason the field is seen as an area of low interest. One scholar who agreed strongly said, "Perhaps it is more critical to generate a good paradigm by working backwards from the international area rather than forward from the marketing area."

Such a new perspective seems appropriate, for 78% agree that there is still a lack of internationalization of the business school, and 90% see it as important. A scholar from Europe said, "In Western Europe there is a need

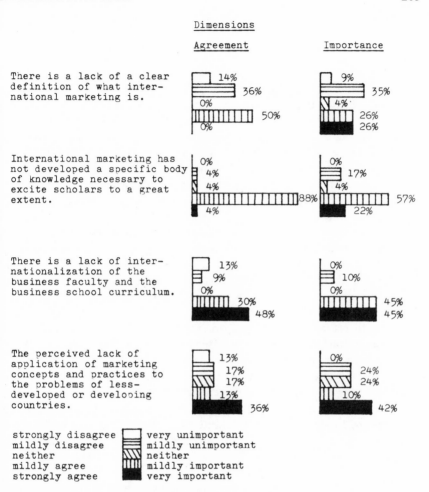

Figure 12–2. The Discipline Content

for more international education in marketing in order to stimulate international marketing activities and also to motivate students with respect to
international marketing as a subdiscipline of marketing." An American
scholar had a similar view when he said, "Internationally oriented faculty
represent a small proportion of total faculty in most U.S. schools, and if the
majority of all faculty does not find the area important, then it is difficult to
stimulate much interest."

For the remaining two statements there was no such agreement or
consensus. The panel members are equally divided on both the agreement

and importance dimensions concerning the notion that there is a lack of a clear definition of international marketing. Perhaps this diversity of opinion is best summarized by a scholar who said that the statement does not really reflect what is essential, namely making it a required area for business education and promoting scholarly journals as outlets. Another panel member indicated that the lack of agreement among scholars has probably had impact on the overall current status of research in the field. A major criticism of the current research in the field is that it is devoid of a strong theoretical base and, consequently, is mostly descriptive in nature [4].

For the final statement in this category, the lack of application of marketing to problems of developing nations, there appears to be a fair amount of uncertainty based on the distribution of responses. Thirty percent disagree with the statement, 17% neither agree or disagree, and 49% agree. In terms of importance, 24% feel it is unimportant, 24% express the opinion it is neither, and 52% feel it is important. This range of responses with no clear consensus was probably why one member said, "Marketing issues in less-developed countries are of a less sophisticated nature (very down to earth, very little data, etc.), which is one important reason why marketing scholars stay away from problems like these." Perhaps marketing scholarship, like direct investment, has tended to stay away from these countries, not because marketing is not applicable or not important, but because the payoff to scholars has been low.

Overall, it is interesting to note that there is basically no difference in the responses between U.S. and European scholars or between the European scholars themselves. For example, the agree-disagree responses to the statement of the lack of a clear definition of international marketing were evenly distributed among U.S. and European scholars. In summary, the findings in this category tend to support the major AACSB-AIB recommendations and efforts to internationalize the business faculty and raise funds to support international business research efforts. Perhaps more emphasis needs now to be placed on research efforts and financial support. The failure to develop a specific body of knowledge in international marketing is related to the next category, which concerns the difficulty of doing internationally oriented research.

Research Difficulty. In this category, there are three statements related to the problems associated with research in the international marketing area. Here there appears to be a consensus of opinion for all statements on each dimension. Seventy percent agree and 65% feel it is important that no organization exists to encourage international marketing research. Perhaps this is changing, for the first issue of the *Journal of International Marketing*

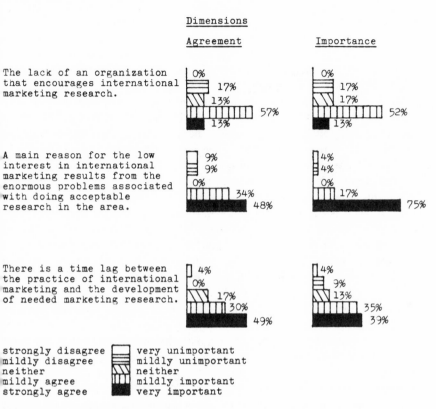

Figure 12–3. Research Difficulty

was recently published and the Marketing Science Institute is beginning to explore research issues for international marketing.

Eighty-two percent feel that a main reason for the low level of interest in international marketing is due to the enormous problems associated with doing acceptable research in the field. Eighty-three percent think it is important, with 75% responding that it is very important. Such strong feelings probably come from what is the present focus of much research in the field. For example, one scholar put it in perspective when he said, "When the area is rather difficult to research both conceptually and practically, it is understandable that most colleagues try easier routes. A good deal of this seems to be conditioned by the overall preference for narrow empiricism results and clinical research, which is less appropriate in international marketing."

The final statement in this category concerns the time lag many perceive between the practice of international marketing by business organizations and the development of marketing knowledge by academics. Seventy-nine percent of the panel members agree that academics tend to lag behind business in this area, and 74% feel it is important. One professor on the panel summed it up by saying, "In a number of European countries, the relatively low business-academia interaction accounts for a slow adoption by business faculties. While this is less in the United States, there seems to be also a tendency that the large MNC's have learned to do their own thing without help from academia and to keep it, resulting in a reduced business-university transfer of knowledge."

This situation is closely associated with what Tesar calls the three stages of international marketing development [27]. The initial stage concerns studying aspects of the foreign market environment; stage two of international marketing concerns the crossing of national boundaries; and stage three involves MNCs' conducting marketing strategies simultaneously in several national markets. Professor Tesar contends that business is already in the third stage of its international development, while most marketing educators are only in stage one. He recommends faculty assignments in MNCs for the purpose of research, collection of teaching materials, and for participation in their international training programs.

Overall, this category is one with substantial agreement on why international marketing is perceived as an area of low interest. Given these reasons and a strong sense of agreement, there appears to be several important implications for change. First, the AACSB-AIB recommendations that international business research be given more financial support should receive increased emphasis and be broadened in scope. The time has now come to conduct summer workshops on research in international business, including of course marketing and other functional areas. As part of this process, it would be critical to include as participants consulting companies who specialize in the international area as well as marketing research directors of large MNCs. In this whole process we must never forget to include colleagues from business institutions around the world.

Second, while many sensible and sound recommendations came out of the AACSB-AIB report, *Business and International Education*, it is time to make some of them real. Perhaps it is time for the AIB, in partnership with institutions in Europe, to establish a permanent organization similar to its clearinghouse proposal that supports and encourages teaching and research in international business. Such an organization would become a real and valuable resource for academics and businesses.

Finally, if conducting research in an international area like marketing is more difficult than doing domestic research, then it seems reasonable that

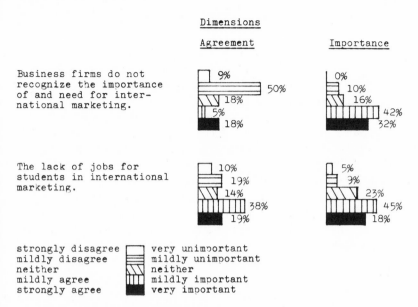

Figure 12–4.   Business Perspective

such international research efforts should be afforded more weight by business school deans when it comes time for performance-evaluation of faculty. In addition, the editors and reviewers of the so-called leading marketing journals should seriously evaluate the relevance-importance criteria for manuscript acceptance in light of what appears to be an overly high regard for narrow empiricism and clinical research.

Business Perspective.   This group contains two statements. One is related to business's recognition of the importance of international marketing, and the other concerns jobs available for students in the field. In the first statement, most (59% of the panel members) disagree with the notion that business firms do not recognize the importance and need for international marketing. Most of those who tended to agree, 23% of the members, indicated they clearly had small firms in their countries in mind. One panel member implied that it might not be business firms that do not recognize the need for international marketing; it is most academic marketers. This finding supports the remarks of Professor Tesar cited earlier.

The second statement or reason is this category deals with jobs available for college students. While 57% of the members agreed with this as a reason for the relatively low level of interest in international marketing, 29%

disagreed. It should be noted that most of those disagreeing were European scholars. Many of their comments implied that young students who speak several languages are hired by a home country firm and placed throughout Europe. For example, one scholar said, "We do not agree—students and business here (in Holland) are interested in jobs which are filled by young international-oriented students." An American panel member said, "No one hires anyone in this area. International marketing is like history—nice to know, but is not job-related." The latter quote closely parallels Loudenback's findings that international marketing education is of little or no benefit to those American students taking their first job [18]. However, several members indicated that while this may be true at the undergraduate level, it is not so for MBA's. One member proposed a solution but questioned its feasibility for colleges. He suggested that the simplest way to create marketable skills is to emphasize export and import skills rather than the present strategic thinking. On the other side, 63% of the members felt it was important, while 23% indicated that it was neither important nor unimportant.

Overall, the findings here suggest that business firms are interested, but students do not get jobs in the area. The implications are that perhaps what educational institutions are teaching is irrelevant for business. If so, it is not only necessary to help educators teach the international dimension of marketing education, but it becomes critical to determine what needs to be taught. This would require greater cooperation and interaction with business firms. As indicated in the previous category, we as academics not only lag behind in practice→ to→ research, but also in education→ to→ job relevance.

Interest in Marketing.   This fourth and final category contains three statements that are more or less self-evident. In round I of the Delphi study, several panel members, from both Europe and the United States, suggested that the low level of interest in international marketing is a function of the low level of interest in marketing as a discipline. As shown in figure 12–5, most or 82% of respondents disagree. On the other hand, 88% agree that the interest in international marketing is less than domestic marketing, while 70% feel it is important. This supports the authors' assumption that international marketing is an area of relatively low interest.

The final statement is an interesting one. While several European members suggested that the perceived low level of interest in international marketing is an American view, the majority of members who agreed with the statement were U.S. panel members (63%). On the other hand, most of those who disagreed were Europeans (23%). It probably is not significant, at least in this study, for 41% of the members felt it was unimportant, while

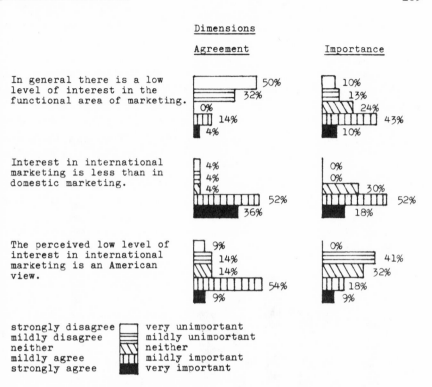

Figure 12–5.   Interest in Marketing

32% said that it was neither important nor unimportant. It could be interpreted to mean that U.S. marketing scholars who have a strong interest in the international orientation view their other colleagues in marketing as not interested in this dimension.

Part II—Research Projects

After the completion of the second round of the Delphi process, there were 50 research projects divided into ten major subject areas (see appendix B, part II). These ten areas concerned theory, education, the macro-environment, buyer behavior, research, product, price, place, export/import, and marketing management. During round III, the members of the academic and business panels were asked to review and judge which they felt were most important. Ten projects were to be selected on the basis of the potential of the project for the advance of the field of international marketing and the potential impact of the project, that is, its potential business, social, economic, or political significance. In the ranking process, a weight of ten was given to a proposal that was ranked first; a score of nine for a project ranked second; a weight of eight was given to the proposal that the same expert had ranked third; and so on.

The result was a fairly wide degree of dispersion of votes or choices for both academics and business people. For the panel of academics, 48 projects

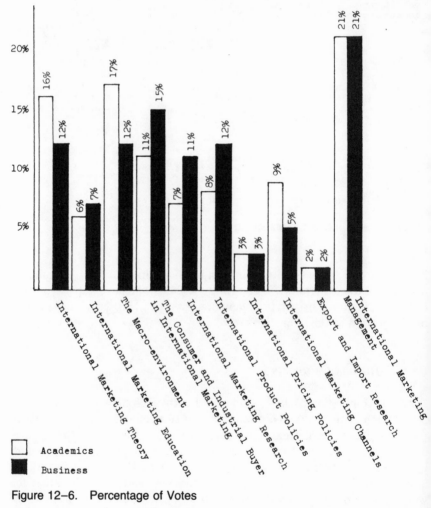

Figure 12–6. Percentage of Votes

received at least one vote, with certain projects receiving as many as eight selections. For the business people surveyed, 45 projects received at least one selection or vote. This dispersion of votes by subject area is diagramed in figure 12–6. This figure shows that the differences in votes or choices between academics and business people is not as great as might be expected. There is equal percentage distribution of votes across the areas of education, pricing decisions, exporting/importing concerns, and international marketing management. Business people have a larger distribution of votes than academics in the areas of buyer behavior, research, and product decisions. Academics have a higher percentage of choices in the area of theory and the macro-environment. However, these differences are not statistically significant (chi-square test).

The importance ranking of the projects for the two different groups are shown in tables 12–1, 12–2A, and 12–2B. The ranking of the top ten projects during round III by academics, in descending order, was 2, 1, 22, 10, 3, 5, 42, 12, 43, and 15. For business people, the ranking of the top ten projects, in descending order, was 15, 39, 42, 18, 2, 48, 11, 5, 12 and 22. While the rankings and projects are not identical, there are more similarities than differences. Out of the top-ten ranked proposals by each group, six are identical in terms of being selected, but not in rank order (table 12–2A). Only four projects were not identical (table 12–2B). If there are major differences, it does appear, and in terms of rank order, that academics tend to rank the development of theory as more important than business people. This seems reasonable and is not an unexpected finding. In the top ten projects, academics had four theory projects, ranked 1, 2, 5, and 6; while

Table 12–1. Importance Ranking of Top-Ten Projects

| | Academics | | | Business | |
Rank	Project	Area	Project	Area
1	2	Theory	15	Buyer Behavior
2	1	Theory	39	Export/Import
3	22	Research	42	Marketing Management
4	10	Macro-Environment	18	Buyer Behavior
5	3	Theory	2	Theory
6	5	Theory	48	Marketing Management
7	42	Marketing Management	11	Macro-Environment
8	12	Macro-Environment	5	Theory
9	43	Marketing Management	12	Macro-Environment
10	15	Buyer Behavior	22	Research

Table 12–2A. Project Similarity

Academics			Business		
Rank	Project	Area	Rank	Project	Area
1	2	Theory	5	2	Theory
3	22	Research	10	22	Research
6	5	Theory	8	5	Theory
7	42	Marketing Management	3	42	Marketing Management
8	12	Macro-Environment	9	12	Macro-Environment
10	15	Buyer Behavior	1	15	Buyer Behavior

Table 12–2B. Project Non-Similarity

Academics			Business		
Rank	Project	Area	Rank	Project	Area
2	1	Theory	2	39	Export/Import
4	10	Macro-Environment	4	18	Buyer Behavior
5	3	Theory	6	48	Marketing Management
9	43	Marketing Management	7	11	Macro-Environment

business people had two theory projects, ranked 5 and 8. Overall, the results suggest more similarities between business people and academics than differences. One caveat, however, the sample sizes in both groups were quite small.

During round III, comments were solicited from all respondents. Because the academic panel members had been instrumental in developing these 50 projects, they made no additional comments. This was not the case for the business people, however. Their comments can be divided into two major areas: one concerning new and different projects and the other dealing with the nature or tone of the 50 proposals.

In addressing what is needed, one business person made the point over and over again that what we all need is, "How to find decisionmakers." Another individual made the same point by saying, "The decisionmaker is extremely important, and I have spun my wheels too often talking to the wrong person." While many recognize that marketing knowledge is important in operating around the world, some indicate that other aspects of doing business internationally is more important. One respondent said that he felt the study of political and business systems is the most important of all.

Another indicated that what is of a real need is uniform, accurate data on competitive activities, government regulations, and bribery by competitors. One businessman took a great deal of time to outline what he saw as the greatest need of all—more fundamental, practical knowledge, such as how to clear customs, determine duties, the impact of doing business between favored and non-favored nations, currency differences, freight forwarding, freight cost, etc.

In terms of the nature of the projects, many of the comments were expected. One businessman said, "The topics are too academic and pretty obvious—would be interested in more practical topics." Another said, "The list is not very original, current, or creative." On the other hand, one business respondent said, "The list is quite complete, even though in my opinion, there is too much emphasis on market research *per se*."

One thoughtful individual said of these projects, "They seem to be assuming or pushing toward universality, whereas understanding country-by-country diversity seems to me more useful." This business respondent also said, "Much work in many of these areas has already been done by some of the American multinationals—although the data have not been published." This supports the contention of one of the academic panel members who indicated earlier that large MNCs have learned to do their own thing without help from academia. Finally, this business respondent indicated that to investigate many of these projects properly would require enormous funds.

Overall, there appears to be substantial agreement between business people and academics in terms of what projects are important. Six of the ten most important ranked projects were identical. While there are similarities, academics tend to prefer projects that are more theoretical than practical. Business people, on the other hand, emphasize buyer behavior, export/import, and marketing management projects. These plus their comments tend to emphasize the practical over the theoretical, which is to be expected. One final note of interest: promotion is not one of the subject areas identified as in need of research, as indicated by a complete lack of any research project or proposal. It should also be noted that there were no comments from either academics or business people concerning the absence of promotion projects.

Conclusion

This chapter attempts to determine and evaluate the reasons why many academic marketers perceive international marketing to be an area of relatively low interest. Also, this study developed a list of 50 possible international marketing research projects that spanned ten subject areas

The future prospect, in examining these reasons and developing research frontiers, is to begin to explore ways to substantially increase the interest in international marketing.

The reasons that emerged during the Delphi process, using a panel of international marketing scholars, were classified into four categories. They were the content of the discipline, the difficulty of doing research in international marketing, the perspective of business firms, and the interest in marketing. During three rounds of the Delphi study, 50 research projects were developed. The ten projects judged most important were selected by the panel of scholars, as well as a limited sample of business people. The study and future efforts based on this work hopefully will hasten to spread the international orientation that is much needed, not only in marketing, but in all functional areas of business.

References

1. *AACSB Accreditation General Policies, Procedures, and Standards: 1978–1979.* American Assembly of Collegiate Schools of Business, St. Louis, Missouri, 1978.

2. Bernhardt, Kenneth L. and Bellenger, Danny N. "The Graduate Marketing Curriculum: The Attitudes of Managers and Educators." *1978 Proceedings of the Southern Marketing Association,* Robert S. Franz, Robert M. Hopkins, and Al Toma, (eds.), 1978, pp. 195–98.

3. *Business and International Marketing.* A report submitted by the Task Force on Business and International Education to the Government/Academic Interface Committee International Education Project, American Council on Education, Washington, D.C., May 1977.

4. Cavusgil, S. Tamer and Nevin, John P. "State-of-the-Art in International Marketing: An Assessment." *Review of Marketing 1981,* Ben M. Enis and Kenneth J. Roering, (eds.), 1981, pp. 195–216.

5. Daniels, John P. and Radenbaugh, Lee H., eds. *International Business Curriculum Survey.* Academy of International Business, 1974.

6. Drucker, Peter. "Marketing and Economic Development." *Journal of Marketing,* January 1958, pp. 252–59.

7. Farley, John U. and Wind, Jerry. "International Marketing: The Neglect Continues." *Journal of Marketing,* 44 (Summer 1980), pp. 5–6.

8. Ghymn, Kyung-Il and White, Georgia Kenyon. "Multinational Marketing Education—Where Does it Stand Now?—An Examination of Business School Curriculum, Textbook, and Journal Content." *1981 Proceedings of the Western Marketing Educators' Association,* Gerald Albaum et al., (eds.), 1981, pp. 11–12.

9. Goodnow, James P. "International Business in the MBA and BBA Core Program." *Journal of International Business Studies,* 4 (Fall 1973), pp. 75–82.

10. Gordon, T. J. and Helmer, Olaf. *Report on Long Range Forecasting Study.* Rand Corporation, September 1964, No. P–2982.
11. Grether, E. T. "The First Forty Years." *Journal of Marketing,* 40 (July, 1976), pp. 63–69.
12. Grosse, Robert and Perrett, Gerald W., eds. *International Business Curricula: A Global Survey.* Academy of International Business, 1980.
13. Helmer, Olaf. *Analysis of the Future: The Delphi Method.* Rand Corporation, March 1967, No. P–3558.
14. Helmer, Olaf. *The Use of the Delphi Technique in Problems of Educational Innovations.* Rand Corporation, December 1966, No. P–3499.
15. *International Dimensions of Management Education.* A report by a special Brookings panel. The Brookings Institute, March 1975.
16. Kennington, Don. "Long Range Planning for Public Libraries—A Delphi Study." *Long Range Planning,* 10 (April 1977), pp. 73–78.
17. Kotler, Philip and Levy, Sidney. "Broadening the Concept of Marketing." *Journal of Marketing,* 33 (January 1969), pp. 10–15.
18. Loudenback, Lynn J. "The Relevance of the Concepts We Teach to Marketing Careers." *Relevance in Marketing: Problems, Research, Action,* Fred C. Allvine, (ed.), American Marketing Association, 1971, pp. 10–15.
19. Luck, David. "Broadening the Concept of Marketing—Too Far." *Journal of Marketing* 33 (July 1969).
20. Marley-Clark B. "The Delphi Method and Urbanization." *Long Range Planning,* December 1974, pp. 81–83.
21. Murphy, Patrick E. and Laczniak, Eugene R. *Marketing Education: Current Status and A View for the 1980s.* American Marketing Association, 1980.
22. Nehrt, Lee C. "A Report of the American Council on Educational Task Force on Business and International Education." *AACSB Bulletin,* 14 (Fall 1977), pp. 40–43.
23. Nehrt, Lee C., Truitt, J. Frederick and Wright, Richard W. *International Business Research Past, Present, and Future.* Bureau of Business Research, Indiana University, 1970.
24. "Planning for International Marketing." *Business Journal, EWU* 7 (Fall 1981), p. 15.
25. "Statement of Clarification of Domestic and Worldwide in the Curriculum Standard IV." *AACSB Bulletin,* Winter 1978, pp. 31–32.
26. Stem, Donald E. and Lamb, Charles W. "Marketing Curriculum: An International Perspective." A paper presented at the Northern Universities Business Association Conference, Seattle, Washington, October 1978.
27. Tesar, George. "Marketing Abroad Forges Ahead, But Education in International Area Lags." *Marketing News,* 11 (July 1977), pp. 7, 12.
28. Tesar, George. "Tripartite Program in International Business Education." *Marketing News,* 11 (November 4, 1977), p. 7.
29. *The Internationalization of the Business School Curriculum.* A program of Planning and Workshops sponsored by the American Assembly of Collegiate Schools of Business, March 1979.

30. Wedley, William C. "New Uses of Delphi in Strategy Formulation." *Long Range Planning*, 10 (December 1977), pp. 70–78.
31. Panel Members Were: Dr. B. Bakker, Erasmus University, Holland; Professor Erwin Dichtl, University Mannheim, West Germany; Professor Jerzy Joseph Dietl, Lodz University, Poland; Professor Eric Langeard, I.A.E. AIX-Marseille, France; Professor Dr. P. Leeflang, University Groningen, Holland; Professor Malcolm McDonald, Cranfield School of Management, England; Professor Dr. Matthew Meulenberg, Landbouw Hogeschool, Holland; Professor Pedro Nueno, I.E.S.E., Spain; Professor Dr. J. Van Rees, Technische Hogeschool Eindhoven, Holland; Dr. J. Reuyll, University Groningen, Holland; Professor Kenneth Simmonds, London School of Business, England; Dr. Helmut Soldner, University of Augsburg, West Germany; Dr. Maciej Stalmaszczyk, Lodz University, Poland; Professor Heinz Weinhold, Hochschule St. Gallen, Switzerland; Professor J. J. Boddewyn, Baruch College, New York, N.Y., U.S.A.; Professor Phil Cateora, University of Colorado, Boulder, Colorado, U.S.A.; Professor Gerrit De Vos, University of Massachusetts, Boston, Massachusetts, U.S.A.; Professor John Farley, Columbia University, New York, N.Y., U.S.A.; Professor Robert Green, University of Texas, Austin, Texas, U.S.A.; Professor Warren Keegan, New York University, New York, N.Y., U.S.A.; Professor David L. Kurtz, Seattle University, Seattle, Washington, U.S.A.; Professor William Lazer, Michigan State University, East Lansing, Michigan, U.S.A.; Professor Jacque Picard, McGill University, Montreal, Quebec, Canada; Dr. John K. Ryans, Jr., Kent State University, Kent, Ohio, U.S.A.; Professor S. P. Sethi, The University of Texas-Dallas, Richardson, Texas, U.S.A.; and Professor Vern Terpstra, University of Michigan, Ann Arbor, Michigan, U.S.A.

APPENDIX A

DELPHI STUDY - PART I

(ROUND 1)

In recent years the conviction has grown in some quarters that international
marketing will be of increasing importance in the coming decades. Yet, on
the other hand, there appears to be a decline in the number of studies done in
the area. This is dramatically demonstrated in the following figure that is
the result of a content analysis of the Journal of Marketing (JM) over a 40
year period - 1936 to 1975. It shows that about 5% of JM articles in the early
period were concerned with international marketing, peaked at 13.7% in the 60-
63 period, and declined abruptly since then.

FIGURE 1

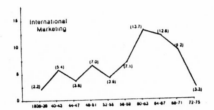

Source: E.T. Grether, "The First Forty Years," Journal of
Marketing, 40(July 1976), p. 66, published by the American
Marketing Association.

The recent work by Myers, Massy and Greyser, Marketing Research and Knowledge
Development: An Assessment for Marketing Management. Prentice-Hall 1980, also
supports the notion that international marketing is an area of "low interest."
It was probably such a background that lead the editors of JM in the Summer
1980 issue to say:

"In stark contrast to the importance and growth of international
marketing is the lack of high quality research in this area. This
is clearly reflected by the manuscripts JM receives. During 1979,
only 9% of the manuscripts submitted had an international focus,
of these, only 10% were of adequate quality to be accepted, and 27%
are still in various stages of revision."

This state of affairs appears to exists not only in marketing, but in most
functional areas of business. The efforts to internationalize the business
curriculum, the business faculty, and their research have been of increasing
concern for the American Assembly of Collegiate Schools of Business (AACSB) and
the European Foundation for Management Development (EFMD). At the June 1980

AACSB/EFMD International Conference in Paris, this was a major topic of discussion. At the EFMD follow-up meetings in Nijenrode in January 81 and at Athens in May 81, workshops were conducted on how best to approach the problem of internationalization. Therefore, while international marketing is presently considered an area of "low interest," it has plenty of company.

(a) Considering the entire field of marketing, do you feel it justified that international marketing is considered an area of "low interest?" (Please check one of the following).

——————   ——————   ——————   ——————   ——————
strongly   unjustified   uncertain   justified   strongly
unjustified   justified

(b) What do you see are the reasons for international marketing being considered an area of "low interest"?

_____

_____

_____

_____

_____

_____

As we have stated, our purpose in this effort is to determine the desirable and future direction for future research in the area of international marketing. Therefore, during the first round of the Delphi process, we ask you to prepare a list of topics or areas of international marketing that you consider to be in greatest need of research. Please follow the instructions listed below:

1.   Limit your suggested topics to a total of five.

2.   Limit your discussion of each topic to three paragraphs.

     i.   In the first paragraph, a brief statement of the problem.

     ii. In the second paragraph, a short discussion of the research
          methodology.

     iii. In the third paragraph of each topic, a statement of why the
          topic or problem is important.

APPENDIX B

SUGGESTED RESEARCH PROJECTS IN INTERNATIONAL MARKETING

INTERNATIONAL MARKETING THEORY

1. Where is international marketing theory?

   Problem: There exists very little theory in international marketing aside
   from that which has been adopted from international economics. The lack
   of such theory makes it difficult to do much more than resort to case-by-
   case description when studying the subject.

   Methodology: There are a number of different possible approaches, however,
   the research methodology should most likely be borrowed from other disciplines and adopted to marketing. International marketing theory could be
   developed from comparative research. On the other side, it might be advisable to use segmentation techniques with application of taxonomy methods
   since this approach tends to be more dynamic than comparative methods.
   Overall, a connection needs to be found between marketing and behavior theory, decision theory, and ethics. One must not over look business history
   that could provide helpful insights.

   Significance: Regarding the substance of international marketing it is
   necessary to realize that decisions are made based on conditions in diversified macro-marketing environments. This macro-marketing-economic viewpoint circumscribes or conditions international marketing decision to a
   much greater degree than domestic marketing decisions. Under this view,
   it is not really clear what the functions of international marketing are.
   Therefore, a sound theoretical base is necessary for the future development
   of the field. A macro-view seems essential where one examines conditions
   fostering the different flows-mostly information, innovation, technology,
   and techniques - between different countries.

2. Are marketing concepts universal?

   Problem: The most important direction for research in IM is the testing of
   the universality of concepts that have been developed and tested in other
   countries, principally in the U.S. Rather than approach IM research from
   the perspective of developing "new theory" in IM and a "new body" of IM
   knowledge, a more fruitful approach would be to develop the hypothesis that
   marketing is marketing the world over and that the weaknesses in marketing
   knowledge is our failure to test marketing principles, concepts, theory,
   etc. beyond domestic markets. While the state of the art of marketing
   knowledge is far from completely developed, there are some principles, concepts, etc. generally accepted as being of value in understanding the market processes, e.g., buyer behavior, product life cycle, diffusion of
   innovations, family life cycle, market segmentation, etc.

   Methodology: Since there are a whole host of concepts, principles, generalizations, etc. taken as "truths" in domestic (U.S.) marketing, a reasonably good place to begin to test the universality of marketing concepts is
   to test these ideas in multi-cultural context. The first task is to select
   concepts, principles and/or generalizations that are reasonably well accepted as "truths" in the U.S. market and test their applicability in other

223

cultures, i.e., is what we teach in the U.S. meaningful in other cultures? Some items to consider are:

(a) Maslow's Need Hierarchy.
(b) Small reference groups and their influence on consumer behavior.
(c) Post-purchase dissonance.
(d) Fashion cycle.
(e) Fashion adoption, i.e., trickle down, trickle across, trickle up.
(f) Price-product quality relationship.
(g) Product diffusion.

In all cases, replication in other cultures of studies already done in the U.S. and/or comparative studies done in two or more cultures would be appropriate.

Significance: An important contribution of such a study such as this would be to focus attention on the direction research in marketing should take. If, indeed, the "truths" we teach in most U.S. marketing courses are not valid in other cultures, then marketing scholars need to re-examine the present direction of research and concentrate more on cross-cultural comparisons in order to develop universal concepts. Perhaps it also should be stressed that the typical marketing core course in the U.S. is a domestic U.S. marketing course and that if students are to understand marketing as a universal discipline, an international marketing course which includes domestic (U.S.) marketing is needed as a core course in business education. On the other hand, if most of the "truths" are valid except for a few minor cultural adjustments, international marketing scholars will want to concentrate their research efforts on further developing marketing theory rather than wasting research effort on seeking an international marketing theory.

3. What is the role and meaning of marketing worldwide?

Problem: Testing present marketing concepts against "different sets of socio-cultural and political values" will not be sufficient. Consideration about the role of marketing in different societies and as part of various economic systems will have to be added. How do societies account for their economic needs, what is the corresponding organization of their productive capabilities? What exchange systems follow from these determining factors and which universals of marketing can be found there, along with more culturally determined variations?

Methodology: Apart from other social sciences, already comparative management research appears to be farther advanced than the state of the art in comparative marketing. Presumably, a number of approaches tried in comparative management studies would lend themselves for adaptation for comparative marketing research purposes.

Significance: An initial assumption that the meanings of basic marketing and decision making concepts are universal could bias much international marketing research and practice. To establish universal meanings and differences we must investigate the basic roles of exchange, markets, choice, influence and innovation as cultural phenomena. We need to also establish the real meanings of marketing concepts within a culture and compare these concepts across cultures.

4. Is the "international" dimension researchable?

   Problem: The sterility of international marketing research can be related probably to the sterility of "the international" as a researchable problem and, to some extent, perhaps to the sterility of available knowledge in marketing in general.

   Methodology: A connection should be found between marketing and behavior theory, decision theory and probably ethics, at least.

   Significance: In a similar way to show the findings of Mayo, Barnard Herzberg and others have led to the development of practical approaches to organization of work, (job enrichment, organizational development), more consistent with the characteristics of people, fundamental research in marketing could lead to newer, creative approaches to meet the needs of our markets.

5. What is the relationship between economic growth and development of modern marketing practices?

   Problem: Modern marketing practices are generally defined in terms of mass marketing, using indirect selling techniques, scientific market segmentation and creating high brand identification and brand loyalty, uniform product quality, and heavy capital investment in marketing effort. What is not clear is how the application of modern marketing practices is related to the rate of economic growth in different countries. In other words, is there a high correlation between economic growth and application of modern marketing practices, or do different countries follow different development paths and adapt to various marketing techniques that are uniquely culture-based?

   Methodology: One research approach is to develop models that would help us cluster countries based on various economic factors and evaluate the extent to which they lend themselves to similar marketing strategies. Another approach is for two or more experts to join forces and develop a concept and a methodological framework for empirical research which could be carried out along these lines by a number of participants in their respective countries. Their findings could then be drawn together and evaluated by the colleagues in charge of the project.

   Significance: The answer to this question is critical for our ability to predict what type of marketing techniques would most likely be useful given a particular state of economic growth. Although there are "limits to growth", it would, nevertheless, be tremendously interesting to find out how modern marketing practices affect the development of an economy. The quality of research done on the macroeconomic level, as of this time, is not very useful for purposes of governing public policy on marketing.

INTERNATIONAL MARKETING EDUCATION

6. What is international marketing education?

Problem: A big problem for marketing is determining whether or not to teach a course (s) in international marketing. If so, then we must determine what to each, when to teach it, and how to teach it. At present, most class outlines are boring, uninteresting, extremely varied and often have more to do with international economics, international politics and cultural than with marketing.

Methodology: Survey of Academics around the world who teach the subject, and of students who have taken international marketing courses in various countries. The objectives of the survey will be to establish whether the international marketing course had any impact on their career. Survey of Multinational executives whose purpose will be to establish what is the material they think should be taught in an International Marketing course.

Significance: The importance of the subject is self-evident. In order for normative approaches to be developed, we teachers must agree on the ground rules.

7. Are students de-motivated to study international marketing?

Problem: This problem is especially important for developed countries, mostly the United States. Stays abroad often have a negative impact on the careers of managers (re-entry problem). The ensuing hesitance to spend some time in foreign countries may be one reason for concentrating efforts on the domestic market. Yet in developing countries and especially in centrally - planned economies, there is a very strong motivation to study international marketing. The main factors are good pay and high prestige of jobs in foreign countries.

Methodology: Comparison of the careers of (marketing) mangers who went abroad with those who did not. It is also advisable to interview students about their preferences concerning future jobs, as well as managers of big companies operating in foreign markets. From the background of the sample of multinational companies, it would be possible to compare working conditions in home and foreign countries.

Significance: If too many top people in marketing are parochial-minded, this will seriously affect the interests of a country in need of export sales.

8. What are the career profiles for international marketers?

Problem: A lot of faculty have been discouraged since their students can not get jobs in this area. Firms have used experienced people from within the company (international experience is often part of a job rotation system) or hire foreign nationals. In short, there are no beginning jobs in this area.

Methodology: Survey the career profiles of contemporary international marketers. Also survey company hiring plans in this area.

Significance: If no beginning jobs exists, perhaps the best we can do is
teach an "appreciation of" international marketing. And many people think
that this would be better if it was integrated into traditional courses,
rather than setting up a separate course.

THE MACRO-ENVIRONMENT

9. What are the determinants of trade between developed-developing and East-
West countries?

Problem: There are perhaps two subjects here. Of course there exist many
similarities between developing and East bloc countries, but at the same
time there are many dissimilarities, mainly on the area of decision making
process and institutional environment. As a result, the scope of this research project should be broadened: considered should not just be trade
(exporting/importing), but all alternatives of international business/mar-
keting involvement. Thus we would look after the determining factors for
the different forms of international business involvement (besides exporting
also licensing, joint ventures plus wholly/partly owned direct investment
operations). What favors trade, licensing, joint ventures, direct investments, and what combinations of them (as practiced simultaneously by MNEs).

Methodology: This type of study creates the need for some traditional techniques - company survey, library research, cross-national research based on
comparative studies. Additionally, there needs to be a stronger political
science/public policy aspects input. The recommended framework of integration would be an approach leaning heavily toward the recently emerging concepts or early foundations of macromarketing (management). One of the
methodological problems to be dealt with is that at times different assumptions have to used in developing countries than in the developed ones.
Also motivation in centrally planned economies and criteria of market segmentation in developing countries may differ. Many irrational factors on
the macro and micro economic level need to be taken into consideration. It
seems necessary to develop comparative studies concerning management systems
and allocation of marketing decisions in the countries of the East bloc.
There are very big dissimilarities.

Significance: The problems are very important from the social and economic
point of view. In order to stop economic recession, diminish social and
political tensions, decrease the role of big powers, etc., it is necessary
to create effective demand for the Southern Hemisphere.

10. Public policy toward international marketing?

Problem: Very little research has been conducted on public policy toward
international marketing, despite the fact that coping with different legal
systems is one of the reasons that international marketing is a separate
field within marketing. Advocated is a stronger differentiation between
macro and micro-marketing aspects. On the macro side, we need more knowledge about the interrelationships between macroeconomic policies of host
countries or regional groupings (especially with regard to foreign trade
and international business activities) and the corresponding strategy alternatives in international marketing to serve foreign markets (entry st-
tategies). Again, recent progress in the area of macromarketing (management) seems to hold great potential for respective extensions to the

international field. Micro emphasis would be more on the laws and regulations impacting upon the marketing mix variables (advertising, direct
selling etc. regulations).

Methodology: Research should be conducted on the impact that different
types of laws and regulations have upon marketing activities and upon
demand. This would include various types of import/export regulations and
law regarding aspects of marketing strategy. The ground work should start
by drawing on the work of Boddewyn/Hollander (Public Policy Toward Retailing - An International Symposium) and related publications by Behrman,
as well as the growing literature on macromarketing (e.g. annual proceedings of the seminars on macromarketing in Boulder, Journal of Macromarketing).

Significance: The findings of such research would benefit the teaching
and practices of international marketing. In addition, they would contribute to the development of the field of marketing in general, since they
would help us understand the relationship between types of regulations and
marketing consequences.

11. What are consequences for marketing cost due to differences in legislation
     between countries?

     Problem: Legislation with respect to elements of the marketing mix is in-
     creasing in Western countries in order to protect the consumer and to in-
     fluence competition in markets. When such legislation with respect to pro-
     duct content, package, information and advertising differs a great deal bet-
     ween countries, it will decrease efficiency in marketing. Differences of
     legislations in this respect might even increase opportunities to use such
     an instrument for protectionistic purposes.

     Methodology: Investigate for a specific, rather than a homogeneous group
     of products, legislation with respect to the marketing mix, import, after
     sales service, warranties, etc., for say two European countries or an im-
     portant West Europe country and the United States. Use a survey to dete-
     rmine how exporting firms experience this problem and what costs are invol-
     ved in this respect. Also ask what marketing solutions are practical for
     specific problems.

     Significance: The results of such research could help governments establish
     efficient consumer legislation.

12. What can international marketing contribute to developing countries?

     Problem: Develping countries have a different combination of needs, re-
     sources and socio-economic environment than developed countries. Yet, they
     have huge markets. It is important to obtain marketing concepts, methodo-
     logies, and techniques that fit their cultures and contribute to the de-
     velopment. Besides the "marketing and development" approach concentrating
     on domestic progress in less developed countries, international marketing
     can also contribute significantly to the advancement of developing countries
     by helping to improve their position in the world markets. To assist LDCs
     to sell the products of their growing industries in the developed countries

and elsewhere should thus also become an important challenge for international marketers. Therefore, the task mentioned under 13 (competitiveness of countries and their industries) should also be performed for developing countries: what are the factors and industrialization necessities which increase the competitiveness of LDC industries in the developed countries and world markets in general?

Methodology: At the current stage of knowledge in this area, exploratory research, probably based on case studies, might be the most appropriate methodology. The narrowing of the field could be done restricting cases to one industry or to a region (Latin America, Middle East). With special emphasis on feasibility studies for LDC export industries and export promotion policies without neglecting domestic development necessities and social priorities.

Significance: This is important because the maturity of markets in the industrialized world, combined with the abundance of resources and the need for all types of goods in developing nations, create the opportunity for another era of worldwide industrial growth with the possibility to reach a higher level of social justice.

13. What are the factors that account for the competitiveness of industrialized countries in the third world?

Problem: What accounts for the fact that some (industrialized) countries are more competitive than others in third world countries?

Methodology: The problem calls for carrying out productivity analyses both with regard to production and distribution. This includes studying the image of products and services that country A enjoys in country B. It may also lead to comparing the economic and social structures of the countries concerned. Empirical research done in various countries will require groups of indigenous researchers. So this research proposal offers an excellent opportunity for experts from various countries to cooperate with a view to finding a better solution to an eminent problem than could be found by a colleague working on his own. (irrespective of the amount of funds at his disposal).

Significance: The advantage of possessing knowledge of this kind is that it leads to an increase in productivity through a more sensible selection of markets, followed by larger sales and lower costs (due to a decrease of fixed costs per unit as well as the impact of the learning curve).

14. What is the impact of doing business with planned economies on marketing organizations?

Problem: Doing business in countries having centralized economic systems implies often that purchasing is concentrated a great deal. Individual western business companies are often too small to develop satisfactory bargaining power and to offer the assortment of products. Consequently, cooperation of companies in joint ventures for such projects is necessary. What is the marketing experience in such joint ventures and what can we learn from their experiences?

Methodology: Analyzing the way marketing is organized in such types of joint venture projects. A basic description of the marketing organization in a number of selected cases. Attempt to find a model or check list for marketing organizations in joint ventures aiming at sales in centralized economic systems.

Significance: Knowledge of weak and strong points in such arrangements and suggestions for improvement.

THE CONSUMER AND INDUSTRIAL BUYER IN INTERNATIONAL MARKETING

15. Does the current state of knowledge in consumer behavior apply in the international area?

Problem: There is such as enormous need for consumer research in the area of international marketing. For example, the whole area of consumer behavior is in great need of research. I am not sure I can identify one particular area of consumer behavior being more important than another. The state of the art in international marketing research is so deficient that any contribution in the consumer behavior area would be tremendously important. Many of the consumer behavior concepts that we take for granted in domestic U.S. marketing may well explain consumer behavior in other cultures. However, we do not really have much evidence that is true. As a consequence, a whole host of studies that would simply validate the applications of various consumer behavior theories in other cultures would be tremendously important to understanding that area of marketing.

Methodology: The research methodology that would be used, in my opinion, would be the same that is used in comparable studies in the United States. In other words, my thought is that there is a need to take research done in the U.S. and replicate these studies in other cultures, (using the same methodology if applicable), with the intent of determining whether or not the concepts are valid elsewhere.

Significance: I believe that this direction for international marketing research is important if we are to truly understand whether or not the principles that we have developed mainly in the United States are truly universally applicable to other cultures, what adjustments to our knowledge should be made to enable the marketers of the future to understand behavior in whatever culture is being investigated. What I have said about consumer behavior would also be applicable to industrial buyer behavior as well. There has been some limited amount of work done in this area, but again, for the most part, it is very sketchy and not complete. Almost any kind of effort would be important in expanding the knowledge of international marketing.

16. What is the role of international buyer behavior studies?

Problem: The marketing concept tells us that the consumer should be the focal point of marketing decisions. Yet, very little international research has focused on either industrial buyers or on final consumers. Worse still, many people seem to implicitly assume that the models of buyer behavior which exist are universal in their application, despite the fact that they have mostly been developed in the United States.

Methodology: Empirical research should be conducted which tests the validity of current buyer behavior theory in an international context. This would call for replications of past studies in different national contexts. Also, multi-country studies should be designed which test the validity of certain aspects of buyer behavior models outside of the United States and which, in general, explicitly consider the environmental (i.e., national) factor in the research.

Significance: The above-mentioned research would not only contribute to the development of the field of international marketing, but it would also contribute to the overall field of marketing through the removal of some of the culture-bound principles which exist in the field.

17. Is there an international model of consumer behavior?

Problem: A basic problem in developing international marketing strategies is a lack of generalized model of consumer behavior that could be applied across different cultures. While we have made considerable progress in measuring differences in buyer behavior within a culture, there have been very few systematic efforts at understanding buyer behavior between different cultures.

Methodology: The research needs call for a thorough grounding in not only social psychology but also cultural anthropology to understand socio-cultural variables that impact different types of purchase behavior.

Significance: Without the development of effective and operational cross-cultural buyer behavior models, international marketing would be limited to "marketing in foreign countries" without any effort at cross-fertilization of ideas and cross-utilization of marketing strategies.

18. What roles does culture differences play in preference for goods in different countries?

Problem: The extent of an cultural basis for different relative preferences for consumer and durable products held in different countries. Classical image studies and analyses on the development of preferences reveal the nature and size of differences that exist between different countries, at best. What is needed, is a theory explaining "the reasons why" respectively a method to identify the higher ordered factors that can account for such differences.

Methodology: There are many ways of researching this topic. Comparative study of two or three countries in depth or analysis of multi-country patterns over time are the two extremes.

Significance: Each country's consumers adopt durables in different orders of priority. Some tentative studies have shown underlying cultural norms differ, but no significant comparative study has been done either into the patterns of the motivations. As the consumer durables producers are increasingly competing on an international front, knowledge of country differences is quite fundamental to their strategies.

19. What are markets and consumers like in Middle-East countries?

Problem: A fundamental study on consumer behavior in some important Middle-East countries. It seems that there is much information and experience on Middle-East markets, but fundamental studies in this field are scarce.

Methodology: A fundamental study in a specific Middle-East country on consumer behavior, attitudes, habits, decision making for a product group, e.g., food. Methods of research might include survey, group discussions and observation.

Significance: The research results should be of help to exporters in developing marketing programs in cooperation with the local distributors and in developing their specific marketing programs.

20. What is the decision process for industrial buyers across countries?

Problem: Cross national comparisons of decision process involved in industrial purchasing.

Methodology: "Microsegmentation" of the potential market of an industrial product. Comparison of decision participants involved.

Significance: Assist in industrial market segmentation and choice of communication targets.

21. How to identify market segments?

Problem: Cross national studies of consumer behavior to enable identification of international market segments.

Methodology: Would require replication of sound consumer behavior studies in a number of countries in a manner to obtain comparable results.

Significance: Open.

INTERNATIONAL MARKETING RESEARCH

22. How can the available, usable and reliable data that are comparable across countries be organized?

Problem: One of the most critical factors, apart from the development of cross-cultural models of consumer behavior, is the lack of consistent and reliable data from different countries. Every E.C. country has its national statistical data providing detailed information on per capita consumption. The E.C. commission publishes statistics on per capita consumption of various foods products. In many countries there are more refined data on food consumption per household, per age group, which cannot be compared easily between countries. In some countries programs are under way to intensify data collection in this area. The objectives of this research are the establishment of differences between statistics on household food expenditure in various E.C. countries and proposals for harmonisation; and develop proposal for a refined statistical data system on household food consumption, which could be introduced in E.C. countries.

Methodology: Data are currently available from a variety of sources. The most important and easily available data are those collected by different agencies of the United Nations. However, these data are supplied by individual countries and are merely collected and reported by the United Nations. The data, however, are highly inconsistent in their quality and reliability. Other sources such as Business International, and Nielson also collect data. While these data are often superior in quality, they are prorietary in nature and are not easily available to academic researchers. Furthermore, quite often they are not collected with an eye toward their cross-country comparability.

Significance: The progress in international marketing research would be highly constrained without the easy availability of data. One solution to this problem would be a consortium of U.S. and European business schools that would be responsible for collecting data from different sources, standardizing it across different countries, and making it available to researchers in different countries.

23. What are the relations between developments in marketing information systems and international marketing management?

Problem: There is a development towards new devices in information collection and information retrieval, which can be used also for Marketing Information Systems e.g. UPC/EAN, Satellites, View Data Systems. The research objectives are:

----Analyse the growth of EAN in European food retailing.
----Inventory the plans in various E.C. countries which aim
    to combine EAN data banks in a national information system.
----Find out the impact of EAN on product standardisation, on
    rate of turnover of products and on purchasing behavior
    of retail companies.
----What are the consequences of foregoing developments on
    international marketing?

Methodology: Investigation of the consequences of the use of UPC/EAN by West-European retail companies in terms of:

----Amount and quality of marketing information in order to improve
    assortment policy.
----Speed of marketing information and its impact on physical dis-
    tribution. This research might be conducted by a survey of the
    big chains of E.C. - countries.

Significance: The research is important since it informs producers about the consequences of UPC/EAN on the relationship producer-retailer in Western-European countries.

24. How does one construct an international marketing information system for developing countries?

Problem: The need to determine a substitutive method for the building of marketing information systems in developing countries where statistics are incomplete and/or unreliable and market surveys are difficult to manage.

Methodology: The research methodology should be derived from subjective proability and Bayesian decision theory.

Significance: The implementation of successful marketing strategies is very fragile in many countries due to the lack of hard data. The situation could be improved if soft data were available at a reasonable cost.

25. What role can marketing analysis play in international investment decisions?

Problem: Marketing research which could define decision prerequisites for investment in international markets is needed.

Methodology: The kind of study creates many research problems associated with long run decisional and predictive processes. This type of research is by necessity connected with data and concepts from other experts and conditioned by numerous economic and social factors.

Significance: Assist in better allocation of world resources.

INTERNATIONAL PRODUCT POLICIES

26. What are the determinants of product diffusion in international marketing?

Problem: Determinants of new products diffusion in an international environment.

Methodology: Estimation and comparison of the parameters affecting the diffusion of new products.

Significance: Development of international strategies based on sequential product introduction.

27. What are the international marketing strategies for services?

Problem: The development of an internationally acceptable service concept; the building of an international service network has not been supported, so far, with a conceptual framework.

Methodology: We should start with case studies, follow with a selection of hypotheses and test them through managerial investigation handled with the help of cooperative service firms.

Significance: Open.

28. How does one determine appropriate country/product mixes?

Problem: There is a need for studies for product/market/country configurations.

Methodology: Probably best approached by clustering or otherwise grouping summaries of activities of several multinational firms.

Significance: To add an international dimension to the rapidly developing literature on strategic planning.

29. What determines product preference?

Problem: Is not the thinking about cultural differences in product preference too demand-oriented? What is seen as cultural difference may well be the result of (a) a lack of abundance of natural resources, (b) the structure of the economy and the state of capital equipment, and (c) traditional supply. These explanations of differences seem much more tangible than socio-cultural and psychological variables and rest on the thesis that buyer behavior may be more conditioned than inborn.

Methodology: Comparison of the market history of a (durable) consumer product in at least two countries of average purchasing power. Published documents and key interviews.

Significance: Would help explain why certain products and brands have a high market share and what resistance to new product introduction in foreign markets can be expected.

30. International generic demand?

Problem: Identification of similarities in the world-wide patterns of demand for different generic products or services, cross-sectionally and over time.

Methodology: Analysis of basic demand and demographic data.

Significance: Law-like relationships would be of great value in forecasting and in building global strategies. The approach of suggesting patterns such as bell-shaped product life-cycles and then searching for them is very dangerous.

INTERNATIONAL PRICING POLICIES

31. What are appropriate pricing terms in international marketing?

Problem: When should you quote F.O.B. and when C.I.F.?

Methodology: Informal interviews with international marketing managers of some companies (large and small) whose goals will be (1) to try to determine what are the factors which affect the practice of each system of quotation, and (2) to try to suggest some guidelines when to use each system.

Significance: A right system of quotation might save a lot of money for a firm.

32. What should be intersubsidiary pricing terms?

Problem: How can you achieve a maximization of global profits while keeping the concept of subsidiaries as profit centers?

Methodology: Informal interviews with international marketing executives of several companies. With some use of logic one should be able to determine an approach to the problem.

Significance: Will allow better coordination of the total international marketing organization and as a consequence more profits.

INTERNATIONAL MARKETING CHANNELS

33. What is the role of logistics in the international marketing strategy?

Problem: All costs associated with logistics are rising, however, it is not usually recognized as an element of the marketing mix of the multi-national firm. In addition, the logistic system often contains decision makers (such as traders, for instance) that can affect the configuration of the supplier/customer relationship.

Methodology: Research should be undertaken analyzing the cost of trans-portation, warehousing, insurance, financing and the like when dealing with international markets. Also, the analysis must be made when different channel approaches are used: selling through an organization created and owned by the company; selling through distributors; selling through a trading company (owned, controlled or independent).

Significance: This is a very important topic because logistics are a critical factor determining international competitiveness.

34. How can a firm optimize its investment in international marketing channels?

Problem: Management of logistics - optimum matching of supply and demand points in a world of floating exchange rates, trade restrictions, local content requirements, export requirements, etc.

Methodology: Would require investigation/analysis of company practice, identification of constraints and model building.

Significance: Open.

35. What are the international channels of distribution?

Problem: A systematic study establishing the different types of channels available to multinational corporations within foreign nations. Delineate their advantages, disadvantages and conditions under which they should be used.

Methodology: Survey of sizable sample of multinational corporations. Questions should address themselves not only to the description of channels but also to the reason behind choices, the drawbacks experienced by uses of these channels. The analysis of the findings should provide a typology of the choices available. Survey should be face to face.

Significance: The field would benefit from the development of some better classifications of channels within nations. It would also benefit from empirical research on such factors as channel power within the different types of channel systems. Working within a different channel system is perhaps the greatest marketing problem faced by international marketers, both exporters and those marketing directly within a foreign country.

36. How best can a firm select and establish a working relationship with in-
    dependent international channel agents?

    Problem: The problem is how does a company which wishes to expand inter-
    nationally go about selecting and working with independent channel agents.
    There is very little research to guide management in this delicate area.
    What kind of agreements are most affective, under what circumstances can
    agreements be terminated, what can be done to obtain the maximum effort
    and commitment out of agents and so on.

    Methodology: I see the first stage of this study as a descriptive survey
    of company experience.

    Significance: The reason for the importance of this topic is the generally
    high level of confusion which exists today. For example, lawyers are ad-
    vising attendees at seminars that you cannot break an agreement with an
    independent channel agent. This is nonsense because I personally know
    managers who have broken hundreds of agreements and have never experienced
    any difficulties or problems. There is a great gap between what works and
    what is written down as document advice in this area.

37. What is the international distribution center?

    Problem: The concept of International Distribution center is becoming
    more and more popular. However, no study has yet investigated what are
    the problems which go with its implementation. Furthermore, it is impor-
    tant to specify where they should be localized (in the vicinity of pro-
    duction entities, main markets, airports, harbors,.....), what change in
    the organizational structure they require.

    Methodology: Informal and in depth surveys of companies using Interna-
    tional Distribution centers and similar companies not using it should
    provide the input on which to base some sound theory.

    Significance: Open.

                          EXPORT AND IMPORT RESEARCH

38. What is the current state of export/import research?

    Problem: The search for exports is gaining in importance as energy prices
    have contunued to rise. This area has been receiving more attention by
    international marketing researchers, but the research being conducted tends
    to be limited to the attitudinal domain. Other writings in the area tend
    to be highly descriptive and non-academic. Books in the area are more
    like manuals.

    Methodology: Future research in the area should aim at the development of
    principles and techniques of importing and exporting. For instance, re-
    search could be conducted which attempts to develop methods of assessing
    market potential in foreign nations.

    Significance: This area is going to continue to gain in importance, and
    academics with an interest in international marketing should involve

themselves in its development. This research would aid one in reaching conclusions in the following areas:

----Market assessment in the import market.
----Product assessment in the export market.
----Supporting export system development.
----Supporting import system development.
----Testing of export and import principles as well as the deduction of new ones.
----Follow-up introduction of an actual product or a service in the foreign market.

39. How to assess export promotion?

Problem: Export promotion is a specific topic of international marketing and trade. Yet it is not well known what effects it has. We may think of government export promotion as well as the export promotion by private firms. Many countries want to promote their exports and do a great deal of effort to that end. Yet, basically, exporting is more a micro thing than a macro thing and little seems to be known of the effects of world market centers, international exhibitions, general export promotion, joint ventures etc.

Methodology: Open.

Significance: A great deal of private research has gone into this subject but little by academics.

40. What motivates a company to export?

Problem: What induces small and medium-sized private companies to extend their sales territory to foreign countries? Why do comparable firms refrain from doing the same thing?

Methodology: This topic is also compatible with a team approach! A comparative study should be made between two countries in which each researcher surveys a sample of exporting and non-exporting industries. Comparative criteria would include:

----Willingness to take risk.
----Profit expectations.
----Preference of direct or in-direct distribution.
----New product development versus exporting established ones.

Significance: It gives concerned firms a perspective as to where to look for additional sales and growth. It helps to evaluate the effectiveness of public policy measures with a view to promote export trade.

41. What decision processes do companies use in determining entry strategies for new international markets?

Problem: Most of the approaches used for export market selection only solve part of the decision problems firms are confronted with. Besides the economic criteria pertaining to marketing, product and distribution aspects must be included in the evaluative process. Thus, export markets are characterized by three factors: the market, the product and the distribution channel.

Methodology: The relative importance of the three factors, their scale values and combined utility score (or riskiness) can be discovered by subjecting data gained in interviews with managers to multivariate analysis.

Significance: Knowledge on the decision behavior of successful exporters can serve to devise aids to non-exporting firms.

INTERNATIONAL MARKETING MANAGEMENT

42. Strategic marketing planning for international marketing?

Problem: Strategic marketing planning has been a critically weak element in marketing research and marketing management in the United States. It has only recently begun to receive attention because of the awareness of the increasing marketing costs and inefficient resource allocation.

Methodology: The development of strategic market planning for international markets would require identification and development of variables pertaining to: economic and competitive conditions; social, demographic and life style conditions; and, political and governmental regulatory conditions for various countries in a manner that these data are comparable thereby enabling parent company home office staff to develop international strategic marketing plans.

Significance: Lack of strategic marketing is even more evident in international markets where research and strategy development invariably lag behind domestic (U.S.) practices. An obvious conclusion is that ratio of sales to marketing expenditures is generally lower in overseas markets compared with United States for similar product categories. This condition will now have to change because markets are becoming increasingly international.

43. How do marketing managers in different national environments engage in marketing practices?

Problem: Unless we can achieve a good empirical base on this issue, it is unlikely that we will evolve a good theory of international marketing. Therefore, a comparative study of managerial marketing practices is badly needed.

Methodology: My suggestion is to carry out personal interviews in several countries. The survey research should focus on the following: (1) process of decision making for each marketing decision, (2) environmental scanning and adaptation done by the marketing managers, and (3) role of research as an input to decision making.

Significance: It will raise the discipline above the anecdotal level. It will generate a good data base on how managers actually do adapt to their national environments. It will enable someone to generate a good theory of international marketing.

44. Determining global marketing strategies?

Problem: There is very little written on how to decide global competitive strategies. With many competitors and differing market conditions, conventional game-theory approaches are not possible. Global market share objectives are too naive. Some investigation is needed into the patterns that have actually emerged in multi-national competition and the premises on which successful and unsuccessful strategies have been used.

Methodology: Open.

Significance: Open.

45. Do domestic and international marketing management differ?

Problem: Studies of decision processes of national versus multinational firms.

Methodology: A flow-chart description of a sample of decisions, especially pricing, product development and volume plans.

Significance: To help determine differences and the impact (if any) of management practices of multinational and domestic firms.

46. What links are there between strategic management and marketing management in international firms?

Problem: What is the headquarter's role in setting objectives, strategies and marketing plans?

Methodology: A survey method is the obvious way, but it is unlikely to provide the necessary insight. Probably a multi-country study. This might be meaningless unless confinded to one industry and to companies of a certain size. A Delphi study on how best to frame the problem might be possible.

Significance: There are virtually no articles or papers on this subject. This is the type of information top management need most.

47. How to appraise subsidiary marketing management?

Problem: How does a firm build a system of performance evaluation which stimulates the local management while not hurting the total performance of the firm.

Methodology: Informal interviews of international corporation executives should provide the pros and cons of different methods used.

Significance: Establish a better system of performance appraisal at the international level.

48. What are appropriate licensing methods?

Problem: What are the reasons for success and failure of this mode of penetration in foreign markets. There are many forms of licensing agreements and joint ventures. Their success depends on different types of parameters. Type, size, and other characteristics related to the dealing companies. Countries of origin, timing, terms of contract etc. The objective of the study should be to delineate what are the main factors of success.

Methodology: Face to face survey of companies which have experienced positive and negative licensing and joint venture agreements. Disceminant analysis should then be performed on the data gathered in order to find the factor of success.

Significance: Help companies improve their procedures.

49. Successful joint venture management in marketing?

Problem: How to administer a joint venture with a foreign partner.

Methodology: Informal interviews with executives of companies who have experience with joint ventures.

Significance: This information should help companies avoid costly mistakes.

50. Are there international marketing economies of scale?

Problem: Identification of the ways firms can achieve the necessary (production and marketing) economies of scale necessary to survive in the global market place.

Methodology: This study would require first conceptualization and model building.

Significance: Open.

Contributing Authors

Jean J. Boddewyn, Baruch College, City University of New York, New York, USA

Erwin Dichtl, University of Mannheim, West Germany

Hamid Etemad, McGill University, Montreal, Canada

Gerald M. Hampton, Albers School of Business, Seattle University, Seattle, Washington, USA

Warren J. Keegan, Pace University, New York, USA

H.-G. Köglmayr, University of Mannheim, West Germany

M. Liebold, University of Mannheim, West Germany

Malcolm H. B. McDonald, Cranfield School of Management, Bedford, England

Matthew Meulenberg, Landbouwhogeschool, Wagenigen, The Netherlands

S. Müller, University of Mannheim, West Germany

John K. Ryans, Jr., Kent State University, Ohio, USA

S. Prakash Sethi, University of Texas at Dallas, Texas, USA

Kenneth Simmonds, London Business School, England

Helmut Soldner, University of Augsburg, West Germany

Vern Terpstra, University of Michigan, Ann Arbor, Michigan, USA

Aart P. van Gent, Stichting Nijenrode, The Netherlands School of Business, Breukelen, The Netherlands

Jan Van Rees, Technische Hogeschool, Eindhoven, The Netherlands